Give Me
This Mountain

&

He Gave Us
A Valley

A Two-Part Autobiography
by
Helen Roseveare

Two Books In One!
Complete

WEC International

Give Me This Mountain

An Autobiography
by
Helen Roseveare

By the same author: He gave us a valley

First Printing by:
INTER-VARSITY PRESS
38 De Montfort Street, Leicester LE17GP, England
©HELEN ROSEVEARE 1966

First published 1966
Reprinted 1966, 1967, 1969, 1972, 1974, 1975, 1976, 1978,
1981, 1983, 1985

ISBN 0-85110-334-0

Inter-Varsity Press is the publishing division of the Universi-
ties and Colleges Christian Fellowship (formerly the Inter-Varsity
Fellowship), a student movement linking Christian Unions in
universities and colleges throughout the United Kingdom and the
Republic of Ireland, and a member movement of the International
Fellowship of Evangelical Students. For information about local
and national activities in Great Britain write to UCCF, 38 De
Montfort Street, Leicester LE17GP.

This printing by:
BRENTWOOD CHRISTIAN PRESS
4000 BEALLWOOD AVENUE
COLUMBUS, GEORGIA 31904-7217

Contents
Book One

Book Two

And Caleb said: Now therefore give me this mountain, whereof the Lord spake in that day; for thou heardest in that day how the Anakims were there, and that the cities were great and fenced: if so be the lord will be with me, then I shall be able to drive them out, as the Lord said, And Joshua gave unto Caleb Hebron for an inheritance.

Joshua 14:12,13

Introduction

In the following pages I have tried to write an honest, unadorned story of my somewhat tempestuous life. Except in the Epilogue I have not tried to draw any morals. But neither have I wanted to pull any punches. I have tried honestly to thank those who have helped me along the way and also to be very careful not to criticize unkindly others with whom I disagreed. At times this may have made the story a little lop-sided since occasionally I have felt unable to give publicly all the facts that influenced me at certain periods. I do not think, however, that this materially alters the basic story.

I have only once in my life kept a diary, and that was under the special stress of the five months in rebel captivity from August to December, 1964.[1] All the rest of the story comes as my memory prompts me. There may be some chronological discrepancies. There are certainly many episodes that are not included, either because they have been forgotten or else because I did not consider that they helped forward the main theme. Other episodes are mentioned and then never referred to again. They were there, but did not substantially alter the course of the journey.

My life has possibly included more dramatic episodes than many another, but this is not the impression I wish to leave with any reader. Rather, it has been for me a journey towards one definite and glorious goal, 'that I may know him . . .', our God, revealed to us in His Son, the Lord Jesus Christ. I have often felt that my life was rather akin to mountaineering, with a clear goal to reach the highest peak. There may be a fairly long journey to reach the foothills before the real climb can be started. On the way up, the goal is often hidden from view by clouds, or by lesser peaks, but the original sight of the summit keeps us pressing on, despite weariness and even discouragement.

I found frequently that I climbed in glorious sunshine, warm and invigorating, my face set determinedly for the nearest peak I could see. As I reached it, I revelled in the sense of achievement and victory and in the glorious view. I did all I could to encourage others to join me and to help them up over the difficult parts. Then, slowly, my imagination would be caught by the next peak ahead, higher, steeper, but again bathed in sunlight, and eventually the resolve would form to set off upwards again.

Here I made a mistake, many times, as the telling of the story shows. As I went down from the present peak into the valley between the mountains, I was often shadowed by the very peak I had been enjoying. This I interpreted in a sense of failure and this often led to despair. I felt I was going downwards into the 'slough of despond'. I see now that I was wrong in this 'feeling'. The going down was merely an initial moving forward towards the next higher ground, never a going back to base level, so to speak. The shadow was only relative after the brightness of the sun; the valley could provide a period of rest for working out the experiences previously learnt, a time for refreshment preparatory for the next hard climb. Had I understood this meaning of the sunshine and shadow in my life rather than interpreting my various experiences along life's way as 'up' and 'down', I might have saved myself many deep heartaches.

I trust, despite this failure, that readers will be able to enter into the joy of this wonderful pilgrimage and the satisfaction of a life spent seeking to know the One who alone gives life. I am in no way offering my story as an example for others to follow. There are many mistakes that I hope may warn others. There are streaks in my nature that I am glad to see the Lord is dealing with, and I should hate others to think that they ought to emulate them. I think especially of the tremendous ambition to be a success in anything which I undertook that so often drove me to set for myself standards which, under all the circumstances, were not really required and which, if I had been more perceptive, I should have known I had no chance of achieving. No, it is not an example; but maybe it will be an encouragement to some on the journey to realize that others have passed the same way.

• • •

Events in Africa move fast. Although this book is being reprinted only a matter of months after publication, already some of the place-names are out of date. Leopoldville in the following pages should now be Kinshasa, Paulis Isiro and Stanleyville Kisangani.

End Notes

1 Published under the title *Doctor Among Congo Rebels* (Lutterworth Press and Christian Literature Crusade, Fort Washington, 1965).

8

1
Getting To The Start

'Either you join us, or you go down by yourself: it's your own affair.'

The nursemaid moved away. I swallowed hard, my eyes misting with tears. Five minutes before everything had been so different as I had run and scrambled up the wooded pathway with my elder brother, gathering wild flowers, happy in the flickering sunlight, chattering and unconcerned. I had noticed Bob's face set in a quiet determination and had wondered. Then we came out from the trees at the top of the ghyll and stood on the flat rock overlooking the rushing stream, silenced, as always, by the noise of the waters and a sense of power and awe at its depth. Suddenly, quietly, so unexpectedly, Bob drew back a few paces, ran and jumped the ghyll. My eyes followed him with silent admiration, and yet with horror glancing down at the fury below. He had done it—our much-discussed exploit of jumping the raging torrent from the rock. Determinedly I drew back, clenched my fists, closed my eyes, ran up to it—and stopped dead!

Bob had run on into the woods, suddenly a man, alone, successful. Then the nursemaid struggled up, carrying my four-year-old younger sister. She stepped over the narrow channel with one easy stride, and told me to hurry up and join them; they couldn't wait all day. Then she moved on, to follow Bob down the pathway the other side.

Despair, loneliness, tears, *I could* not do what Bob had done, and jump across. The more I longed, the greater the noise and depth and width and horror. I was terrified of that water. With a wild sense of defeat, I turned and rushed back down the hill, burning tears of shame choking me. What would he think? Would he play with me again? I was just a sissy, a girl, afraid—yes, that was it—afraid of water and heights.

This longing to be accepted, this need to be loved, to be wanted, so often a part of childhood, came early to me. There was that day in Cornwall two years before, when suddenly a hush fell on the crowded beach, and Mother noticed all eyes being drawn in one direction. Way up the sheer face of the cliff on a narrow ledge, unable to go up or down, she saw the round, diminutive figure of her four-year-old, trying to defeat this sense of inferiority, longing to shine in the eyes of her adored six-year-old brother.

As a child I was endlessly active, restless with animal spirits, always in mischief, with an urge to excel, to be noticed, to be the centre of the group, an inner need to be admired—and life often seemed very hard and unsympathetic. Often blamed for trouble that was not of my making, I would despise the others in my heart for not owning up to clear me of the accusation.

School soon absorbed much of my excess energy, but the work came easily. Books were a fascination, so much so that, when my younger sister whispered, 'Read to me, Peggy', in the dark of an evening, I could forget the whipping I had earlier suffered unjustly. Lying side by side, by torch light, under the blankets, we devoured many of the thrills of Long John Silver, the White Rabbit, Pooh and Henry Esmond, and the world took on new silvery lights of happiness and mystery.

This air of mystery laid the foundation of Sundays. I loved this day and the sense of difference—dressed tidily, walking up the steep, narrow road past the curio shop, where two white stone cherub book-ends smiled at me each Sunday as I ran ahead of the family, till I had saved enough to make them my mother's birthday present. The cool, dim building, with high, carved wood pews; the thin, tall candles flickering below the amazing coloured east window; the vases of austere white lilies; the choirboys in surplice and ruff, the acolytes and servers, the cross and incense; the priest in his beautifully embroidered linen vestments; the pealing organ and rich strange music that filled the building right up to the great carved dome; the long, difficult words folded into the lilting chants; the sermon with its grave cadences; all these I loved, absorbing almost unconsciously a lasting impression of beauty and solemnity. Then home we would go to a family dinner, so often the only day Dad was with us, and after that off to Sunday school, held locally at the teacher's home. I vividly remember that wonderful day (my eighth birthday) when she talked to us of India, and we cut out pictures of Indian children and stuck them in our 'Missionary Prayer Book'. It was then that the quiet resolve was made. When I grow up, I will go to tell other boys and girls about the Lord Jesus—a child's determination that never faded.

Odd incidents stand out clearly like beacons, all pointing to the absorbing necessity of being loved and wanted. There was the day I had a new dress, in velveteen, plain, dark, with three silver buttons set obliquely each side of the chest—just what I longed for, quite different, smart, commanding. I recall a visit from an American cousin to my school when I was ten and my being sent for by the headmistress who introduced me as 'an exceptional pupil with a brilliant mind'! I had to look up 'exceptional' in a dictionary afterwards, and was very puzzled to know if it was complimentary or not, but it had obviously impressed these important relatives!

The following year, exam-time came round and I woke up feeling ill one morning. Despite it, I struggled to school, starting on a glorious, straight-forward maths exam—and then was violently sick after completing only one of the ten questions. I shall never forget the bitter disappointment of having only 10 out of 100 for my best subject, or the subsequent radiant joy when it was not included in the averages and I once again received the form prize for the year. These little things mattered so much.

During these years three memorable summer holidays added to the scenic background of life. The first—through France and Switzerland, then south to Pompeii—had the added joy that my beloved godfather, 'Uncle Ray', accompanied us in his own car. I glowed with happiness at being specially 'his', sometimes travelling on my own with him. The second, with family car and camping equipment, took us through Germany (where we joined the crowds in Berlin to watch the Olympic Games), Hungary (and the Budapest Music festival, with everyone in national costume), Bulgaria (with its back-to-front writing, and nods for nos), to Istanbul (all minarets and tramcars). But it left less impression. The third stands out clear in my memory—the majestic beauty of Norwegian fjords girded by mighty mountains; the deep clear depths; the coastal steamer. Up and on we journeyed through to the far north, where we saw the *aurora borealis*, splendid in all its magnificence of heavenly colours. There were reindeers and moose; Laplanders, shy and colourful; and the sharp cold of the Arctic. Then back again, through festoons of lakes and stately crimson pines, reflected in glory in the evening sun. Last of all came a few days in Leningrad—travelling by train; guarded by soldiers, sight-seeing by permission!

11

Then it was my twelfth birthday—and boarding-school. I insisted on changing from my pet name, Peggy, to my real name, Helen. The former now seemed childish, an obstacle to my determination to be a success, to grow up, to be popular. For here at boarding-school, too, the urgent 'need' was to impress, to be loved, to be wanted—a need that grew steadily stronger through these formative years. My vivid imagination found plenty of food for exaggeration in all the experiences of recent holidays, magnifying out of all proportion the happenings and personalities. I boasted of my introduction to Hitler at the Olympic Games in Berlin—weaving truth (that we *saw* Hitler at the lighting of the torch) and fiction (that I was introduced to him) so cleverly that I myself failed to remember where one ended and the other started. Linked with all this, there was a funny sort of feeling in the back of my mind that I had been sent to boarding-school because I wasn't wanted at home. I do not now think this was true, or fair to my parents; but these are the things that eat their way into a child's mind. It became a must to be popular, to impress; I was hungry to be loved and wanted—and yet I just wasn't that type. And so I lied, and magnified still further my fabulous stories—and it didn't work. In fact, it had precisely the opposite effect, and I found myself more 'unwanted' than ever.

There were growing needs at other levels too, not least the demands of a quick mind. I found a great urge in me to lead, and there just had to be an outlet for this. Even as a child I could see in a flash a possible line of action—how it could be accomplished—and its consequences! This led me into endless mischief—a scheme for 'escaping from the school block if a fire broke out in the basement cloakroom', for example. Needless to say, the route—through the gymnasium window, across the tiles behind the sewing-room, down a drain-pipe on to a small flat roof over the music wing . . .—had to be demonstrated; and the severe reprimand that followed when we were found halfway was well merited! I wanted to lead in 'good things', too, but seemed to lack the opportunity and outlet for the healthy, buoyant energy of youth.

Then, again, the urge to learn began to burn in my heart. I would have learnt anything they put in front of me! I longed to grasp knowledge, particularly proven facts, mathematical and scientific, with their orderly reasoning and accurate method. I wasn't, at that stage, interested in the 'end', or the out-working; I just longed to assimilate knowledge for its own sake. With this went a 'need' to win, to dominate—not others, but the facts themselves—to get a 100 per cent not in order to defeat other pupils, but simply for the satisfaction of knowing I had mastered the subject. If I didn't succeed, if I didn't gain the form prize, I'd failed—failed myself. And I probably also felt, deep down, that if I didn't do well I would fail to win the love and respect of my parents and brother, always so deeply important to me.

I joined the school dramatic society. As a youngster at home I had always been fascinated by acting and had organized productions of various plays which were performed in an oasthouse loft with footlights, curtains, stage props and everything else all meticulously correct. The actors were my sisters and any local friends I could inveigle to join us. Proceeds were in aid of mission funds. The school dramatic society, however, was a very different kettle of fish. But still I must be good at everything; I must succeed and be in the limelight. Even though I dreaded every moment of every rehearsal and, when it came to the actual performance, dreaded being in front of people, scared that I would make a fool of myself, yet this inner sense of need drove me on.

Somehow, in the middle of this, I became conscious of God. I've no idea what I thought of God, or who I thought He was; but there was Somebody, God, who was bigger than everything around me—and I needed Him. I needed something big. I needed Someone who was so big He could be bigger than me! And so God came in—and I was confirmed, along with the rest of the Upper IVths. It may not have meant very much. I'm sure I didn't understand the real meaning or full significance of it. But it was a sincere intimation that I realized my need for God. In a stumbling way, it was the conscious start of my search for Him. I *had* to take hold of this God. Confirmation appeared to be the way people got God—so I was confirmed. God knew—and accepted—and leant towards me to draw me steadily nearer Himself. I wasn't 'converted', it's true. But I'm not sure that God is as interested as we sometimes seem to be in the precise order of the steps that lead to true conversion. At any rate God drew near to me in it all, because He knew that my decision to be confirmed indicated a search for Him, for Someone bigger than myself, Someone I could draw on and depend upon, Someone to deal with all my complicated 'needs', all the complexes and worries that burdened my heart.

Sure enough, shortly afterwards I began to get guilt-stricken about the everlasting troubles I was in—talking in prep., talking in corridors, talking after lights-out—all necessitating a journey to the headmistress on Monday morning. Mounting that dreaded flight of stairs from hall to platform before the assembled school was a weekly affair for me! Not that I was really so much worse than the others. It was just that, when asked, I *had* to own up. Our school was run on a principle of trust and honour, with no staff supervision, particularly of prep. periods. The form monitor, a girl appointed each term from her own class, was responsible for maintaining discipline. I didn't even need to think when the inevitable question came; I knew perfectly well I must have talked, because I always talked. My great friend Kath and I used to sit together in class. The Monday came when Kath was ill and mine was the only hand that responded to the Form Mistress's 'Anyone talk in prep. on Saturday?' Oh, she said, so you're talking to yourself now, are you? But at break she sent for me, and over a cup of hot milk and a slice of marvellous currant cake in her little study, she had a heart-to-heart talk with me about the stupidity of breaking rules, the value of hard work, and above all, the preciousness of strict honesty. She taught maths, and from then on I was her star pupil!

There was a growing hunger for honesty from this time on. I had to have Someone big enough, above it all, outside, so to speak, who could cope. And I gradually became conscious that I could reach Him only if I were absolutely honest.

At this time, too, came a hunger for beauty. It was wartime, and everything was rather drab—plain white china, blacked-out streets, school uniform clothes—and the tragedy of war. My school was in North Wales, but my home was in Kent. I used to travel through London, and many times saw the blitz, and its awful horrors that, along with the poverty and filth, shocked me bitterly. I remember travelling back to school one day, crossing from south to north London in a bus, when an air raid occurred and panic broke out. Before we could even halt, women leapt from the moving bus, running for shelter in the nearest building. Suddenly a bomb fell on that very house, which crashed in a blazing mass. I watched with horror as Civil Defence men tried to reach the screaming women.

Young though I was, I was deeply upset by the meaninglessness of it all, feeling that something was fundamentally wrong. Surely Somebody was big enough to get all this into focus. I didn't then know who this Someone was. It was just a search going on inside me for Someone who could cope with all the world's needs as well as with mine. There was a growing consciousness that everything seemed so useless, so pointless. One went on talking in prep. and reporting to the Head. And on the larger scale, bombs fell and men and women were being killed. Others were hungry and nobody was really bothering to provide them with food. People in other lands had so little, and no-one seemed to care. We read the newspapers, we discussed in school current-events lessons—and through it all was this growing impression that life was meaningless. Where was it all leading? As I tried to probe deeper, I became scared. There was no-one to turn to, no-one to guide one through the rocks.

All this led to an intense reaching out after the Unseen, a developing perfectionist attitude that shrank alike from the sight or sound of destructive suffering, unalleviated poverty, and superficial insincerity. In the summer of 1941 I cycled from school to attend an SPG[1] summer school.

Shyness kept me from joining in many of the activities, but I'll never forget the short, daily, devotional sessions led by the chaplain, Father Charles Preston, a 'brown' monk of the Anglican Franciscan order. His face shone with an inner light. His words were always quiet and kindly, never tinged with sarcasm or frivolity, obviously utterly sincere and quietly satisfied. He drew me. He was never hurried or impatient. We sat in the still hush of the chapel and he talked of God, and my heart was filled with longing. Our surroundings melted and he carried me away into the great mysterious Presence of God, and showed me the nail-pierced hands and the out-poured love and the wooing heart of the Saviour.

One evening, with an inexplicable hunger after God, in absolute simplicity and forthright honesty, I made my first 'confession'. An overwhelming sense of release poured into my heart that now God knew all. He knew the very worst about me, and it was now up to Him. The burden of sin and failure and shame rolled away. I went back into the nave of the chapel walking on air. In the dim light I knelt and read that lovely hymn:

> 'Take my life, and let it be
> Consecrated, Lord, to Thee . . .
> Take myself, and I will be
> Ever, only, all for Thee.'

I meant every word. I walked out quietly into the moonlight, across the grounds, and a great joy flooded my whole being. I felt I could have jumped over the rooftops!

Home I went again, to put much right, with apologies and a real effort to be useful and part of the family. Then back to school, to pull with authority instead of against, to apologize for past wrongs, and above all to make an all-out attack against the spirit of lying, driving myself to confess every time to the one concerned, till very shame began to close my lips against the fantasies. I became a school prefect, and the head of my house. I longed to lead, and to lead well and rightly. I longed to be respected, not now for myself, exactly, but that I might lead others to put God first.

I tried earnestly to help others, to be kindly, to be sincere. I was an ardent Anglo-Catholic, regular at the confessional and the mass, every part of me stretching out after the Unseen Power who could meet all needs. And yet I was acutely conscious that *He* was not doing so. The needs were getting bigger; the hopelessness was more hopeless; the futility of life itself at times became almost unbearable. Whilst in church, I could lose myself to all the problems, bathed in the strange mysticism and pious ritualism; but on leaving the service, I had nothing—no power, no companion, no help to answer the daily needs and meet the daily problems.

It was this sense of emptiness and futility which led me to become a cinema fan in my holidays, to try to escape from the pointlessness of life. Every week-night and twice on Saturdays, if there were seven different films, I would try to lose myself in a make-believe world—anything to drown reality. Sometimes I would even go twice to the same film rather than suffer the boredom of an empty evening. There was a great emptiness, a great void in my life.

I helped at times at the Franciscans' headquarters in Peckham. Because of the blitz there were no Sisters living in that area, but I loved to stay in the guest-room of the Order's Home. There was a lovely church opposite, very still and quiet, in the midst of the rush of traffic, the whine of the air-raid warnings, the sufferings and poverty of the people around. Flickering lights burned in the red crucibles in front of each altar. All else was dim, with a vague sense of the unreal. I would creep in, and upstairs to the gallery, along to the Lady Chapel, many times in a day, seeking an explanation, a companion, a comfort to my heart's loneliness. Every three hours, the Franciscan monks had prayers there, and I knelt in the shadows, and drank in of their piety. Then back I would go to the poor tenement building opposite, with its rickety stairs, uncarpeted floors, peeling paint, and its many and varied visitors—mothers in distress for sons missing in the war; mothers in dire need of coal or food or clothing; mothers in depravity, in immorality and loose living—all came, and were helped, and went away comforted. In the evenings, there was the 'Club' for young people, teenagers who had been turned away from the Civic Centre Club for one reason or another, young men and women often from most unsavoury backgrounds. The dancing, endless records, and open rottenness; the weakness, and weariness and emptiness of life—I saw it all, but took no part. I had no interest, no awakened desires, just an apathy.

And all the while God was driving me to see that in myself there was nothing, absolutely nothing of any worth. It became at moments almost a desperate fight—the knowledge that God held the key, the answer; that He could make sense of it all; that without Him, it was a weary, stupid, empty, pointless, useless life. The burden of the world's need was crushing, overwhelming. Only God could meet it, could answer it; and yet, where was He? How could I find Him? How could I become part of His pattern, and lose myself in Him?

End Notes

1 The Society for the Propagation of the Gospel, an Anglo-Catholic missionary society.

2
Climbing To the Top

I left school a few weeks before the end of the summer term 1944, in order to have a short holiday and prepare to go to Cambridge for the 'long vac' term. This was a war emergency measure, enabling doctors to complete their nine-term university course in two years by making compulsory the fourth term from July to September each year, during the long vacation. My father met me in London and took me to a show—one of the Gilbert and Sullivan operas.

It was the time of the V.1 'doodle-bugs' and everyone was tense and fearful. There was little chattering in the streets and shops. When the siren alerted us of an approaching raid, everyone hurried quickly on their own business. Then someone caught the high whine of a V.1 and stood still, looking up. The action was infectious. We almost felt the very traffic stand still and draw in its breath, and all London waited. The whine grew; faces were strained. Each one knew we should make for shelters, but we had done it too often, and even shelters were not proof against these new weapons. A fascination was on us. Suddenly there was a sharp silence—a great pause hung in the air—then an explosion, a rumble, and a gentle sigh caught up and multiplied, as each walker hurried on his way, secretly ashamed of the first thought, 'I'm safe this time.' The urgency of self-preservation amidst all the fear and uncertainty almost pushed into second place the thought, 'Poor beggars, I wonder who got that one?'

And so I reached Newnham College, Cambridge, at the end of July, found my way to Clough Hall, and discovered from a list on the notice-board that I had been allocated room 8a, a small room, usually the bedroom attached to the larger sitting-room. The latter was to be a bed-sitter for this extra term, to enable the new 'freshers' to be accommodated. The place seemed vast and empty and silent. A cold fear of lone-liness clutched at my throat. Why had I come? I felt that I would never fit in to college life. I knew no-one. My trunk was pushed against the communicating door and, to try and calm my yearning to run away and leave it all, I started urgently to unstrap and unpack. Having piled everything on the small bed, and pushed books on the two small shelves over its head, I turned to place things in the drawers of the chest. I glanced at my pale sallow face in the mirror, and the untidy plaits hanging down over my shoulders—and noticed a card stuck in the frame. Leaning forward, with my arms full of clothes, I read, 'If you don't know anyone, and have nowhere to go after supper, come and have coffee in my room, no. 12, at 8 p.m.' It was signed 'Dorothy'. My eyes blurred, and a lump filled my throat. I quickly finished unpacking, my mind excited, homesick and fearful by turns.

A bell sounded, and I slipped into the corridor and watched and waited. Others walked by, chatting and nonchalant, and I joined the stream towards the 'hall'. It was still war days, and food rationing was strict, yet a good meal was served us at the serving-tables, each one collecting what they wished individually. The other students were friendly and would have drawn me into their conversation, but an overwhelming shyness (from a sense of inferiority, or a fear of not being able to hold my own) kept me a grim prisoner. Soon their conversation drifted into their own channels, and my monosyllabic replies became unnecessary. Tears pricked my eyes—my very first day, and I had raised up a barrier that I had vowed should never stand again! I wasn't hungry, yet didn't dare to leave, not knowing the rules. So I made a mockery of eating, following the lead of others.

Back in my room after supper, my loneliness and fear of this vast place with its swarms of intellectual students became so intense, the feeling of being submerged and lost in it all so real, that I lay numbly on my bed and planned how to write home and ask them to let me leave.

I must have dozed from sheer weariness of mental strain. Wasn't that a clock striking ? Glancing quickly at my watch, I remembered the invitation—8 p.m. at no. 12. I ran to the bathroom, washed my face, and made my way along the corridor. Knocking at the door of no. 12, I entered—and Dorothy glanced up, her face red, smoke swirling around her, as she knelt by the hearth, trying to coax a fire into existence! 'Can *you* make a fire?' The straight forward, urgent appeal, the complete acceptance of a total stranger in her room, the absurdity of the smoking pile in the grate on a hot, sticky, July evening—and the barriers were gone! We soon had a kettle on a cheerful blaze, and a group of about eight of us, I think, sat around on chairs, sofa, bed and floor, chatting about everything and nothing. I never quite knew who were newcomers like myself, and who were 'old stagers'. I don't remember much of all the chatter— I believe the coffee tasted a good deal of smoke and paraffin—but I know I slept well that night, with a quiet feeling of security that I had a friend.

Next day, Dot called for me for breakfast; and later took me down town, showing me the quickest way to the Anatomy block: then on to the shopping centre, to see which shops were the cheapest, and which the most reliable, for books, equipment, stationery, and so on. Home we went to lunch: then back again to sign on for afternoon lectures and to arrange about tutorials. She was with me all through that day. That was Dorothy. I am glad to say she eventually got her own degree, as well as helping crowds of us to settle in and to get ours.

The Anatomy Dissection Room! Never will I forget the first day, and my sense of unutterable horror. The very smell of formalin today brings back a wave of memories. The crowds, the noise of chatter and instruments, the growing silence through the morning as concentration mounted, the greasy books propped open on the benches, to show their brightly coloured, tidy diagrams of the pale mess we were handling—and to me, always a sense of unreality, of horror, almost of foreboding. I developed a deep sense of revulsion, that almost paralyzed my thinking capacity. A demonstrator coming round, neatly sorting out one strand from the higgledy-piggledy mass in front of me, and demanding name, description, origin, was one of the daily nightmares of the next three years that began to crush my hopes.

A paralysis seemed to settle over my mind each day at 9 a.m. as I entered the lecture theatre. All I had studied the night before seemed wiped out, like a clean slate. The lecturer's words never penetrated, owing to the gnawing fear that he might ask me a question and reveal my ignorance to all. And by 5 p.m., as I stumbled out of the block, and found my bicycle, joining the stream of humanity, I felt bowed and unable to face any more study. Fortunately, that first term, there were no tutorials, or I really might have given up and gone home!

Then came the first Saturday. What a wonderful sense of freedom! I lay in bed late in the morning, and wandered to the notice-boards after breakfast. Pinned up was a list for any to sign who would like to play cricket in the afternoon. Dare I? I loved it, but I hadn't been any good at school—and here they were probably all excellent. 'Hallo,' said a voice behind me. 'Do you play?' and there was a tall broad girl, with a beaming smile and thick wavy hair. 'I'd like to try', I replied diffidently. And that was the beginning of another friendship—with the cricket captain for the coming year. I was assured somewhat jokingly that if I knew which end of the bat to hold I'd be in the team! We had a wonderful afternoon, about fourteen of us. I wasn't good, by any stretch of imagination, but I was far from being the worst!

After tea, we went on the river in a punt. I was thrilled not only by the actual novelty of the experience and the loveliness of the countryside from Cambridge to Grantchester, but above all by the natural friendliness of the other girls, the very fact that they appeared to want me to join them. We went bathing together in the Grantchester pool. It was all wonderful and new, and I determinedly set about forgetting the past misgivings and fears, my insecurity and need.

On Sunday I got up early and went down town to Little St Mary to early mass. The quiet reverence, the sense of mystery, the peace was all as I knew it—and yet no-one spoke to me as I entered or as I left. I went again at eleven and saw several students there, but again there was no gesture of friendliness or welcome—and none of my little group of new friends was there. The day dragged on, but without the usual happiness of a Sunday. In the evening I went to St Benedict's Church, where the Franciscans worshipped. I spoke to one at the close of the service, mentioning my friendship with Father Charles. He was courteous, but distant—certainly not welcoming, nor proffering any invitation of friendship. I felt hurt and puzzled as I cycled home, and went to bed supperless since I had missed 'hall'. I didn't see any of my new friends about and realized anew the old pangs of loneliness.

And so a pattern began to set in, and with it a sense of belonging, and thus security, a pattern of work and study, mingled with friendships and Saturday outings. On certain days, however, Dorothy and the others didn't join us after hall. When I asked about this one week she told me they had a prayer-meeting daily between early and late hall, and a Bible study together once a week after halls. Would I care to go? Certainly! And so I went to my first Bible study and sat amazed as someone unfolded the mysteries of Ephesians 3, and even more amazed as they discussed it afterwards and freely quoted other parts of Scripture to support their arguments. Going back to our rooms later on, after a cup of cocoa and biscuits, I shared with Dot my amazement at their knowledge of the Bible and understanding of its contents. With a kindly smile she suggested that I should go regularly.

The following Sunday we met at late hall, and she asked what I was doing afterwards. Would I care to go with her to a Christian address? I had cut evening service and was feeling a little guilty at having been caught out, but she made no comment (doubtless having been praying that she might meet me there). And so together we went to the sermon arranged by the Cambridge Inter-Collegiate Christian Union (CICCU), a regular Sunday evening activity during University terms. We left our bicycles in the small courtyard outside—and they were stolen during the service, which rather effaced any memory I might have had of the sermon's subject-matter!

And so my first term passed. I was still closely bound to the Anglo-Catholics, sensing a need of the protection of organized religion and imposed discipline to control the hungry urges of spirit and soul, and possibly also to carry the ultimate responsibility for solutions for the world's great needs without involving me. I went regularly to confessional and mass, found peace of mind in formal obedience, but lacked any friendship or encouragement there. Alongside this were the happy, free friendships with Dorothy, Sylvia and other members of the Christian Union—games and outings together, sitting together for meals and, later, for the Bible studies and Sunday evening services—friendships that were open and clean and healthy. Their lives and faces radiated a happiness and peace that was very nearly infectious, and quite obviously satisfying. It was thrilling, just tasting the wonder of this level of friendship and of communion. Yet some inner fear, or reserve, kept me back from definitely identifying myself with them, so that I always remained just a little apart.

Four weeks' holiday followed, back with the family in our new home in south-east London—a lovely big house and a marvellous garden. And yet I missed my new friends and longed for the next term to start. My school-girl sisters all seemed very young and immature. And I don't doubt that to them I seemed stand-offish and a prig! The first 'V.2s' fell at this stage, and there were sufferings and shortages on all sides. The parish church had been badly bombed and we now met in a hall behind the Methodist church. But I did not appreciate the way the Vicar took the service, and missed so much the elaborate ritualism to which I was accustomed that I was not over-bothered about going regularly.

My second term began with mixed feelings—joy in renewed friendship and dread of the growing pressure of work, augmented by the fear of tutorials. Slowly I began to slip into the habit of joining the CU for the prayer meetings as well as for Bible studies. Then on Sundays I began going to church with them, sometimes Congregational, sometimes Brethren, sometimes Evangelical Church of England. Mr. Kenneth Hooker, I remember, preached the Freshers' Sermon on I Timothy 2:5, 6. I was stirred and challenged. I learned new hymns and choruses, and enjoyed the bright, alert singing. Even now I can remember the first time I sang, 'More about Jesus would I know....' My whole being was deeply stirred. We were sitting round the fire in Sylvia's room for a Bible study one evening late in October. I don't remember the study—the words of the hymn kept repeating in my mind. When the others dispersed, I stayed sitting on the rug, gazing into the fire, with a great longing stirring in my innermost soul. 'More about Jesus would I know....' As we sat, the two of us, in complete, unbroken stillness, it was as though a window opened and slowly, amazedly, in stunned awe, I glimpsed through—a twig sputtered on the fire, and it was lost. Again, urgently, holding on to the moment, willing the very presence of Jesus to become real to my soul, the glory seemed to shine, a light of great brightness. I hardly dared to breathe; it felt as though life was suspended, caught up, breathless. My heart filled with joy and wonder—and it passed. With a sigh, I turned to Sylvia. She was praying. It was already the early hours of a new day. We did not talk; I slipped away to my room.

During that Christmas term I think I reached a mental assent that the presentation of the gospel offered by the CU members was true, though I remained unconvinced that this need clash with ritualistic practice in church worship. I was tremendously intrigued by their love of Scripture, and I began to read avidly. I started at Matthew and slogged through to the end of the New Testament that term. Slowly I became gripped by it. First I read with them, then I read on my own, with a growing hunger to know what it was all about and to know the One who had written it. Everything began to fit into a pattern. I could see that they had something that I did not, and a great desire to have it myself was born. I stopped going to other meetings and other churches.

I went to all the CU activities I could—Bible studies, prayer meetings, missionary study groups, open-airs, church meetings. I agreed to it all in my mind. And the joy of new friends, the great happiness of being an accepted one of this new crowd, made life seem very good. As far as they were concerned they believed I was truly 'converted', and told me so. But as yet I had no peace, no heart satisfaction. The sense of need was still there, with the niggling question, Are you *sure* this is real? I *was* sure it was real *and* the truth; but I was also conscious that I lacked something.

The two other demands entered into fierce competition. One of the SPG home workers came on a visit to Cambridge for a long weekend in late November and especially asked to see me. I did not want to meet her; I did not want to face again the conflicting loyalties. But I could not politely refuse. The evening's talk left me unsettled, unhappy, yet completely unconvinced. Her argument, about the sacraments, the mass and the confessional in particular, no longer rang with authority as in the past. Her plea seemed to rest only on the historical symbolism of the church and not on scriptural reality. She stressed that in the church, symbolized by the priest, was stored all truth and the only means of salvation. The accent was on works, regular attendance at church, full confession, implicit obedience to all church discipline, and the receiving of grace only by the divinely appointed means of the sacraments in the hands of the priest. There was so much I did not understand. I felt so weak and helpless, like a baby, unable to answer her, or to give a reasoned explanation of my newly awakening faith. Why did I no longer need the doctrine of consubstantiation, the real presence of Christ in the elements at the mass? How dared I ignore the church's recognized means of grace? I did not know the answer then. All I had was an indefinable realization that something was missing, something wrong. I Timothy 2: 5, 6, the text of the Freshers' Sermon, came back vividly. 'There is...one mediator between God and men, the man Christ Jesus.' Nowhere in the New Testament had I read of the priesthood being invested in a human priest who could act as a go-between between myself and God.

The following weekend Father Charles came, and I loved him, simply and sincerely. I went to confessional on the Saturday evening, and to services all day Sunday where he was ministering and preaching. Again the old mystical attraction drew me and enfolded me, and my newly awakening soul cried out for fear of being submerged once more.

The other interest which competed for my support at this time was Communism. One Saturday, that same term, I was asked to 'help out' by playing goal-keeper for the Newnham hockey team—and my luck was in! Having practically no previous interest in hockey, I became goal-keeper overnight for the Cambridge University Women's team! Here I met the captain for the year, the quiet, efficient, outspoken leader of the Cambridge University Women's Communist Party! Our rapidly flourishing friendship involved many party meetings, and the learning of the fundamentals of dialectical materialism, and of the ideology that they said could answer all the crying needs of our poverty-stricken and suffering world.

Sundays became a three-cornered battle—Anglo-Catholicism in the mornings; Communism in the afternoons; Evangelicalism in the evenings. The CU made no criticism, neither did they retract the offered friendship. They did not argue, nor seek to persuade; they just went further out of their way to draw me out and help me.

As Christmas approached, news came from home that one of my younger sisters had mumps. We had all had chickenpox together several years before—and I had been very ill with it. Later we all had measles—and my eyesight was permanently damaged. So it was felt best that I should avoid the mumps if possible, and therefore not go home till January. Where then for Christmas? Two kindly Methodist friends, Jean and Mary, each invited me for a week to their homes—and I had a lovely holiday with each, in keen Methodist families. But there were ten more days before the quarantine would be ended.

Dorothy and Sylvia arranged for me to go to a houseparty. They even filled in the forms, looked up the trains, and handed me the timetable of events! So on December 27th I arrived at Mount Hermon Bible College, Ealing, with a suitcase and my fears, to join what turned out to be a gathering of keen Christian women training as officers for young people's camps and houseparties for the coming Easter and summer. I was like a duck out of water! I shared a dormitory with other girls of my own age—including a bright, red-headed girl of nineteen next to me whose brother was a medical student in my year at Cambridge. I remember they all seemed to have plenty of money—and I had practically none! Afternoons were free, and they all went sight-seeing, or to the ice-rink—and I stayed at home, ostensibly to study, unwilling to let them know that I could not afford it! It was cold—the last winter of the war—and coal rationing was severe. We huddled eiderdowns over our knees as we sat in the study room for morning Bible study and discussion groups. I bought a lovely new Bible complete with a commentary.

On the second day we were led in a study through the book of Genesis—shown how to summarize it, get hold of it, divide it up, and then share it with others. I was fascinated and took detailed notes. My ignorance of Scripture was appalling. Our leader told us that the day after tomorrow we would do the same with the book of Romans and suggested that we each try to read through it beforehand. I bought the IVF *Search the Scriptures* (a Bible study course prepared to help students). The next evening, after supper, I curled up by the fire in the sitting-room, and started out into Romans. I read. I studied each suggested question. I wrote the answer in the margin of my lovely new Bible. Time ticked on. I reached the end. With a satisfied sigh, I closed my Bible, uncurled my stiff and cold legs, and slipped quietly upstairs to bed. On the landing I met two girls coming from the bathroom. 'You're late', I said. 'You're early', they rejoined with a grin. I slipped into my bedroom, to find that it was 6.30 a.m. and these girls were getting up for kitchen duty! Later that morning, in Bible study, I fell asleep—and missed the very session for which I had spent all night preparing! But Romans has remained one of my 'favorite' books of Scripture ever since. Through its orderly array of facts, its clear systematic presentation of doctrine, I gripped the essential basic truth of man's need in his lost state of sin and depravity, and of God's provision to meet that need through the substitutionary death of Christ, of His wonderful power to make this provision real and vital to each individual by the work of the Holy Spirit, and, even more, of His amazing desire for fellowship and communion with us, His adopted children, by the daily indwelling and outworking of His same Spirit.

I sat through meeting after meeting and filled an exercise book with notes. I talked things over with many of the staff. I heard the different doctrines being carefully and accurately expounded, supported by Scripture. My mind could grasp it, and begin to take in the tremendousness of its import. I was beginning to get the 'jargon'—and yet I knew in my heart that I hadn't got *Him*.

The last evening of the houseparty there had been a bit of a row at the supper table and some sharp disagreements, largely revolving around denominational practices, particularly differing ways of celebrating the Holy Communion service. I had spoken up, albeit diffidently, in defence of the doctrine of consubstantiation, the 'real' presence of Christ in the elements of bread and wine. Had not Jesus said, 'This *is* my body...this *is* my blood'? But I became heated when laughed at. They asked if I could be truly converted if I was such a Romanist at heart?

I left the room and rushed upstairs, bitterly ashamed of having been drawn into the argument and losing control of myself. I gazed out of the window, and heard the happy chattering of the others down below. My mind went back through that week and all its teachings, through the past term and the multitudes of new influences and new friendships, back to my home and family and childhood. Suddenly, I flung myself on my bed, in a flood of tears and loneliness. With an overwhelming sense of failure and helplessness I cried out to God (if there was a God) to meet with me and to make utterly real and vital to me *Himself*. I raised my eyes, and through my tears read a text on the wall: 'Be still, and know that I am God' (Psalm 46: 10). That was all. Immediately the whole burden fell away in a moment. Be still and know God, whose name is 'I am'. Be still and *know Him*. Stop going to this one and that; stop striving to understand with the intellect. Just be still, and know Him. In that moment, a great flood of peace and joy and unutterable happiness flooded in, and I *knew* that He and I had entered into a new relationship. I knew God, and I knew in that moment that all the theories were true, and somehow He would work them out for me. The steady reading of Scripture in the previous months, the careful listening to doctrinal teaching both at the houseparty and in Christian Union meetings, had prepared the way. For years the Holy Spirit had been opening my eyes to a sense of sin, convicting me of my unworthiness before a Holy God. But now came the wonderful gift of repentance. God poured out His grace in forgiveness, in cleansing from all the uncleanness of sin, and in revealing, at this time, the amazing wonder of the friendship of Christ.

I went downstairs walking on air. Some of the other campers said afterwards, 'Your face was absolutely shining and we knew something had happened.' I went into the sitting-room and joined the rest for the final meeting. We sang a few choruses (I remember that I didn't know any of them!) and then our leader opened the meeting for testimonies. I didn't know what she meant by a 'testimony' so I waited. Silence reigned! She made another attempt to get us talking by pointing out what a blessing it could be to testify to others. Still dead silence! 'Well, hasn't anyone anything to tell of what God has done for her during the week?' I understood *that* and opened my mouth—and suddenly found I'd nothing to say! I who had been accustomed to speaking at any time, on any subject, found I was tongue-tied with an intense helplessness. I just didn't know what to say. I knew something had happened, and as I sat there with my mouth open I eventually somehow blurted out that I had met with God, and He had forgiven me and...that was all! Dr Graham Scroggie, a veteran Christian and much-loved Bible teacher, was there. He wrote in my new Bible Philippians 3:10, 'That I may know him, and the power of his resurrection, and the fellowship of his sufferings, being made conformable unto his death.' He said to me, 'Tonight you've entered into the first part of the verse, "That I may know him." This is only the beginning, and there's a long journey ahead. My prayer for you is that you will go on through the verse to know "the power of his resurrection" and also, God willing, one day perhaps, "the fellowship of his sufferings, being made conformable unto his death." ' And so started for me the thrilling journey of the Christian pilgrimage through this earthly life towards the heavenly eternity.

3
Enjoying The View

I went home next day wearing a bright new Scripture Union badge and carrying a shiny new Bible. In the crowded compartment of the slow Victoria-Bromley train a man diagonally across the carriage from me asked what my badge stood for. A little embarrassed, I explained that members of the Scripture Union undertook to read a set passage from the Bible each day, believing that it was God's book and that it would help them to live good lives. He asked for further explanations. Raising my voice against the noise of the engine and the wheels, I sought to reply—very conscious of the curious, rather antagonistic, looks of the other ten passengers, disturbed in their happy solitude. Rather red in the face, but determined not to run away from the challenge of it, I told him of my conversion the day before, and a little of the battle that led up to it, including my very real longing to know God and to obey Him. Our conversation continued until Shortlands where, with a sigh of relief, I stumbled out—only to find myself followed by my questioner! Quietly he placed a hand on my shoulder and wished me God's richest blessing in my new life. The surprised look on my face made him smile. Then he explained that my brand-new badge and Bible had told their own story and he had deliberately drawn me out to testify in public to help me start out in the way I should go on! I later found that he was a keen member of Christ Church, Bromley, which fellowship I myself soon joined.

Now began a period of great joy. Everything was wonderful. I loved every moment, every meeting, every opportunity for testimony. I had the inestimable joy of knowing that Christ was my Saviour. I joined the CWICCU,[1] and enjoyed fellowship with many new friends. I revelled in the security of being publicly committed. I had, as it were, burned my boats. I gave up going to the cinema and lost my desire to join in many of the activities which were merely the done thing—drink, smoking, make-up and dancing—none of which had ever held any very

29

real attraction for me personally. I wrote to my father and to the board of directors of my school who were paying my college fees, to tell them that I was now studying medicine to be a missionary. In all honesty I felt I must let them know just in case it affected their desire to continue paying for my education. Both wrote back and assured me that they were delighted and would continue to support me.

To be a missionary? I had known for years that I was going to be a missionary. Would my conversion change this? Did I need some further specific call? I had already, however, signified my intention of serving God abroad by joining the Inter-Varsity Missionary Fellowship, and the urge in my heart towards overseas missionary service was growing greater, not diminishing. It began to seem to me the *obvious* Christian duty of one and all. I was puzzled by others' lack of interest in missionary service, their lack of concern for the millions who were in darkness, who had never heard of the love of God.

Bible study was an excitement in those early days. I remember being fascinated by a series of ten Bible readings on the Song of Solomon. Next term we were going to study for ourselves the eleventh chapter of Hebrews—and Sylvia, our Christian Union leader, said that I was to lead the third study on verse 3: 'Through faith we understand that the worlds were framed by the word of God....' I spent hours with her preparing that study, and I learnt more perhaps in its preparation than in all I heard others teach in the subsequent weeks. It set for me the pattern for the future of thorough, accurate Bible searching and digging. It impressed me with my appalling ignorance of Scripture. All I had was just a vague rudimentary knowledge of some of the well-known children's stories, but with no real idea of where they came, nor of their context. Sylvia was studying Psalm 119 in the early mornings of each day and had made a beautiful and exquisitely neat chart of it, on one huge sheet, in all its sections. On this chart she was underlining in different colours each line of thought throughout the Psalm, and one could see a pattern emerging. To watch her studying the Bible in this way, to see her obvious love of it, stirred up in me a great desire to know more. Since my conversion I had also started Dr. Graham Scroggie's four-year Bible Correspondence Course, which meant, roughly speaking, studying a book a month. From 7 to 8 each morning was one of the happiest hours of the day, reading, studying, underlining, comparing, learning Scripture. And slowly it was taking possession, the new affection replacing the old.

Then, too, there was a growing realization of the possibilities of prayer. In April 1945 I went to the IVF Student Conference in Oxford. Again the old shyness of meeting new faces and the fear of being asked things I did not know tended to shut me up within myself. Everything was a bit high-powered. Open discussion groups tended to depress me as everybody else seemed to know so much more than I did! But the prayer sessions were the great moments of each day. God drew very near in those seasons of prayer, and I began to learn the liberty of the outpoured heart. Mildred Mitchell, daughter of the Home Director of the China Inland Mission, was there, and was a great help to me. She and I and another friend with whom I was sharing a room had a long discussion late into the night about guidance. How, we asked, can one be sure of knowing God's will? I remember her summarizing on her fingers in the following order:

1. Daily Bible reading, when He can speak to us through a passage, an example or a warning;

2. Daily private prayer, when we talk the problem over with the Lord; as we wait on Him in quietness, He can speak directly to our hearts;

3. The advice of Christian friends and those of greater experience, who may have had to make a similar decision in the past;

4. One's circumstances, including family or business commitments, health or even finance.

Then she moved her thumb to and fro in front of her fingers and said, 'Peace—in each one, in turn, individually and together. Let the peace of God umpire in your heart; if He is speaking He will give peace and silence other voices.' I still use the same basic principles in guidance today.

Then came the great problem of sport. I had played in goal for the hockey team that season, and now the cricket season was starting. I loved the exercise, and perhaps again I was influenced by the feeling that I could achieve something, gain my blue, prove to myself that I wasn't useless! But it all took time—daily practices down at the nets, and games or matches every Saturday afternoon. So I and other Christians involved began to pray about it and God challenged us to use our sport as a medium of evangelism, and to seek the captain of the team for Himself. That summer our cricket captain was a Christian Scientist.

She and I were great friends and enjoyed being together. As a result I began going to many meetings with her to learn what she believed and, in exchange, she came to a few of ours. Slowly the warmth of friendship offered in the Christian Union, and the obvious sincerity and warmth of conviction, backed up so solidly with scriptural accuracy, began to win her towards our faith. But in particular she was influenced by our growing friendship and intimacy. For me it was a wonderful day in the summer of 1945 when she openly declared herself for Christ and broke away from the Christian Scientists. I believed her to be my first 'convert'—and it was with a deep sense of grief and sorrow that I came to realize a few years later that she was won by my persuasiveness and personality to join in with us, rather than by the beauty and power of Christ. The former could not hold her, nor establish her, nor satisfy her, except along a fleshly level of human friendship. Only the latter could have given her new life, and strength and joy and courage. Many times since I have had to be careful not to over-persuade folk, nor to draw them only by the strength of my own rather dominant personality.

In the summer of 1945 I went to my first camp as a junior medical officer. What an exciting, wonderful fortnight! There were some six Christian women as Camp Officers, and fifty or so junior teenage girls. We had hired a lovely boarding school at Chumleigh, Devon, to give the girls a first-rate country holiday for a fortnight. I remember so clearly VJ Day which celebrated the defeat of Japan and the end of those six long years of war. One of my jobs at camp was seeing to the cleanliness of the toilets—and we had a mild epidemic of summer diarrhoea! At the 8 a.m. staff meeting I mentioned our urgent need of toilet paper to our Commandant so that she could add it to her shopping list. Just then the telephone rang. It was the local Vicar giving us the news of Japan's surrender and warmly inviting us all to a united service of thanksgiving in the village. 'Oh', I exclaimed in horror, 'the shops will all be shut. Whatever shall we do for toilet paper?' The group got down to praise and prayer for all the events of the day and the spiritual well-being of each young camper. Then the Commandant, in her closing prayer, reminded the Lord of our need of toilet paper. I think I was shocked! Certainly I was amazed that one could dare bring such a topic to the Almighty!

Later in the morning we all walked down to the church and attended the united thanksgiving. As we left afterwards, one pleasant-faced man came up to me, and said how very pleased they all were to welcome us to their village and to their fellowship, adding with a smile that he was the local grocer and would be delighted to do anything he could to help us. I blurted out my tale of woe, our need of toilet paper! And in half an hour twelve rolls were delivered to the school where we were staying. Truly God had answered prayer.

Near the end of camp, we had an 'object-service'. The youngsters all went out, two by two, to collect or make some object mentioned in the Bible. These objects were all gathered on the table in the meeting-room, each with a small label giving the Scripture reference of where this object could be found. There was a piece of bread: 'I am the bread of life'; a wild flower: 'even Solomon in all his glory was not arrayed like one of these'; a bunch of grapes referring to those brought back by the twelve spies of Moses' time; a jaw-bone calling to mind one of Samson's exploits. There were many others, among them a lovely plaited ring of thorns. The text attached to this was Mark 15:17, 'And they...platted a crown of thorns, and put it about his head.' At prayers that evening each leader in turn spoke a few words on one of the objects. I was terribly nervous. I had never tried to speak before without hours of careful preparation! I gazed at the table in a sort of numb horror, and the crown of thorns stood out so clearly, I could not see anything else. I was number four to speak—and I willed the others not to choose the crown of thorns! Eventually I stood up to take my turn, lifted up the carefully plaited ring, and then closed my eyes in a sudden wave of nausea from sheer panic. My heart was pounding; my mouth felt dry. Somehow I pulled myself together, and spoke of His suffering in my place, His receiving my condemnation. At last it was all over. One of the staff mentioned afterwards how touched she had been to see my earnest prayer before I spoke—and my heart lurched! Yet in the years ahead, I was to learn that she had been more accurate than I then dared to believe, as I discovered new avenues of prayer, when, as Paul puts it in Romans 8, the Spirit groans within us and our hearts go out to God in wordless prayer as we do battle with the unseen powers of darkness, knowing nothing but a horror and fear of failure.

During the next Christmas term life continued to be very full and wonderful and worth while. I was asked to become an executive member of the Christian Union for the coming year. When reading the doctrinal basis which I would need to sign, I was struck by the statement that I believed the whole Bible to be the inspired word of God. I had not yet read it all, and felt I could not honestly sign this until I had read it right through. This stirred me to a concentrated effort to complete my first reading of the Old Testament by Christmas, before the end of my first exciting year as a newly born-again Christian. I was deeply stirred at the thought of being trusted with leadership. I had always longed to lead, and now strangely I feared it. I felt so unable, yet knew that I could rely on His enabling.

During the term I was asked to go to the home of Dr. Joyce Goodchild at Nottingham to give my testimony at an informal Saturday evening meeting. This was another milestone; my first public speaking engagement! I remember preparing with such infinite care and practising in the bath, speaking to the taps, timing myself exactly to the limits I had been given. What a thrilling and wonderful weekend that was! Every new experience seemed to be just one more part of this new mountain-top of joy, one more view over the glorious surrounding peaks. It was to be the start of a precious friendship, and forerunner of several such meetings in the coming year.

I was chosen to play goalkeeper not only for the University Women's team, but also for Cambridge County Ladies hockey team, along with Olga, the University captain, and Jessie, another Newnham undergraduate. Together we set out for Colchester in the week after Christmas for the week's tournament of Eastern Counties at Clacton. We lived at the Girls' Friendly Society Hostel at Colchester, sharing together an attic dormitory, since Clacton was out of reach of our student allowances! The first night there, I fought, as many others have done, the brief battle with pride and self-consciousness, and then got down on my knees by my bedside for prayer. They were both quiet till I climbed into bed. Then in the dark, Olga (the leader of the University Women's Communist Party!) bluntly demanded the point of what I had done. What benefit did I think prayer was? I knew so little how to explain, but I tried to share my assurance of the truths I had learned during the past year. Throughout the week, at meals, on buses, in the evening round the sitting-room fire, we argued Communism versus Christianity. I felt very helpless and seemed to make no impact on Olga at all. Jessie just listened and watched; but during next term she quietly joined the Christian Union. She was never very dramatic, just quietly sure of Christ's love for her and her love for Him. What a joy and encouragement this was to me, even as I saw Olga slipping away from us and apparently hardening against us.

In July I went to Keswick with Dr. Goodchild. We were to be a mixed bunch, about eighteen of us, in three big bell-tents. Three were girls from Nottingham University, there were Mary and myself from Newnham, and the rest were factory and shop girls, many of whom had been converted during the previous year at Dr. Goodchild's Saturday night At Homes. It was a memorable Keswick for me. Dr. Goodchild, Mary and I went a day earlier than the rest to set up camp. First we had to scythe the long grass! It was blisteringly hot, the end of a heat-wave, and it was exciting pitching the tents and preparing. Food rationing was still severe. That very week, bread, cakes and flour rationing commenced. We managed to procure all necessary permits and bought the week's stores—a tongue, the week's butter ration, etc.. These were placed in large basins in the small stream at the bottom of the field. We went to the station to meet the other campers and returned to find the butter gone, basin and all! We reported our grievous loss to the police, and set about helping everyone to unpack, to make palliasses and to settle in. I felt sure the thief would return for the tongue! As dark fell, I slipped from our tent and sat on the running board of the car, facing a hole in the hedge the other side of the stream, with a large mallet on my knees—my one urgent prayer that the Lord would not let me kill him! I heard him approach; I raised the mallet; he neared the hole; I sneezed! and he fled!

The camp presented great difficulties. In spite of sincere efforts on the part of the student element to prevent it, we found ourselves divided into two groups, university and others. Friendliness was interpreted as patronage; squabbling and petty unkindnesses started and it looked as though the whole purpose of the camp would be wrecked. Then the rain came—and it poured steadily for three days! The field was a quagmire, the stream a rushing torrent; everything was soaking and there was no way of drying it. Then I became ill. Frantically Dr. Goodchild sought for a solution. The Convention secretary came to our aid, and arranged for us to have the loan of the local drill-hall. The IVF men came over and cleaned it out for us, loaned us camp beds and dry blankets, and started a shuttle service to move us in. Now we were all together in one big room around a central table, except for Dr Goodchild in a little side room. And I lay ill on her bed with a mild attack of pneumonia. When everyone was settled in she joined them for a short prayer meeting. Together they praised God for everyone's kindness to us and His provision for us, and prayed for His outpoured blessing and especially for my speedy recovery. Immediately He began to work. Apologies were made, new friendships began as they all mixed together. I recovered quickly. We were all deeply conscious of the Lord being vitally in our midst.

There followed in the summer another and longer camp at Weston-super-Mare, to which secondary school-girls from all over England came. Again it was far from easy. To begin with there were divisions amongst the leaders, some of them denominational in their origin, others arising from differences in their approach to the whole question of discipline. The campers were quick to sense the lack of unity among the officers. Rules were broken continuously and at one stage near-anarchy reigned! Instead of the usual harmless ragging and fun we were faced with vicious and spiteful gang warfare. During that camp, however, I personally began to sense clearly His hand upon me for leadership. There was a new sense of dignity, a great assurance of His will, a fresh vision of what I believed He yearned to do for us and through us. I was conscious that the girls responded to me and appeared to respect me, and this gave me a deeper desire to help them. I was not myself deeply involved in the staff difficulties, since I was a relative outsider. This gave me more time to be quiet and on my own. It was at these times that different girls came to me with their problems, and I was amazed to see how the Lord clearly gave me the words to help them. Then I found a great longing to take a series of Bible studies with any who wanted to come, and I readily obtained permission for this from the other staff. In those meetings I 'found my feet', so to speak, and first began to realize that He was giving me a gift of imparting to others that which was precious to me.

The following Christmas term, at the start of my third year, a member of the CU executive and with a great desire to win other students for Christ, I faced up to His demand for complete, unquestioning obedience. I felt at that time that this involved me in Believer's Baptism as a public testimony to my faith. Asking the advice of certain spiritual leaders at Cambridge, I was deeply shaken by their apparent antagonism, one of them even quoting Galatians 3:1-3 to me. I became clearly convinced in my own mind, however, that for me my spiritual advancement towards maturity in Christ demanded this step of obedience, even though it might lose me Christian friends and valued fellowship. Possibly this was for me the first touch, the first hint, of the years of loneliness that lay ahead, though I knew nothing of this then. I went to Nottingham to stay with Dr. Goodchild for a weekend in November, and at her church I was baptized. It did not mean anything very definite so far as a new experience in grace was concerned—but for me it was a definite step of obedience.

Every third year the Christian Union in Cambridge organized a Mission to the whole university. The time for this was now upon us. We had been preparing for weeks. Every day had meetings arranged. We had given out leaflets and personal invitations and it was easily our greatest concerted effort of evangelism of my three years at the university. On the Saturday previously, Olga had arrived at my room to borrow my hockey tackle (I wasn't playing that year became of the Mission, and also because of my tripos!). In the evening she returned and I offered her a bath—a luxury to her as she now lived in very poor digs as a research student in nuclear physics. She accepted gratefully after a little pressure. Because of the shortage of coal, baths were still rationed. She then joined me round the fire for hot buttered crumpets! We had been praying hard; it was a long time since we had had any contact with her. She was friendly and open, obviously lonely, and enjoying being with us. We invited her to the Mission and she agreed to come.

An amazing week followed. I seemed to live for Olga's conversion. I was round at her digs all hours. I waited for her for meetings. We discussed and argued, I prayed and wept. For the first time since I entered Newnham, I incurred late gate fines—and Miss Chrystal, my hall tutor, was so thrilled to think I was coming out of my shell, she paid them for me! And on the last day of the Mission Olga acknowledged a mental assent to the truth of the gospel. Then a fight began. We read and studied, prayed and discussed together till all hours. I obtained leave to stay up in Cambridge for the first week of our vacation in order to stay with her in her digs. I yearned over her in a way I had never previously experienced. At last she said that unless God Himself revealed to her heart the assurance of her salvation she would not go on believing. Doubts poured into my soul; I nearly lost my own faith. Could God fail her? Was it possibly *not* true? To me, this was just a glimpse of the great agony of identification to which we are called. I held on, almost in blind faith, almost in despair. And just before Christmas peace came. Olga quietly knew a tremendous assurance and depth of reality. She was hungry for fellowship, Bible study, knowledge, everything she could receive. In January we went together to Nottingham and she, too, was baptized.

A few weeks later, at the beginning of the Lent term, Princess Aida Desta of Ethiopia came into my room and said that she had just received a letter from the Headmistress of Clarendon, her old school, telling of their urgent need of a matron as their own had been suddenly taken ill. We got down on our knees and laid this need before the Lord. As we arose there was a knock at the door. Olga came in and blurted out: 'I've given up my job; it seems inconsistent with my faith as a Christian. Pray for me that God will show me what he wants me to do now.' Within ten minutes we were on the phone to Clarendon to ask if Olga would be suitable as assistant matron. That weekend she went to take up her new duties! It was there at Clarendon that she assisted at the annual China Inland Mission Conference and received her clear call to missionary service; and for many years now she and her husband, Douglas Abrahams, have been preaching and teaching the gospel in Japan.

In March I had two amazing dreams on consecutive nights, all the more extraordinary as I very rarely dream. The first was a walk alone across snow-covered fields, very white and dazzling. There was a road up the hill, with a fork, leading down through dark sombre pines. Suddenly a garish farm-wagon, in gaudy red and green, came roaring down the hill, skidded, slewed down into the pine forest, and was soon lost to view. Then the deep impenetrable silence fell again. I drew my eyes away from watching the empty track where the lurching wagon had passed, and turning, climbed the stile and started across the white waste, climbing, climbing. My breath hurt, the cold was cruel, the pure white burned my eyes, the lonely silence weighted the frosty air. I neared the top, strangely fearful, suddenly conscious of a great destiny. Each step ached; each gasping breath tore at my chest. There was a sense of foreboding, of death. To reach the top was essential, yet it spelt death. Then came the final struggle—tremendous brightness, clarity, purity, far distant views. I felt caught away from myself, apart, separate, and I seemed to die, shrivelled in the icy cold, yet reaching out into the blazing light. I woke in a sweat of fear, and yet a sense of tremendous triumph, as though I had been vouchsafed a glimpse into the future. I reached out for my Bible, opened at my daily reading, and suddenly Obadiah 17 shone out with joy, 'Upon mount Zion shall be deliverance, and there shall be holiness; and the house of Jacob shall possess their possessions.' It was a call to an utter dedication, a going forward to possess *my* possessions in Him, my Deliverer, my Sanctifier.

The next night again I was caught up, as it were, in a dream of great vividness and horror. It was a dream of big crowds and pressures and fear. I found myself in the streets of London, being hunted, driven, threatened by evil men, surrounded and impeded by endless traffic. All was noise and bustle and colours, confused and terrifying. Again I woke in fear, in horror, pleading Him to deliver me. And clearly a voice seemed to ring in my ears, 'They need *Him*!', and my life's task was unmistakably clear. He was calling me to seek and to save the lost, to be identified with them as *He* was, in all that wretchedness and humanity, to snatch some from the burning, the fear, the hysteria, and draw them into His peace and grace.

Finals came and went. The last weeks were a frantic rush of study, continuing late into each night. I remember as we entered our Biochemistry practicals—my best subject, the one on which I was relying to pull me up to 2nd class honours—a slip of paper was passed to me. My brother Bob, it said, who was a student at St John's College, was very ill with angina. Everything went from my thoughts. The invigilator, Dr Baldwin, came round to see our prepared notes as to what we intended to do to work out the problem set, in order to give each one permission to use the delicate apparatus—but my paper was blank. He looked at me astonished, knowing my keenness for the subject. I silently passed him the scrap of paper. Immediately seeking permission from the other examiners, he hurried me out, got me into his car, and drove off to the hospital named on the slip. There we learnt that Bob had a mild attack of Vincent's angina and would like a bottle of lemonade! With my heart at rest, we flew back to the labs. and I was given the full three hours from then, and managed to pull off the desired 2nd class honours degree!

July found me travelling once again to Keswick, just two of us, on bicycles with small tents, to camp under Speaker's Rock. It was a wonderful and blessed week. On the Tuesday I went up to the mountains alone and spent all night before the Lord—Miss Ruth Paxson had spoken to a women's meeting on 'That great big capital "I" ' and my heart yearned to know full and utter surrender, that it might truly be 'Not I, but Christ'; that I might fully enter into the experience and understanding of the crucified life, identified with my Saviour. Once again, I became ill at Keswick with a sort of gastric 'flu. After two days in bed others kindly made it possible for me to go home by train instead of bicycle.

Camp followed, an exciting and enjoyable fortnight. But just at the close the sickness caught up with me again. I managed to get home, and arrived on the day my family had left to go abroad for five weeks' holiday. I was to look after the place in their absence! For two weeks I was really ill. The doctor wanted to move me to hospital and to send for my parents, but I dissuaded him, not wishing to spoil their holiday. He then told me that I had poliomyelitis. Slowly the pains and stiffness wore off and I got better. But a great spiritual battle began to rage. During the illness I found I didn't want to die; and now that I was getting better, I didn't want to be a missionary! This shook my faith—my faith in myself, perhaps; my faith in my experience of salvation and, since it followed so hard on the time spent at Keswick, my faith in the validity of my consecration. Yes, He began to shake everything that was shakable, to get me free for Himself. But I wasn't sure any longer what I wanted, nor where to turn.

End Notes

1 Cambridge Women's Inter-Collegiate Christian Union, which in those days was organized separately from the men's Christian Union.

4

Down Into The Valley

Slowly, painfully, there had been growing within me during this past year a sense of incompleteness, a gnawing fear that possibly I wasn't being absolutely honest. Outwardly everything was fine! I was a leader of the Christian Union, a keen promoter of missionary interest, an ardent student of the Bible, as well as being a third-year undergraduate with hockey and cricket blues. Yet there was a feeling of cloaking something over, that somewhere there was a higher level of thinking that I hadn't yet reached, that perhaps I wasn't even looking for as yet.

I was conscious of 'explaining away' certain texts of Scripture, such as 'He that committeth sin is of the devil. . . . Whosoever is born of God doth not commit sin . . . he cannot sin, because he is born of God' (I John 3:8-10). I feared this chapter, with a strange kind of horror. I remember going to a series of Bible studies on the letters of John, and hearing what was no doubt an excellent and scholarly explanation of such passages based on the tenses of the verbs in the original Greek, and so on. Though the interpretation was completely satisfying for the one who taught us, deep inside myself I was not personally convinced. I was frightened of indulging in spiritual dishonesty, of accepting explanations just because they suited me, suited what I wanted to believe, and in this way quieted the qualms of my conscience.

Then again, there were 'expressions' of our faith, certain words and phrases used to express conservative evangelical thought, which doubtless were perfectly accurate and scriptural, but which I suddenly realized had no definite spiritual content for me. I remember so clearly with Olga, in the days which led up to her conversion, how precise she was. 'How do you know it is true?' she would query. 'He is in my heart; He has changed my life', I would reply. 'But how?' 'I received Him as my Saviour; I am cleansed in His blood.' Slowly there entered a gnawing doubt. Was this just evangelical jargon? Was there a reality behind the shadow of words? Olga's conversion became desperately important to me, not only for her own sake, but for mine also. Should she be truly convinced of Him in her head as well as her heart, I would be sure, because I knew that she would not be converted merely through an emotional need (as possibly I had been). And yet at the same time I felt ashamed of this mental attitude of clutching at a straw to convince myself.

It was a method of 'establishing assurance'. Assurance is one of the great glorious truths of the evangelical faith, one of God's great gifts to us from Calvary. Scripture assures us that we may know Him, that we may know that we have eternal life (I John 5: 13). I lacked this assurance as a permanent reality in my life. At one moment I lived in it and enjoyed it, testified to it and taught it to others. Then would come a wave of depression and fears and doubts 'lest that by any means, when I have preached to others, I myself should be a castaway' (I Corinthians 9:27). I had to persuade myself. I had to encourage others to persuade me. I had been baptized as a public committal and testimony, a burning-of-my-boats. It was to me an act of obedience, but it was all part of my effort to receive assurance. I claimed the promises of Scripture, 'He that hath the Son, hath life', 'Lo, I am with you always.' I underlined them in my Bible. These were the facts on which my assurance stood, and still I lacked it as a consistent permanent experience. I accused myself of trying to work up what could only come down from above.

Again there was a certain 'exclusiveness' in the outlook of many Christians I knew that an inner voice urged me to question, the attitude that this was the truth and there was no other. One part of me accepted this utterly. I was deeply convinced mentally of the absolute reality of the truth and value of the Scriptures. But beyond this, I was not so sure. How much was tradition? The phraseology that we used to express the truth—was it not too small to include the whole greatness of truth? Was it not possible that others, though using such different phraseology, were actually describing the same truth? I had experienced a tremendous sense of liberation when He revealed Himself to me. I left the Anglo-Catholic way of worship. I felt the terminology of the mass and of consubstantiation was unscriptural and sadly misleading for hungry souls who were seeking Him who by His own blood 'entered in once into the holy place, having obtained eternal redemption for us' (Hebrews 9:12). And yet, as I looked at the life of Father Charles, humble, gracious, consistent, severe and yet withal gentle, he revealed Christ to me. How was this reconcilable?

Another growing fear was that of excusing behaviour with which I knew I ought to be dissatisfied. I suppose this was the outcome of various conflicting doctrines. On the one hand, there was the grand sublime teaching of our eternal security, of our assurance that He who had undoubtedly saved me on Calvary would equally certainly perfect the work and bring me into His eternal presence; that He who had caused me to be born again, adopting me into His family, had promised never to forsake me, never to cast me out, never to loose me from His hand. All this was of grace, infinite wonderful grace, received by faith but never won by works. Yet on the other hand equally, I read that to him who overcame to the end would be given power (Revelation 2:26). To him also was the promise given that his name would not be blotted out of the Book of Life (Revelation 3:5). I read also that there shall in no wise enter into heaven anything that maketh a lie (Revelation 21:27). And there was the story of the unforgiving servant who, although previously forgiven his debt, was delivered over to his tormentors till he should pay every penny (Matthew 18:23-35). Much of the teaching of Scripture was undoubtedly conditional. There were great 'if' passages.

In the mental strain which resulted from all this, I tended to call certain sins weaknesses—or human frailties—and thereby to excuse them. It was nicer to speak of exaggeration, probably due to over-enthusiasm in a good cause, than to speak of lying. Yet I felt I was practising mental dishonesty in making such excuses for myself, and trying to establish assurance. Again it was nicer to speak of 'warm friendship' than 'inordinate affection', and thus to vindicate the over-exclusiveness of affection between two of us that shut out a third, or at least made her feel uncomfortable and unwanted. It was easy to excuse myself in my own heart with such arguments as 'Surely the friendship could not be sin? Were we not being blessed in witness to others?' Or again, 'Was I not a Christian Union leader, respected and honest, and no-one appeared to criticize my behaviour?'

Then slowly there dawned a sense of exhaustion. The joy and excitement of the first three years suddenly seemed to drain away. When I left Cambridge and started at West London Hospital there was not the same fellowship. At the same time there were new temptations and difficulties. Working in a small group instead of in huge classes, I could no longer hide in the crowd and avoid the questions I so dreaded. Work began to get on top of me; unhappiness, loneliness, fear, inferiority, all began to be acutely present. At the same time Bible study and prayer became perfunctory instead of joyous. I no longer wanted Christian fellowship but had to stir up the desire. Witness continued, but with no real faith or expectation of seeing results. Looking back it is easy to realize that at least part of the explanation lies in the fact that, like many of my fellow medical students, I was suffering from overwork and strain, resulting from a very full programme. I did not understand this at the time, however, and so thought that this exhaustion meant spiritual failure.

Throughout this difficult period, a coming-down from a mountaintop in order to strike out for another peak, as I could see later, I had a horror of being thought inconsistent. I'll never forget going to Oxford in June 1945 for the Varsity Cricket match. It was to be played on Saturday, but rain caused the match to be postponed. On Sunday morning, on our way to the cricket field, Mary and I met the Rev. W. H. Rowdon, our own vicar from St Paul's, Cambridge, who was the visiting preacher at St Ebbe's that morning! We were carrying our cricket bats over our shoulders. When he stopped to speak to us, asking where we were going, I remember the surprised tone of his voice when he said, 'Playing cricket on a Sunday?' We continued to the match in sober silence. We had given it no thought! We were part of a team, away from home. Could we have let them down overnight? The match started with no joy for us. Oxford women batted first and made 173 for 8. Then Cambridge, believe it or not, were all out for under 30. I was opening batsman and carried my bat for a duck! But my heaviness and dissatisfaction of heart had nothing to do with the score. Were we wrong? Others inferred we were. I must be personally convinced. Was *God* telling me not to play games on a Sunday? Ironically, I remembered my school days when, as an Anglo-Catholic, I refused to take part in House sports on Ascension Day, taking a lone stand against much determined opposition. Was I not willing to take the same stand now for love of my Saviour as I then took out of reverence for my God?

All these gnawing problems, and the sense of possible dishonesty, led to an almost desperate effort to convince myself. Olga's conversion had been a tremendous buttress to my faith, but could it still be possible that it was all emotionalism, a myth, a soporific? Could it all be untrue? I was urgently aware that I must know the answer, one way or another. I daren't ask openly. I was afraid others might think as I thought, and my questioning might undermine their faith. If one started to question, might it be the start of a snowball, till the whole fabric of faith was shaken?

So the determination grew to teach others, and in this way to convince myself! I threw myself whole-heartedly into summer camps—Varsity and Public Schools in 1947, Inter-Schools 1948, Barbican Mission to Jews 1949, and so on. On Sundays I became a Girl Crusader leader. I loved it. We had our class at home where I was living while studying at the West London Hospital, in a room behind the garage. Two boy Crusaders came in one week to help me cement the floor and clean the place up. Next week, two or three of the thirteen-year-old girls came and helped me paint the doors and windows. Then we made forms and table, using sawn logs for the legs. We drew and painted big thermometer-charts for our inter-group class competitions. Days were full and the girls were as keen as I was. The preparation involved for the regular weekly class was good for me.

One Sunday, arriving a quarter of an hour before class, I overheard two twelve-year-olds earnestly discussing the pros and cons of cinema-going. A great yearning grew in my heart not to fail these youngsters, and so our 'Keenite Class' came into being. My only free afternoon was Saturday, so it was given out that any twelve to fourteen-year olds who would like to do regular Bible study could come to my home on Saturday from 3 to 4 p.m. Some of the other leaders were skeptical—Saturday afternoon for a Bible study? But they came! They crowded our small room! I can see them now. The twins, the one thin and wiry, the other round and cosy; Jean, bright-eyed and keen; two little scraps, probably only elevens. Each week anything from eight to sixteen of them would turn up. We set out on the Minor Prophets! I have never learnt so much about the prophets as through those weekly classes—their historical order and setting, spiritual content and purpose, personal application and reality. I loved teaching those youngsters. And yet there was still a haunting fear that I was not willing to be weighed up by my own standards.

Ward services in the West London Hospital were another outlet. There was no nurses' Christian Union at the hospital then—we started one a year later—and there was little fellowship in witness. I obtained permission from the Board and Matron and the Chaplain to conduct these services, covering three or four wards each Sunday. I didn't really believe I would see conversions. It was an act of duty, the kind of thing a Christian medical student should do. I carried a little portable harmonium, set it up in a ward and gave out hymn sheets I had bought. Then, playing with two fingers as best I could, I sang a solo (because no-one sang with me!), I led in prayer, read from the Bible and preached a short message. Then gathering up the hymn sheets and folding up the harmonium, I would move on to another ward. I spent two hours doing this every Sunday evening for almost three years, constrained by a 'must', a deep personal challenge to fulfill this duty even though at times it was an unpleasant one. Others joined me in this service: a fellow student, Pauline Bousquet, our Casualty Officer, Derek Rose, and at times people from my home church.

There came the day when I accepted the challenge to go to the men's wards as well as the women's. I started in the men's orthopedic ward. What a mistake! The occupants were sixteen fit and healthy young fellows, some with their legs strapped up in the air following a motor-cycle accident, and others of similar kind. 'What hymn shall we start with?' I never made that mistake again! 'Roll out the barrel', from the far end of the ward! I gallantly plodded through No. 7, 'Fight the good fight', whilst they lustily roared 'Roll out the barrel'. In the second verse a boot landed on the harmonium. Through the third verse I prayed earnestly what I should do, especially with regard to the boot! At the end of the verse, I picked up the boot and hurled it back down the ward. I didn't play cricket for Cambridge for nothing! The fellows were so impressed that a mere girl could chuck straight, I had no further trouble at all. They all listened quietly, even intently. And then the thrill; after the service one young lad in his early twenties gave his heart to the Lord! My first known convert in those ward services. It challenged me deeply. Why had I not seen others? Why did I not expect conversions? My coward heart answered hesitatingly, Because your life does not measure up to Scripture, 'Be ye holy; for I am holy.'

It didn't really matter what people thought. It didn't matter what it cost. One just had to be all out for Him. Sometimes there was a sense of desperation in my heart that days were closing in, and it was our responsibility to tell the heedless and careless, the indifferent and the sarcastic, or else their blood might be demanded at our hands. With it all came this tremendous challenge to holiness. We must be holy. I fought against the apparent cost involved, the realization that I must give up anything that got in the way of 'Jesus only'.

In the wards and in front of other doctors I was very conscious of inferiority, or rather a fear of what others thought. This crippling shyness just had to be subdued and overcome by a daily dying to self, by a vigorous painful effort. Yet there was very little success. Almost crushed, and deeply discouraged, I was invited one day by a nurse to accompany her to see a film. I asked no questions. Coming off duty from casualty at 6 p.m. I joined her and we travelled together to Richmond. We arrived at the theatre late and found it packed out. We stood at one of the doors craning our necks and, taking turns to be in front, were able to watch a little. The film was *Three Miles High*, an amazing record of courage and endurance, of magnificence and beauty, of challenge and determination, filmed in the Himalayas on the Tibetan border. It told the story of twenty years of missionary endeavour against tremendous odds. Immediately, something deep within me stretched out to join this team, to throw in my lot with such people. Major Leonard Moules of the Worldwide Evangelization Crusade was showing the film and was at the bookstall afterwards. I hung around till most people had left, and then went to speak to him. We talked and my heart thrilled. He gave me literature and he invited me to his Mission Headquarters. At last we parted and I returned to hospital, but with a new joy, a new certainty, a new challenge.

Then the struggles redoubled! I had been twice to the Keswick Convention. The addresses I heard there had offered me just what I wanted, all that I was striving after, but they didn't show me how to enter into this wonderful full life. It was all there, the challenging ideal of this glorious life of holiness and victory, of purity and of power. But there seemed no way of bridging the gap from my despair to this liberation. I agreed to all that Keswick had offered me. I agreed to all the teaching of Scripture. My whole being acknowledged that this was the truth, but—there was always that 'but'—my heart wasn't involved in it all. Every part of me cried out that there must be heart involvement, communion within this truth. It was quite plain that mental assent without heart involvement was ultimately impossible.

I was filled with a tremendous desire, a great hunger after Him. I must go on at any cost. I no longer cared what it would mean, or what it might involve. I was willing even to leave my home and join in mission life at WEC Headquarters while still a medical student at the West

47

London Hospital. There at Headquarters I lived in a hot-house of spirituality. Students from Emmanuel College, Birkenhead, from Cliff College, from Swansea, Redcliffe and Mount Hermon Bible Colleges surrounded me, all keenly devoted to His service. Talk at meals was largely of the Lord. I listened in also to organized discussions on different doctrinal and theological matters such as the difference between Arminianism and Calvinism, pre- and post-millennialism, foreign and indigenous missionary strategy, and found myself profoundly ignorant. I joined prayer meetings for revival which went on into the small hours, alive and on fire with a passion for souls and the zeal of the Holy Ghost. I watched lives that were real, earnest, separated, that radiated light and warmth and truth. I longed to be fully one of them. I pleaded with the Lord. I trusted and stepped out in faith, claiming the promises. I tried to fulfill every formula that each one testified to in their own experience. And still my heart felt cold. Sin in my life seemed to mock at my endeavour.

Looking back, it is easy to smile at the intensity of feeling and also the excessive introspection. Yet how extremely real it was at the time. I readily grant that chronic introspection of this type can become very unhealthy, mentally as well as spiritually. As has often been said, a carrot cannot grow if it is continually dug up to see how it is getting on. Nervous individuals can make themselves chronically ill by taking their temperature four times a day and noting each little rise and fall. Likewise, persistent introspection can work one up into a highly tense state of spiritual sickness.

I fell into most of the traps possible. I made myself almost ill through my preoccupation with my own holiness—or rather lack of it! It took a long time to recover from that mistake, which need never have been made. Of course, I never can be holy! How simple, when one realizes that the Lord knows me as I am in all my weakness, loves me, and waits to impart Himself, His own holiness, His life, living in me.

Each conviction of sin was good in so far as it led me to trust the only One who can deal with sin. But if the sense of failure only made me more acutely conscious of my own miserable state, it had achieved nothing. The Lord allowed a growing realization of failure in each of the different realms mentioned, in order that He Himself might fill the vacuum. He longed that I would become more preoccupied with Him and less with myself.

5
Trudging On

For four years I had known that there was something wrong with my voice, some trouble in my throat. Where previously I had been a member of various choirs I was now no longer able to sing in tune. There was a growing huskiness, a feeling of a 'potato in my throat', accompanied by a slight difficulty in swallowing. I was vaguely afraid, but did not seek advice. Now rapidly the condition worsened, and it became virtually impossible to speak above a strained hoarse whisper. At times I was reduced to using a pencil and paper when I wanted to converse. In March 1950 I entered my own hospital where I was a student for an operation under the ENT specialist for 'benign nodes on the vocal chords'. I was given a small single room adjoining the women's ward. When I came round from the anaesthetic that Friday evening, the walls were cheerfully panelled with large amusing diagrams of the war-time celebrity and such slogans as, 'Wot! No talk-

ing?' An attendant nurse hastened to impress on me that on no account must I make any attempt to speak. Anything I wanted must be written down. The vocal chords must be completely at rest for four days following the operation.

The Tuesday following, while I was alone and resting, a wonderful thing happened. Slowly, an intense awareness developed. Someone was with me. My heart thrilled; the room seemed charged with His presence; a great sense of *light* was borne in upon me. For two or three hours I was deeply aware of a wonderful companion spirit, not hearing anything, nor seeing anything, but just knowing.

Later, lunch was brought in. The vision dimmed, and yet something had occurred, a new start had been made. From that morning, a hatred of sin was born. Till then I had hated the consequence of sin, the shame of failure, the fear of exposure. But somehow I lacked a hatred for the sin itself. In fact there was a curious liking for it; in its way it was pleasurable. I wished to be freed, and yet I wanted to enjoy it. Suddenly I now knew an intense hatred of all that had crucified my Lord. It was the turning-point for me. The downward path from the peak of happiness, with its puzzlements and questionings, was arrested. Suddenly the next peak stood out clearly ahead. The encircling mist had lifted and left the way clear and inviting. He who was calling me on to service overseas was standing there, gently smiling, promising His presence and companionship and enabling, telling me to look forward and upward, not backward or inward. Suddenly the months of struggle and longing were over; I was satisfied. Not that my doubts were exactly explained; they no longer seemed to need explanation.

The next day the surgeon visited me. He stood at the foot of the bed and commanded me to speak. I had been longing to do so for five days but now found nothing to say! The moment was deeply important to me. Could I speak? At last, fearfully, expectantly, I tried. A deep wave of disappointment and nausea swept over me as I made a noise like the barking of a dog. He examined me carefully, and then curtly said that the operation appeared to have been a failure, but that if I liked to come back in six months he would see if he could help me. With that he left the room; the sister and nurse followed him. I was alone, deeply alone. A wave of giddiness, darkness, heart-ache, came over me. My medical career, let alone my missionary career, was in the balance. My head reeled under the cruel blow. Stunned, miserable, I just lay, tasting the bitterness of the empty future, the mockery of all that had led up to that moment.

Slowly another voice began to force itself through the night in my heart. 'Can you not trust Me?' it seemed to whisper. 'Did I not meet with you only yesterday, beckoning you on to Myself? Why are you so fearful?'

My heart rebelled. Was I not crushed, unable?

'Have you not used your voice for your own ends, for your own glorification, for years? I will give you a new voice for use in My service.'

I just lay there quietly, and slowly peace filtered back into my heart. I felt that His promise was not only with regard to my natural voice; that was just a kind of token. It was to be my whole life, my inability to be holy, my longing after *Him*—all this He was promising to indwell and fulfill.

That Friday I went home. It was Good Friday, and my mother's birthday. Roughly speaking, my condition was much the same as when I entered hospital. When I spoke it was in a strained hoarse whisper. In the evening of Easter Sunday I went to church with my sister. The Rev. Tom Darlington (who was a missionary in China during the Boxer Revolution) was preaching. It was a powerful sermon, appealing to us to let God the Holy Spirit have His way in our lives, taking possession, infilling, making holy with His holiness. Afterwards a group of my old friends gathered outside the church, discontented and unsatisfied. One challenged me directly: 'Helen, do you know what Mr. Darlington was preaching about in your own experience? Is this really something for us now, or only in old age after years of suffering and trial, such as he himself has gone through?' Clearly, without a moment's hesitation, I said a joyous *'Yes!'* ringing with assurance. And suddenly I realized He had healed! An amazed hush entered my heart, a tremendous feeling of awe. *He* had touched me. I looked forward, upward to Him from that moment, and knew that I must always go upwards and onwards, whatever happened in the world around. His call was to live always unto *Him*.

Six months later I went to see the specialist in outpatients. He was honestly amazed when he first examined me and asked if I had been treated elsewhere. I assured him that I had not sought help at any other hospital, and I tried to testify to him of the power of God to heal. However he merely commented that such cases were known, on occasion, to show considerable regression, and the matter was closed.

Finals followed in three months. What a grind it was! Parts I and II of my final MB comprised some twenty examinations—papers, practicals, orals—a fortnight's gruelling nightmare. The results were read out a short while after I had left my last oral, and though I had passed Part I, I had failed Part II. It was a blow and disappointment, and yet there was the certainty that in six months I would try again and by His grace succeed. So I began a six months' 'trial of endurance', studying all hours, from an early 6 a.m. rise until after midnight. Harry and Gladys Jones came home from Congo that autumn. Mr Jones needed immediate surgery for a large gastric ulcer and came back to us at Mission Headquarters for post-operative care. About this time his wife developed bilateral pneumonia. I had the privilege of caring for them and spent many hours in their room. We talked much about the work which they had had to leave and that was the start of my knowledge of the need of the Congolese.

The day came to go again to Cambridge for Part II finals. We read Isaiah 58 in the early morning, the chapter of my missionary call, especially verses 6-11. I remember Harry taking up verses 13 and 14 and praying that I would keep holy the Sabbath day in the coming week, and that *He* would cause me to rejoice in Him as a result. This time He crowned the effort with success. What a thrill, ringing home to say I was through! A doctor!

There followed ten days' wonderful holiday at a Christian guest house near Bournemouth where the Joneses were now recuperating. There was a Salvationist there, an elderly man, I remember, and he had no jersey! I knitted him one, incorporating the Salvation Army badge of Blood and Fire. I gave it to him as a New Year gift, but really it was a 'thank-you' to the Lord for seeing me thus far.

Harry, Gladys and I had wonderful times of prayer and Bible study together, as well as many walks and discussions. It was a time when I could think over many questions that had been shelved during the years of intensive study. Gladys Jones was a trained church worker. Together we discussed and prayed over many problems, particularly such matters as hurtful friendships, inordinate affections, the loneliness of the single woman missionary, and the battles involved in this loneliness.

On 15th January 1951 I returned to WEC Headquarters as a candidate! I really felt I was getting somewhere at last. It was Monday when I arrived, and I moved into one of the rooms on the first floor of the hostel, sharing it with another candidate, a girl from Sweden. On Tuesday, after breakfast and washing up, I was told to go and wash the cement floor of the toilets and bathroom on the women candidates' floor. I found a bucket and brush, and set to. Strange as it may sound it was almost the first time in my life that I had done a household chore. I was always the trainee-doctor till that moment! I scrubbed out the first toilet and started on the second. A candidate entered the first with muddy shoes. The floor was still wet. When she left, I returned and did the first again. Meanwhile, someone else entered the second. This continued for some little time with a rising sense of frustration. I'd never get them clean! I'd fail, my very first day in training, to achieve the task I was set. Tears pricked at my eyes. I scrubbed on, muttering, 'Devil, get out of here! Devil, get out of here!'

Someone came in, and standing still a moment watching me, heard my muttered comments. She laughed and startled me. 'Now I understand why our cakes are all burnt today!' she exclaimed. 'We're in the kitchen underneath, and you're sending the devil down to us!' She left amused. But there was another quiet spectator, Elizabeth, who was in charge of the candidates and who had given me this task. After a short pause she gently asked me why I was so upset. I explained the cause of my frustration. 'For whom are you scrubbing this floor?' she replied. 'Why, for you, of course; you sent me here.' I've never forgotten her answer. 'No, my dear. If you are doing it for me, you may as well go home. You'll never satisfy me. You're doing it for the Lord, and *He* saw the first time you cleaned it. That now is tomorrow's dirt.' It was quiet, godly wisdom that has followed me through many years in Congo.

My six months at Mission Headquarters were wonderful days! Early morning rising at 6 a.m.; serving tea to missionaries on furlough; a quiet hour of prayer and Bible study; breakfast and washing up; family devotions, worship and prayer until 10.30; coffee; then 'chores' till high tea at 5.30 p.m.; and those amazing thrilling evening meetings when I learnt what *prayer* meant, labouring, believing, claiming, rejoicing—all across the world from Colombia to the Philippines, holding on for missionaries and nationals, governments and projects, in persecutions and triumphs. They were tremendous meetings! And so to bed by 9.30 p.m., worn-out and happy.

Chores! What memories there are! I was put in the laundry for most of my six months with Ruth, a grand girl who had just completed her course at the WEC Missionary Training College in Glasgow. Elizabeth showed me the first day what was expected—through the bath (soaking), to the boiler (boiling), to a tub (rinsing), up through the mangle (beware of your fingers!), out on the lines (beware of the mud!), back through the rollers, and so, neatly piled, into the airing cupboards—some thirty-six sheets, pillowcases and towels plus white overalls and the men's shirts for the first day. Starching of collars was an interesting extra! Somewhat fearfully, yet believing for the best, I made a start (merely adding my own personal laundry to the vast pile, to save time) and went through the exercise exactly as instructed. A distracted Elizabeth arrived somewhere around 3 p.m. when all the sheets, *etc.,* were nicely out on the lines in the back garden. 'What *have* you done?' I glanced round fearfully wondering if I'd set the house on fire inadvertently. 'Everything is *green!*' I learnt that you don't mix coloureds and whites—the only white articles at the end of my first day were my green ankle socks, shrunk to child's size with happy boiling!

Ruth and I soon discovered how to work the rollers with a minimum of effort. She fed the clean sheets in, and they passed out on to a board balanced on my outstretched legs as I perched on the table, reading aloud to her—always from the very *best* books in the WEC library!

I was tried for one week in the kitchen, but that was disastrous. Saltless solid lumps floated in a tasteless soup served up as porridge; Welsh rarebit came out like chewing gum surmounted by a sickly yellow sauce. The male candidates could stand no more, and despite grumbles of a 'stiff-necked people' (from over-starched collars) I was duly returned to the laundry.

Norman Grubb, our home-base leader, had recently visited Ruanda and the work of the Church Missionary Society and came home deeply moved of the Spirit at the work of revival he had witnessed there. He spoke many times in morning prayers of the way of the cross, not only for conversion, for the start of our walk, but also for the daily continuance of that walk: 'keeping short accounts with God', the immediate confession of sin, as soon as the conviction registered, listening to the still small voice of the Spirit; the quick claiming of the cleansing of Christ's blood and renewal through forgiveness; the restitution to any offended brother; the joy and happiness of 'walking in the light'. My heart was stirred. I wanted all God had for me. With this renewed desire for close, continuous fellowship with the Lord came an increased sensitiveness towards sin. I began to feel the sinfulness of pride and selfishness and lack of prayer burden, as well as of exaggeration, or deceit, or quick-temperedness. The open way of sharing and fellowship became precious and vital. The candidates were brought into an even deeper unity and joy.

Whilst staying as a student at Headquarters I had made a deep friendship with another girl candidate. We were drawn very close to one another. The urge of affection grew. I found myself hurrying home from hospital to be with her. Then slowly I knew that I was on a slippery path that I had walked before; a demanding friendship that did not want a third person to share it with us. I can thank God now that there were faithful senior friends on the staff who understood, and who separated us. Then the other left for the Far East. I saw her off—and a great blank filled my life for weeks.

Now that I was a candidate my face was set to join her in her missionary sphere. I had been at Headquarters only ten weeks when the staff clearly and firmly told me I could not be accepted for that field. I understood—and thank God, by His loving grace, I agreed and knew that they were right. Then where was it to be? I was a qualified doctor; I was living in a missionary training school. But so far I had no knowledge of where He wished me to serve. Every week missionaries on furlough from any of thirty different countries pleaded for more workers, and almost all of them added, 'specially we need a doctor'. The need was on every side. I could see it clearly! I longed to serve, in turn, in at least six different places. But how could I be sure which it should be?

Daily I asked the Lord for clear guidance, for a definite word from Himself. One Tuesday in April 1951 I tore off the block calendar in the dining-hall and was puzzled by the text there: 'Repair the house of the Lord' (2 Chronicles 24:4; 34:8). Why had this been chosen? I pushed the slip of paper in my pocket and forgot it. On Thursday I received a letter from an old school friend (who had been converted in recent years, a fact of which I was unaware). She enclosed that same tear-off calendar slip saying that the Lord had urged her to send it to me. Amazed, I went and read carefully through those relevant chapters but still could not see what the Lord was saying to me. On the Friday at morning Prayers, the leader of the leprosy crusade of our Mission read that same verse, from the same calender slip, telling us how the Lord had burdened her through it in special prayer for Congo, our oldest field in the Mission, with over 1,500 leprosy patients in our care, and over a quarter of a million Congolese looking to us as a Mission for their medical care, as well as for spiritual and educational help. And yet, after thirty years of pioneer work and earnest prayer, we still had no doctor to offer them. Surely this lack was as a 'breach' in the wall of the church of God in Congo, and *He* needed us to be burdened to 'repair the house of the Lord'.

I could not get away from it. Three times in one week the Lord had spoken. But I did not *want* to hear. Not *Congo*, Lord! Anywhere else but there. But I'm an evangelist, a preacher, a pioneer. I want to go to a people who have never yet heard the message of salvation. Congo is an established church, a ministry to Christians.

On Sunday, as I made my way to my own home church, I prayed again earnestly that He would speak so certainly that I could not be mistaken. The vicar read the story of Balaam and his ass (Numbers 22) and he preached on verses 31 to 33! 'Three times the Lord has clearly spoken to you', he said. 'But you do not want to heed. You want something special and dramatic. Beware! He may not be patient for ever. Heed his voice in His thrice-repeated message and obey—and He will bless.' I went home very soberly, but completely convinced that He would have me to serve in Congo.

On 27th June the Mission quarterly staff meeting was taking place. Amongst much other business five candidates were being considered for acceptance into the Mission. I was called to the kitchen, and asked to carry some fifty cups and saucers to the hall next to the library where they were meeting. The swing door into the hall was stiff and heavy. Gingerly I leant on it, pressing, balancing the heavy tray. Very slowly I edged my way in, and carefully along the narrow hall. Suddenly I realized that I was overhearing the staff meeting. I could not hurry! I tried to close my ears, but inevitably I listened for two long agonized minutes to myself being discussed. Lowering the tray on to the table, I fled—back down to my beloved laundry, my face scarlet with shame as I realized what others thought of me—proud, always knowing better than others, unable to be told things or warned or criticized, difficult to live with, and so on.

I carried a basket of sixteen sheets upstairs and hung them on the eight lines criss-crossing the garden. Turning to walk back for another load, I heard a sharp twang. Swinging round dismayed, I saw my precious day's work lying bedraggled in the mud. Suddenly the Lord showed me the funny side of it, and with a rush of laughter, I said aloud, 'Hallelujah!' Those in the staff meeting had seen the disaster from the library windows and had come hurrying out to help. They were suddenly arrested and puzzled, as they heard my exclamation followed by a chuckle of dry humour. It was infectious, and grins slowly spread from face to face. When they returned to their discussions my fate was sealed. I was accepted, a sense of humour being considered heavier in the positive balance than all else in the negative!

That morning my Scripture Union reading had been Psalm 60.

Verse 2 had gone straight to my heart, 'heal the breaches thereof'. It was the same phrase! Called into the august presence (the meeting consisted of all missionaries who were then on furlough, together with the home staff, about forty of them all told) I was asked if I had any special Scripture to read first. Asking for Isaiah 58:1-11, I was suddenly shaken, as the reader went on and read also verse 12, 'Thou shalt be called, The repairer of the breach.' After various questions, and loving exhortations and warning, I was given the right hand of fellowship to become a member of the mission.

I had a short holiday, and in September sailed for Belgium to learn French at the Colonial School in Brussels to be followed by a course in tropical medicine at the Medical School in Antwerp. They were eight memorable months. The very first day, knowing practically no French at all, I attended a dictation, with about 140 other missionaries, designed to divide the class into two groups. I understood nothing at all of what was read to us, but wrote down the sounds as best I could. We duly heard the results, and I was listed in the 'forte' class (the strong ones!)—presumably because seventy folk, wishing to be in the 'faible' class, had handed in blank sheets. I attended our first lecture without understanding a single word, till suddenly I heard my own name! My neighbour told me to stand up—and then everything seemed to happen till I was in tears, the lecturer shouting in fury, and the class torn between sympathy and amusement! Never mind, that Professor taught me French in four gruelling months, and I can never be too thankful.

In Antwerp, there were more lessons to be learnt. I lived with our missionaries, Mr. and Mrs. Boerop, and what an atmosphere of sacrificial love there was! I had three weeks in bed with jaundice, following a savage dog-bite when cycling home from school one day. They couldn't do too much for me. Then I followed it with mumps! Their kindly concern knew no bounds. Their teenage daughter Joke and I shared a room, which by day became dining-cum-sitting room. Their boy, now a missionary in Europe, helped his Dad in a hundred and one jobs about the house, and in the Bible shop in the front room.

Then Joke became very ill. There was no extra money available. They trusted me to care for her. Two other missionary doctors on the tropical course kindly came and visited her also, giving their services freely. It was an anxious ten days, of high, swinging fever, interludes of delirium, much pain and increasing weakness. She needed penicillin, but we had no ready money available. All extra money had been spent on me during my four weeks of sickness. We were down to 'brown bread and sugar' meals. Urgently, importunate prayer was made. Each injection of penicillin was 'prayed-in' individually, being provided by the local chemist only as we produced the necessary francs. Yet all the time there *was* money in the shop from the sale of Bibles. I was puzzled; my faith was sorely tried. Their radiant quiet confidence and unswerving loyalty to principle, and through this, to their Lord and Saviour, was a tremendous lesson to me. Joke got better. My course ended. I left their home deeply blessed spiritually by their faithful sacrificial fellowship throughout those six months.

Deputation work followed for three months, then a round of farewells to friends and family. There had been a most generous response in many meetings that enabled me to buy the necessary personal needs and medical equipment for the years ahead. Shopping, packing, labelling; visits to consul and shipping agents; vaccination and inoculations; the time passed all too quickly.

And so the great day dawned! I remember at the evening fellowship at Headquarters, Thursday, 12th February 1953, giving my testimony and thanking the staff for 'putting up with me' for the past three and a half years. This was greeted with a resounding 'So you should!' which put me right off, so that I couldn't say any more! The following morning, Friday the 13th, saw me off at Liverpool Street Station at 9 a.m. to catch the boat train to the London docks. I recall the great crowd of staff and candidates on the platform, the last 'phone call to Mother to say goodbye, the accordions and hymn singing, the handshakes and tears. Then the whistle, the green flag, and we're off!

6
Made It!

The *Dunnottar Castle* sailed late, leaving early next morning as
dawn broke over the grey mist of London dockyards. There were seven
of us in our party which consisted of two returning missionary couples
going out for their third or fourth term of service, an American and his
wife from the home base setting off for a six-month tour of our African
fields, and myself. With morning Bible studies and prayers, hours spent
happily in language study, writing letters and reading, and informal
Bible studies with interested passengers in the evenings (the newly
appointed Bishop of Kampala led us through the Epistle to the
Romans), our days were happily full, as we steamed through the straits
of Gibraltar, to Genoa, along the length of Italy, across the Mediter-
ranean to the Suez Canal, in ever-growing heat to Aden, and at last to
Mombasa, in Kenya.

The journey had various highlights—principally the excitement as
we rounded the easternmost point of Africa. A radio message requested
us to change course to due south, instead of south-west, following the
coast. A sick sailor on an oil-tanker needed urgent medical care and we
were the nearest ship carrying a doctor. We steamed steadily south to
the Equator and next day met the tanker. We all watched the short,
early-morning drama of the visit of our doctor in one of the lifeboats,
and his return with the sick man suffering from appendicitis. Then our
steamer began a large swing to steam westwards for Mombasa.
Suddenly the note of the engines changed, and there was another alter-
ation of course. All on deck waited to know the reason. Eventually we
spotted a white fleck on the horizon. We steamed slowly towards it and
then watched, fascinated, the real drama as several men were rescued.
Now in the last stages of despair and agonized thirst, they had been
adrift from the Seychelles Islands in a small fishing boat with no stores,
compass, or sail, for over nine days. Had we not gone off-course for the
oil-tanker, no ship was likely to have seen that tiny distress-signal shirt,
and those men must all have perished. How wonderful are the ways of
God, directing a great liner carrying hundreds of passengers to the very

spot in the ocean where nine pathetic men so urgently needed help! The hearts of all of us were strangely moved that day as once again we swung westward and steamed for Mombasa.

Africa! Customs formalities, unbearable heat, arguments and noise, flies and thirst—and at last the train for Nairobi. We had a carriage to ourselves—three double-bunk bed compartments, and one large four-bunk compartment for me and all our luggage. Excitement? I couldn't eat or talk. I was barely able to think for it! I rushed from side to side of the compartment so as not to miss anything. At each station on the long slow climb up from sea-level to 5,000 feet I leapt down, to stand on African soil, to read the name of the station and its height, to sense the *feeling* of Africa, its smells, and ways, and moods.

We spent a week in Nairobi at the Church Missionary Society's guest house, and for the first time the realization of *fear*—in those days it was fear of the Mau-Mau. No-one was sure who was friend, who foe. Even a faithful, willing house-boy might have been forced to take the bloodoath, and your life might be in danger.

Up country again to Namasagali—then the lake steamer to Masindi. The heat and dust, the gorgeous frangipani flowers, the leisurely pace, and the horror of seeing someone's precious tea-chest containing a china dinner service haphazardly and unconcernedly tossed from the boat to quay, or quay to boat, with a resounding thud, remain indelibly imprinted on the mind. On again to the edge of Lake Albert. I recall the small steamer, the customs formalities, the happy, indiscriminate mixture of French and Swahili. And so we reached the last lap of the journey. It was stiflingly hot as we crossed the lake, not a breath of wind. Mosquitoes and flies owned the atmosphere, and I felt suffocated under my mosquito net. Out on deck at 5.30 a.m. I watched, straining, for the first glimpses of the Congo as a glorious sunrise broke across the lake, bathing the mountain range in golden crimson light. I was home!

It was a deeply thrilling and moving moment, a climax to all that had gone before.

The Mission truck was there. Jack Scholes, my field leader, was at the jetty side, a distinguished-looking man with shining white hair. Beside him were two Africans, and Jim Grainger, his right-hand fellow-worker. They joined us on board for breakfast, everyone full of chatter and news. There were letters of welcome from all the missionaries—almost overwhelming to a newcomer! One from Jessie Scholes to me quoted Zechariah 2: 5, 'For I, saith the Lord, will be unto her a wall of fire round about, and will be the glory in the midst of her.'

Customs formalities completed, we loaded up the truck and were off!—up that tremendous, breath-taking escarpment of countless hairpin bends and magnificent views back over the lake. We stopped at an Africa Inland Mission station for lunch—and what a welcome they gave us! Everyone made me feel I was coming home! Then on again to the Brethren station of Nyankunde, where we were to stay the weekend. There I met two missionaries who had been with me in Belgium. We played some strenuous tennis—*not* what I had expected in Congo! We arrived at 5 p.m. and that evening an urgent call came for the doctor, but he was away, and I was asked if I would care to go. As we approached the distant forest village we heard the awful death-wailing. We entered the round mud hut, circling between the outer and inner wall in growing darkness, our eyes smarting from the wood smoke, till we reached the centre. Slowly we became accustomed to the dark and the noise, and I knelt beside the still figure, stretched on the earthen floor, already chilling and stiffening, surrounded by naked women (his wives and relatives) rocking to and fro on their heels, wailing abysmally.

After a weekend of rest and fellowship we set off again. Five of us went with Mr. Scholes in the two-ton lorry, and two with Mr. Grainger in a three-quarter-ton pick-up. Down from the mountains and wide-open grasslands we drove, into the endless forests, crossing rivers, passing village clearings, on, on—two days of travel, till we reached Ibambi as dusk fell on Tuesday evening, 17th March 1953. My reading that morning had been in Genesis 35: 'Arise . . . go up to Bethel and dwell there....' Truly I felt this was my Bethel and, like Jacob of old, my one desire was to make an altar there to God for worship and service.

Trees were decorated in welcome. There was even a floral arch as we approached the home up the long avenue of palms—a red banner with cotton-wool words 'Welcome to Ibambi'. We were surrounded by a great and growing crowd of Africans and whites. I remember the talk and noise, the laughter and singing. First to greet us came Jessie Scholes, with her 'Welcome *home*, dear'. Then Pasteur Ndugu, senior elder of the African church, stepped forward to welcome us all, and myself in particular as the 'new' missionary, in the name of the church.

'We, the church of Jesus Christ in Congo, and we, her elders, welcome you, our child, into our midst.' I never forgot that moment, or those words. What a privilege for a young missionary to be 'their child', one of them, to be cared for, nurtured, loved and taught by them.

Everything was so new, so strange, so exciting. The early morning tea at 5.10 a.m. so as to be able to be ready to go over to the Bible School for morning prayers at 6.30 a.m.; those wonderful morning Bible studies (that term in Hebrews), and the struggle to get beyond the language barrier; breakfast and family prayers followed, and at 9 a.m. over to the dispensary—an empty room in the old Mission Office building, with cement floor, tin roof, wide verandah and large windows. It had so little equipment—just a camp stool and table, some tea-chests with boards across as shelves, a handful of basic medicines, and a few slips of paper hurriedly torn up from an exercise book for report cards. We had no common language but made up for it with an abundance of goodwill. And suddenly there were swarms of patients! noise, heat, smells, waves of nausea, everyone talking at once, crying babies, running sores.... It was dusk before all had drifted away, and I was left cleaning the room, sorting out what there was of drugs, frantically making lists of what we urgently needed, almost overcome by waves of weariness and in the background a slight dread of inability to cope. Then came supper, family Bible study and prayers, cocoa, and so to bed about 10 p.m.

So began the routine—at first with no helper, Congolese or European. But it was a beginning. The Scholes were thrilled, as I was, in the vision the Lord began to unfold, even in those early days, and did all they could to help and encourage me in what seemed a monumental task, the creating of an official and efficient medical service for the church in our Heart of Africa Mission[1] area.

One day that first month there was an evening call to go to see a catechist, Abamangi. Jack Scholes kindly drove me out to the village, some twelve miles off the main road. As we went he talked to me of Mission ways, of the Lord's dealings, of the possibilities of success as a missionary. 'If you think you have come to the mission field because you are a little better than others, or as the cream of your church, or because of your medical degree, or for the service you can render the African church, or even for the souls you may see saved, you will fail. Remember, the Lord has only one purpose ultimately for each one of us, *to make us more like Jesus.* He is interested in your relationship with Himself. Let Him take you and mould you as He will; all the rest will take its rightful place.'

At Easter I went with the Scholes to Poko, 120 miles north, for the weekend conference. I gave my testimony in Swahili! It was my first public attempt to use my new language. After the service, I met Elizabeth Naganimi, a widow of about my own age, a sweet Christian woman with a great desire and longing to serve the Lord. He spoke to her that weekend, and she soon came to join me as my first helper and close friend. Oh, the laughs we had in those early days together as she spoke Bangala and I stumbled through Swahili, and neither of us understood a word of each other!

Following the conference came four weeks working at the Red Cross Hospital at Pawa, fourteen miles north of Ibambi, travelling to and fro daily, learning more of tropical diseases, their diagnosis and treatment, and the necessary laboratory work involved. One day, on the rounds, I noticed a teenage boy dying of tetanus. Dr Kadoner mentioned that he was from our Mission. I went back after the ward round and tried to speak to his parents, with my few halting words of Swahili. When I felt they understood, I laid hands on the boy's head and prayed (in English!) in the name of our Lord Jesus Christ for his healing. As I prayed, I felt the fever leaving him. I was awed, and a little fearful. Next day, I asked Ida Grainger to go with me and talk to the parents in Swahili and to pray with them. She did, and learnt that the boy had slept peacefully all night, without another fit. He was, of course, receiving all possible treatment and serum, but it was clear that the Lord had chosen to heal him.

The following week one of our church catechists, an elderly faithful warrior, was taken to the Pawa hospital with an obstruction, for urgent operation. The next day, when I arrived, I met his two teenage grand-daughters from our Ibambi girls' school, on the hospital verandah in tears. Slowly, there and in the ward, I heard their story.

The old man had not had an operation; he was merely written up for four-hourly sulfonamide therapy. When the local nurses arrived at 6 p.m. they offered him his pills in exchange for one of his grand-daughters for that night (almost all our Congolese nurses are men). 'I'd rather die', the old man exclaimed, sending his girls away. They had gone to a neighbouring village, to Christian relatives, and returned next morning to see their grandfather. I was shocked and deeply horrified. I called Dr. Kadoner to the bedside, and tried to explain in excited muddled French; but he shrugged his shoulders as much as to say that he knew these things went on but had no power to prevent them. 'Is not this Africa?' Every part of me refused to accept this, and I vowed, God willing, to have a Christian hospital, run by Christian nurses, where all should see and know Christ's love and purity. The old man died next day.

In May Mrs. Scholes was taken ill. I woke at 2 a.m. and heard her husband moving about, and then heard vomiting. I called out quietly to see if he needed help. She was unconscious, with a fever of over 105°. We made up an injection of quinine from crushed tablets and did all we could. By 6 a.m. her temperature was only 96°, but her blood pressure had fallen to within dangerous levels. I stayed with her all through the next three days as we fought first cerebral malaria, then blackwater fever, with intense weakness, hours of semi-consciousness, vomiting and feeding problems. How I longed for a nurse to help me! How very ignorant I felt as a mere doctor when it came to urgent nursing procedures. For two months we nursed her, and cared for her, and slowly watched the Lord heal her and restore her to us. It knit us together in a deep bond of love. From then on they treated me as one of their own children whom they had had to leave at school in England.

We went away together for a two-week period of rest and convalescence during Bible School vacation, south to Bomili (80 miles) and on to Opienge (a further 140 miles). There we met the Revival. How can one ever hope to explain what we saw and experienced of the mighty working of the Holy Spirit? Senior missionaries and African church elders had been praying earnestly for years that the Lord would graciously pour out upon the Congolese church floodwaters of revival in the Holy Spirit; and suddenly the answer was upon us.

At Opienge, we were at first spectators, puzzled, a little afraid and uncertain, as we saw and heard much that was unusual and foreign to us. Slowly He brought to our hearts the peace of conviction that this was of Him, that He was in control. Meetings were alive with a new power: the building was crowded out as never before. Some were shaking violently, others crying out for mercy, yet others singing and praising the Lord. There was much noise. Humanly speaking we might have felt it was confusion, yet He revealed that it was Holy Spirit order. Hour after hour, in church, on the compound, at the home, to Africans or to

Europeans, men and women were confessing sins, seeking forgiveness and cleansing, going away full of a mighty joy, their faces radiant with new-found peace. Jesus Christ was being glorified. Sin was being put away. Many were being burdened to pray for the unsaved, to go out in teams of witness preaching the gospel. Surely this was never of the devil! God forbid! Only the Holy Spirit glorifies Jesus.

We returned to Ibambi, arriving on Friday afternoon, 27th July. There we heard from the other missionaries that for two weeks an amazing work of repentance had been going on all over the station compound, many being convicted of hidden sin and seeking out Europeans and church elders for advice and counsel, for confession and restitution.

That evening we gathered in the Bible School for the Friday evening fellowship meeting at 7 p.m. Jack Scholes led the meeting. After some hymn singing and a time of prayer, he stood to minister the Word before opening the meeting for testimonies. Almost immediately a mighty wave of Holy Spirit power swept through the hall. There was a great rush of noise. We looked around amazed, possibly shocked. Then we felt puzzled, even afraid, as we saw apparent confusion. Africans were on their feet, their arms raised above their heads, calling on the name of the Lord. Others were shaking violently and crying out in apparent pain where they sat. Yet others were thrown violently down, across the forms, on the cement floor, yet without physical hurt. Another rushed wildly to the front and threw himself on the ground, crying violently. Some just sat looking round, stupefied. Some children cried, clinging to their mothers. We prayed, and all felt the conviction that this was of God. The Holy Spirit was in control. We must keep our hands off, and let Him work.

Slowly the pattern changed—tears became laughter, crying became singing, shaking of conviction became trembling with joy, as sin was confessed, cleansing claimed through the blood of Christ, and the Spirit took possession. The singing! It was such singing as we had never heard! The whole congregation was slowly drawn into the rising crescendo of joy. In the small hours of the morning we began to make our ways home. On all sides the singing continued. Others drifted back, drawn to the fellowship, and worship and singing continued all night and all next day. The station was alive with a new thrill of His presence.

In the weeks, and even months, that followed, a great burden of prayer came upon the church, a yearning over sinners and unsaved loved ones. Many saw amazing visions, of heaven and all the glories of His presence, of hell and the great horror of His judgment. All were seized with a sense of urgency in witness. Schoolgirls would go out in small groups before dawn, to testify to Jesus in some outlying village before getting back again for school. Stories were legion of His power, dealing with backsliders, dealing with outsiders, convicting, cleansing, converting. All had a hunger to hear the teaching of the Word, and a joy in testimony. There was no waiting for people to arrive for services; they used to *run* to church ten minutes or more before time, and start singing! There was no waiting for people to testify; they queued up. Work on the station went ahead and everywhere there was singing. They were tremendously thrilling days.

At the start, the work was mainly amongst Christians who had hidden unconfessed sin in their hearts and lives, secret drinking, hasty tempers, adultery, impure thoughts, prayerlessness or coldness of heart. Many times as these things were laid open and confessed, my own conscience smote me. Were not the same things, certainly coldness, prayerlessness and impatience, present in my own life? Yet I did not then find release and joy. I joined in their joy, but I held myself largely apart from the work of the Spirit. One African confessed to exaggeration leading to untruthfulness, and I left the meeting bewildered and unhappy. I spoke to the Scholes. I confessed my own fear that I too exaggerated, possibly unintentionally, maybe in circular letters—more by what was omitted than by what was actually written. But I did not find peace and joy. My fellow-worker, Elizabeth Naganimi, deeply involved in the Revival, was radiant. Her shining love often rebuked me and I almost feared to be with her. She walked very closely with the Lord.

One day during this time, as the work of the Spirit spread all over our Mission field, station after station sending in wonderful reports of His mighty dealings, John Mangadima, a student nurse at the Red Cross Pawa Hospital, arrived at Ibambi. He said simply that God had sent him to work with me in the church medical service. Later we heard of the great blessing he had been in the camp of leprosy patients at Pawa and of his shining testimony to the doctors there that earned him his dismissal. We also learnt of his quiet acceptance of God's ways. Through his testimony at the Government post where he went to have his labour card stamped and endorsed, a woman, Mama Damaris, was converted and brought to repentance and faith in Jesus Christ. She arrived at Ibambi next day with a glowing face. Asked where she came from, she could only say 'Hell'. Who are you? 'A woman from hell.' Where are you going? 'Heaven.' And the woman from hell joined our ranks to become in the years ahead our chief midwife in charge of the Nebobongo maternity unit.

In the three months before Christmas seven other senior school-boys joined me at Ibambi, all keen to train as nurses. So was born the vision of the nurses' training school. As I toured our large field area, visiting eleven of our fifteen stations, I became more and more convinced that my main ministry must be to train Congolese nurses to run dispensaries and clinics at each station. They would be nurse-evangelists, preaching the gospel to their own people, gathered through their need for medical care and aid. 'Repairer of the breach.' This seemed clearly the meaning of the phrase which had been so prominent in my missionary call—to supply a Congolese medical service to their own people, staffed by keen, well-trained church workers, of a similar standing to the church, Bible-school-trained, evangelists.

In January 1954, we held our missionaries' conference at Ibambi, when all gathered together for prayer, Bible teaching and spiritual refreshment, and to discuss our programme for the coming three years. I looked forward immensely to this gathering, and to meeting all my fellow workers. Yet I was not unconscious of underground tensions and a sense of anxiety. There were those amongst us who were not in sympathy with the way He had chosen to send and reveal revival power in our midst. There were personality clashes and hidden jealousies. There were determined views on many subjects that seemed not to be in accordance with the general policy.

During the conference, both Dr. John Harris, who had arrived in Congo only four months after myself, and I were asked to give some idea of our medical vision and proposed programme. John was keenly interested in the welfare of leprosy patients throughout our area of responsibility. I was keenly interested in the training of national work-ers to accept this medical responsibility. We outlined our plans; we sought permission to go ahead. Then came the question: Where should the nurses' school be located? It seemed obvious to me (and therefore subconsciously I expected it to be obvious to everyone else!) that it should be at the centre, at Ibambi, where we were already firmly established. So it was a shock to realize that some were strongly opposed to having the medical centre stationed at Ibambi—anywhere else, at all costs! After hours of discussion, it was eventually agreed that it *should* be in the Ibambi *area*, but not actually at the station. It was suggested we move it to Nebobongo, seven miles north, where for many years we had had a large camp for leprosy patients and maternity work.

I was somewhat stunned. I felt so sure it was not His will to make the medical centre a separate work from the Mission, under separate administration with all the problems that my quick mind could see clearly following such a move. However, I was encouraged to wait quietly and let the Lord resolve the problem in His own way and time. There was no immediate hurry.

I remember at that conference the wonderful daily Bible studies led by Jack Scholes, from the first eleven chapters of Leviticus on the four 'basic tenets' of the Mission, faith, holiness, sacrifice and fellowship, as revealed in the sacrifices, the types of Calvary. One illustration which he used about a carpenter stands out clearly in my mind today. The man had completed preparations to make a cupboard, each board cut accurately to size, planed and aligned. Now he gathered up nails of various sizes and different heads, for the final assembly. Holes were bored to receive the heads: the nails were placed in position in turn, and then hammered home, covered over with wood filling, and the whole varnished, so that in the completed article no nail was seen, only the cupboard as a whole. Were we willing to be nails, in the hands of the Master Carpenter? Would we grumble at the painful blows of the hammer, or would we remember that the hammer was held by the nail-pierced hands? It was He, not our circumstances, nor our fellow-missionaries, who was choosing us to take our hidden place in His church.

The conference ended; days of tidying up followed; station routine recommenced. Then, on 20th January 1954 our nurses' school started, with a membership of eight. It was a very humble start. I was not fluent at Swahili, and used no French. The boys were from all different standards, from John Mangadima who had done one year post-primary school[2] and was keen to go ahead, to Joseph who had only completed 4th grade primary[3] and been out of school for some years with practically no desire for academic advancement. I had no notes to help me, no idea of what such a course should include, no indication from the Government as to official standards or syllabus.

We built our first two wards, a lovely whitewashed mud building with a thick thatch and large shuttered windows. On one side was a twenty-four-bed ward for women and children, a hall for consultations and drug cupboards, and three small rooms, for maternity, minor surgery or special cases. All these were to the right of our dispensary. On the left we built a small eight-bed men's ward. The church members did most of the work, helped by nurses and patients. Catechists and evangelists came in to roof it. It was officially opened, named 'Bethany' and dedicated to the Lord's service in September 1954.

One day in this same month I was sitting on my verandah during the lunch-hour rest period when I was presented with a whimpering six-month-old baby, sturdy, healthy, but hungry! The agitated aged relative, who almost threw her at me, told me that her mother had died that morning. They had tried to bring her to me, but were prevented by flood-waters. He pleaded with me to adopt the child, so that she might be brought up to love the Lord. If I refused, her other relatives would take her and she might never hear the gospel, So 'Fibi' (Swahili version of Phoebe, 'moonshine', light reflected from the sun) entered my home and, in a few days, my heart, to become my own little girl. The sudden weaning, linked with my own ignorance of milk mixtures and sugar measures, led us into three dreadful weeks of endless crying, diarrhoea, skin rash, losing weight, and frantic disturbed nights. But slowly we got to know each other, and to enter on our new life together.

I was ill in late November with a severe attack of malaria. Elizabeth Naganimi took little Fibi, and from then on became her nanny, her most precious friend, her faithful tutor in things temporal and spiritual. I had to be at Bomili for Christmas, to attend the confinement of one of our missionaries, although I was hardly fit for the journey. On arrival, I developed jaundice, and an unhappy three weeks followed. So many memories crowd those days. I recall eating a red-hot pepper by mistake; the birth of a white baby in a village surrounded by forest, seventy miles from the nearest hospital should aid be needed. I remember the love of our Ibambi evangelists and their wives, eight families who were working in the Bomili area as missionaries to help this much smaller church to get established.

So back to Ibambi for another year of work. The nurses' training school was going ahead. Arthur Scott, one of our missionaries who had trained in Belgium as a Health Officer, had sent me the notes he had prepared over the years for training African nurses. These, with Dr Chesterman's textbook for African dispensers, made the basis of our new textbook, painstakingly typed out for each of our eight students each evening for the following day's lectures. Then Miss Roupell, another missionary, became very ill. I drove her to Stanleyville, along some three hundred miles of Congo roads, to have an electro-cardiogram and to see a heart specialist. After that we had a tremendous epidemic of infective hepatitis; then another of a severe kind of measles. Days were always full. But God gave the ability to cope with ever-increasing responsibilities. Greek traders brought their children to me with tonsillitis, or for general check-up during their school holidays. Africans poured in from every side, demanding a surgical service, midwifery care, eye specialist work, plus all the multitudinous stream of medical cases. The work grew and grew; the vision clarified; I was happy.

In October 1955 five of my nursing students were ready to go for their state examinations. We were all terribly nervous! I managed to provide each of them with new khaki shorts, a shirt, and a clean white apron. I drove them up to Pawa in my Chevrolet van. They were subdued—very strange for Congolese! We were ushered into one of the rooms at the back of the large laboratory buildings where the Red Cross nurses had their schooling. There we were joined by some twelve of their students who were all talking off-handedly in French. Our boys felt awkward, knowing only the local Swahili. But they were the better dressed (small comfort to my heart)! A government doctor came from Wamba, eighty miles to the east, the Red Cross doctors were there, and myself. For their oral examination the boys came in singly, my students politely being offered first place. Each one had from five to fifteen minutes' questioning (in Swahili, I was relieved to hear) while the doctors chatted casually amongst themselves, and seemed to give scant attention to the answers. I dared not look at my boys. I was frightfully anxious they should do well. At last it was an over and the results were read out. Yokana of Ibambi was first with 95 per cent! Mangadima was third with 85 per cent; two other Ibambi boys had passed, and one was deferred till next year's exams. It was wonderful news! We set off home, singing triumphantly the whole journey, wild with excitement.

Our medical service for the Congolese church was launched. Our first Africans were qualified as State assistant nurses. We were established! The future looked settled. I went to bed that night, radiantly happy, flushed with success, heady with the first draught of popularity.

End Notes

1 The registered name of the WEC in Congo in colonial days.
2 Equivalent to third form in British secondary schools.
3 Equivalent to the top class of the British primary school.

7
Further Vistas

Christians often seem to have the impression that 'becoming a missionary' is some form of metamorphosis by which a radical change of nature is achieved. Someone, possibly deeply stirred at a missionary meeting and challenged by the need of some less-privileged people, feels constrained to offer for overseas service. Almost inevitably this 'offering' comes to be regarded as a 'holy call' to a sacrificial vocation. The whole idea becomes wrapped in a veil of romantic splendour, so that even the candidate may fail to observe the unreality of it. The tendency of congregation and friends well-nigh to hero-worship the missionary only increases the dilemma. Looking at the situation honestly and critically, many may know that, mentally, physically or spiritually, the candidate is unsuitable for missionary service. Some would-be candidates do not even have a burden of prayer for the peoples they hope to serve, nor have they ever sought to bring their immediate friends and neighbours in their own country to a knowledge of their Friend and Saviour, Jesus Christ. Yet they vaguely hope that as soon as they board the steamer or plane to take them to a foreign land, something mystical will occur and transform them into their image of a 'missionary'.

Nothing can be further from the truth! I believe that, at its simplest, a missionary is one sent by God to live a Christian life, usually amongst people other than his own. It is living which counts. This may include formal preaching, but it will certainly include personal relationships, and these often have to be worked out under most trying conditions. For example, many missionaries discover that it is far from easy to adapt themselves to a completely different climate. The native foods may be hard, not only on the digestive system, but also on the aesthetic tastes. The language barrier may constitute a difficult problem, especially in early years. One cannot choose one's friends. Two missionaries of vastly differing backgrounds, likes and dislikes may be thrown together for several years with no choice of other companionship. One is often

74

expected to do jobs for which one is not trained, and which may be actually distasteful. Yet in all this, one is called upon to reveal Christ, to live a Christ-like life, to be a 'missionary'.

It is then that one realizes it is not the journey in the steamer that changes one's nature. I did not escape from myself by going to Congo. Rather, I came to know myself better, perhaps more as others had already seen me. The ordinary trials and frustrations of life that meet us all were just as real in Congo, and, in some ways, were more pronounced, as there were fewer ways of avoiding or circumventing them. For myself, it was only as I allowed the Lord to show me my own pettiness, or wilfulness, or pride, in different circumstances and problems, that I became willing to let the Lord teach me of Himself. 'Take my yoke upon you, and learn of me', the Lord said: 'for I am meek and lowly in heart.' What happened in the two years following my first taste of success as a missionary doctor shows simply how very much I had to learn of Him, for surely no-one merited the description of Christ-likeness less than I, if it was to involve the phrase 'meek and lowly in heart'.

The day after I returned from taking my students to Pawa for their State nursing examination, Jack Scholes came over to the dispensary to see me at midday. He informed me that the Mission field committee, then in session at Ibambi for their quarterly meeting, felt that the time had come to implement the suggestion made the previous year at the field conference that the medical programme of the Mission should be run from Nebobongo. They would like me to make preparations to move there that week.

I felt as though I had been slapped in the face. Stunned by the sudden overwhelming realization of what this decision would involve, battle royal raged in my heart. Standing surrounded by my first achievements—nurses, buildings, outpatients—I envisaged the gruelling task ahead, and resented the apparent thoughtlessness and thanklessness of this demand, coming at this particular moment. Rebellion flared up within me, and I determined to withstand what I felt was a bigoted, even stupid, committee blunder, sure in my own soul that it was totally detrimental to the over-all vision of God's will and pattern for the Mission medical service.

Mr Scholes agreed to my impassioned demand that I might come over and see the committee that evening. All day the fire smouldered in my heart. My mind seethed with bitter criticism against the 'committee', unhappy in the certain knowledge that the decision was made, in part at least, because of personal antagonisms. I therefore felt quite justified in arguing that it was not in His will. With the clinics finished, hospital clean, school over, I washed and changed, going over and over what I intended to say. My arguments and proofs were all ready. I thought I knew what they would reply, and I had already planned how I would prove their arguments false. A fellow-missionary who was staying in my home at the time tried to calm me down, but I was in no mood to listen. I went across the compound, seething and unhappy.

I had to wait. Mrs Scholes suggested we pray together. Never! Pray? with my heart aflame and my tongue poised for battle? Impossible! Quietly she herself knelt and prayed for me out loud. Slowly the fire died out, a hopeless helplessness flooded me, a feeling of 'very small littleness', and I began to see the pointlessness of battle. Then she talked with me, of Jesus, and His deep, deep love. 'He that toucheth you toucheth the apple of his eye' (Zechariah 2:8). It was not the committee, not a group of fellow-missionaries, but the Lord Himself—through them, it was true—who was sending me to Nebobongo. He had a great purpose, possibly a difficult, even dangerous, way; but He would go with me. At Ibambi He could not do for me what He wanted to do, to make me 'more like Jesus'. It was His hand, His nail-pierced hand, that held the hammer (even the committee!) to fulfill His purpose, to drive the nail fully home to take its place in the building of His church. '*All things* work together for good to them that love God, to them who are the called according to his purpose' (Romans 8:28). When called to the committee I listened quietly to their proposals and was given the grace to agree. And looking back now how glad I am that the Lord overruled and constrained me to obey.

On 30th October 1955, I left Ibambi in the Mission truck with all my possessions to go seven miles north to Nebobongo to take over the responsibility of station leadership and the development of a Mission medical service. Evangelist Agoya and his wife Taadi, with their six children, went with me. They had had to return to Ibambi from their work at Bomili after eighteen months' missionary service as Taadi was desperately ill with her sixth pregnancy, and we had grown very close to each other, as sisters in the Lord, during those anxious months.

So started a new life. Mr and Mrs Coleman and their young family had left for furlough the previous week after caring for Nebobongo for a couple of years. I joined Florence Stebbing, a capable nurse and midwife, who had already had some four or five years' service at Nebobongo. The work generally was in a discouraging state. In 1953, the Belgian Red Cross Hospital at Pawa had closed the large and flourishing leprosy colony that Mission nurses had supervised at Nebobongo since 1940, taking over a thousand of the camp family to their own new centre, some nine miles further north. The remaining two hundred patients had scattered to surrounding villages, refusing to be coerced to this Roman Catholic hospital, preferring to forgo treatment. The beautiful colony, with its rows of homes, neatly-laid-out gardens, and flourishing acres of food crops had reverted to jungle. There was almost nothing left to be seen of it. The station workmen, many of them previous camp patients, were drifting away, as Nebobongo was no longer considered a treatment centre. However, the small, neat, brick-built maternity unit, with its ten beds and well-equipped labour ward, continued, due to Florence's constant care and love, staffed by a group of pupil midwives whom she trained with endless patience.

There was also the orphanage, consisting of two long, low, brick buildings, filled with small wooden beds, each with a separate room at one end for the five Christian women who cared for the thirty-eight noisy, happy toddlers! What a sight to see them all in an open verandah, on forms by the low wooden tables, with folded hands and bowed heads singing 'Grace' before the steaming bowls of rice, plantains, and manioc leaf were handed round! They were all ages, from nought to ten, most of them dressed in bright-coloured cotton rompers. Each of the five women carried on her hip, slung from one shoulder, one of the newest arrivals, still bottle-fed.

The station layout was interesting. Our land lay all to the north of the Paulis-Ibambi road, half a mile of road-frontage on a sharp bend. Opposite us, to the south, was forest and dense undergrowth, sloping away down to a stream and marshland. Florence took me on a tour of inspection. We started at the Paulis (eastern) end of the roadway. All the land to our right was cleared, rising from us in a fairly steep embankment to a half-mile-long, flat plateau-top, parallel with the road, 120 yards back, and mostly only about 50 to 70 yards wide before falling away again, plunging downhill at both ends to streams and freshwater springs, and centrally leading away to the old colony for leprosy patients. We left the road by the first entrance, and climbed up to a very nice, almost square, brick-built home with grass thatch roof where Florence was living. It had four rooms, a kitchen and bathroom and, out behind, a cookhouse. Walking along the plateau-top, westwards, we looked down the steep hill to our right to the African workmen's village, some twelve homes, many of them urgently needing repairs or renewal. To our left there was a large mud-hut home where maternity patients waited for their babies, and this house, too, was obviously in very bad repair. Continuing to our right, we passed a lovely church building, low brick walls and pillars, and newly thatched, standing on the rough cement floor of the old home of the founder of the leprosy colony, Mrs Edith Moules, who had started the work at Nebobongo in 1940. The church could seat about eighty to ninety, and was also used for primary schooling for the orphans. A few were in there as we passed, being taught the rudiments of reading, writing and arithmetic by one of the pupil midwives. But one had the impression that teacher did not know much more than taught, and probably very little was getting across. So we came to the maternity compound, with brick-built, grass thatched buildings for normal and infected cases, and houses for the midwives.

The station was divided into two by the road that ran north-south through the middle, from the main road back to the old leprosy colony. Crossing this, we came to the second large European home, where I was now to be installed—a house with some eight rooms and bathroom, and a verandah. There were no Africans living within hailing distance of either of our homes, our cooks and their families lived down in the village. Opposite my home, across the wide drive, there was a coffee plantation (where today the primary school stands). Further westwards was a large open courtyard, with two long, low dormitories for the orphans, their kitchen, and the open verandah for meals. On again we came to a long narrow stretch of level wasteland.

We went to inspect the water supplies, scrambling down to the streams through rough undergrowth, along narrow muddy tracks. They were in bad shape, dirty, overgrown, full of insects, the sure source of sickness. We made our way towards the leprosy colony, but all was overgrown. Even the roads were hard to decipher in the new jungle, and we stumbled home not a little discouraged.

That evening, I met the whole family in church for a welcome meeting. We eyed each other speculatively. My mind was full of housing problems, water supplies, feeding, clothing, administration, sanitation, counting how many there were and trying to calculate what it was going to entail. They for their part were wondering if I would stay, whether they were going to have security again and jobs, if I would work in with them or shout at them and throw my weight about. But slowly, together, we thawed out towards one another, and it would seem that we all decided that first evening to trust Him to work it out for us, to unite us as one family and make a success of the new venture.

Next day, with Agoya and two of the senior station workmen, we got down to it. We walked all over the ground a hundred times, with paper and pencil and tape-measure. We drew up plans and discarded them, and started all over again. Eventually it began to take shape and a new vision crystallized. I sent a message to the church elders responsible for the work in our area, asking them to meet with us and discuss our plans. First, we wanted them to seek out relatives for as many of the orphans as possible, or else Christian friends who would adopt them into their homes, as we felt that to make a start with the hospital we must take over their buildings and build more around them in that courtyard. Second, we wanted to build a completely new workmen's village in a healthier spot, on the long level stretch of wasteland at the western end of the station. Third, we wanted them to find us a teacher for our children, the orphans who would stay with us, the children of the evangelist and the workmen and the nurses. Fourth, we wanted them to find us a team of eight willing Christian workmen to make bricks down at the old brick-kiln, ready for new hospital buildings.

They agreed and we all set to with a will clearing land, cleaning water-holes, digging new toilets, planting food gardens. It all took time, and it was a full year before we began to see results for all our labour. We made many mistakes, needless to say: sharpening the teeth of the long double-handed saw without setting them first, for instance; building the firing-holes in the kiln too widely spaced so that they fell in, so losing us 17,000 of our first 22,000 bricks; miscalculating the volume of hewn trees for kiln firewood on the Government return sheets involving us in tremendous expense; building a new dispensary as a roof on pillars only, with no walls, so that it was blown away in the first hurricane storm. But we learnt!

There were more serious mistakes, too. Out of twelve orphan children who were taken home to Christian relatives or adopted into various homes, eight came back to us, unhappy and underfed, and we had to re-think our programme for them. We realized that we could not sacrifice them to the cause of progress in another direction. We were unable to obtain a school teacher for them, so I taught them myself for three hours every morning. But I taught them as I knew how, and when they took exams to go to the central Mission primary school at Ibambi, to pass up from our grade 3 to their grade 4, they all failed. I had used English methods and these were unacceptable in a Belgian colony.

Letters came from other missionaries asking why I couldn't visit their stations, as I was the Mission's doctor, not just Nebobongo's. I regret to say I was annoyed and wrote indignant replies reminding them that they had sent me to Nebo, and pointing out that having, as I did, station responsibility, I was up to my eyes in work—administrative, building, and educational, as well as medical. I urgently needed a chauffeur-mechanic to relieve me of all the endless driving for weekly food-markets, and for emergency patients. One day a young man arrived with his wife and two little boys from the Wamba station, saying he had heard I needed a chauffeur and he wished to offer for the job. We were thrilled! We showed him a house in our new village, and everyone welcomed the family and helped them to settle in. Next day at morning prayers, there was a call for the ambulance. I called Daniel to me, passed him the car keys, named a student nurse to go with him, and gave him the scribbled note of appeal with the address. He just stood and looked at me. Well, I asked, what do you want? I then discovered he had never even sat in a car before! He had come to be *taught* to be a chauffeur mechanic! He learnt—and I learnt a lot, too, in order to teach him! But he became my most valued friend during the next three years and an extremely good chauffeur.

More serious still, I was working almost round the clock. My days began at 5.30 a.m. in the hospital wards, and rarely finished before 10.30 p.m. in the office. In addition there were frequent night calls, emergencies that broke in upon an already tightly packed programme, operative responsibilities that sorely tried me and left me tired and worn out afterwards. As a direct consequence my quiet times alone with God in the morning, drawing fresh strength and inspiration and guidance, began to peter out. I still did regular Bible study as I taught for three-quarters of an hour every morning in church before the day's work began. But it was becoming automatic. The joy was slipping away. The desire for prayer fellowship with whites or Africans began to fade. One knows how closely physical tiredness and spiritual ill-health are linked, and this tiredness faces so many missionaries who have to cope with the problems of under-staffing and overworking.

Little things began to make me irritable. I remember one day, a Thursday, when I did an eye-clinic in the morning at 9 a.m. I had got the house ready, darkened rooms, instruments out, and two patients came. After they had gone I waited a little while, had coffee, and then another came. After that, and a further wait, I cleared up everything and prepared to go to the hospital for ward-rounds. At midday an old lady was led to the verandah of my home. My houselad came to tell me that she wanted her eyes tested. I was annoyed and asked where she came from. It was from a nearby village, so I refused to see her, saying she could have been in time for the 9 a.m. clinic and must come back next week. I turned away and went in for my lunch.

Shortly afterwards my senior dresser, John Mangadima, came to me. He was grieved, and rebuked me for turning the old lady away. 'Could you not see that she was blind? She has waited all morning at the roadside for someone to come to lead her to the Christian doctor who heals people. She is a soul for whom Christ died—and you have harshly turned her away. Would He have done so?' Since then, I have always lifted my heart in a quick, silent prayer as I go to answer the door, that I may receive every visitor, whatever the hour, in His name and for His sake, showing His love and gentle kindliness and courtesy.

Meanwhile the work grew on all sides. We urgently needed extensions in the maternity compound where some forty babies were being born each month and some twelve pupil midwives were in training with three qualified girls in charge. We urgently needed more room in the hospital compound. By this time we had two wards, one with eighteen beds in it for women and children, and one with eight beds for men—and yet we often had as many as fifty patients at a time needing hospital care. The out-patients had to be seen on the verandah, sometimes as many as 150 at a time, with nowhere to sit for morning prayers, or for treatments, and no shelter when it rained. The other building, which acted as laboratory, pharmacy, theatre and a place for sundry other 'odd jobs', leaked badly and also needed a damp-course built in.

We had no hospital village for the countless patients who came from far-distant places and needed daily clinic treatments. Our own new station village was growing apace; there were already two neat rows of eight houses each. But the number of student nurses and young workmen grew faster than the village. We had several acres of land under cultivation, with large crops of peanuts and rice, manioc and plantains, paw-paws and pineapples. But still we had to buy nearly one ton of food each week for our ever-growing family. Once again we had over thirty orphans in our care, but at least two of the women who cared for them were now too old, and really too weak, to continue their work of drawing water, cutting firewood, and endless laundry and ironing, cooking and feeding, as well as mothering and spiritual care.

We now had over thirty children of primary school age in the four first grades, as well as twenty student nurses in the three years of their course; and all the teaching fell on me! The administrative work, involving Government forms, accounts, reports, letters, grew at about the same pace, and yet all had to be done somehow, usually after 10 o'clock in the evening, often with many mistakes made through sheer weariness. But where could one call a halt? To which department could one say 'No'? Everyone had a claim. Needs abounded; our reputation had grown, particularly for eye clinics and maternity work and tuberculosis, and patients came to us from as much as 400 miles away. Could we refuse them?

It is easy for Christians at the home base to say that a missionary should not do too much, and should take one day off in seven. In theory we all agree. But when one is a doctor, single-handed, with no other medical help for 50 or even 150 miles in any direction, it is hard to put into practice. How urgently every missionary society needs new recruits to share the work-load. This would seem to be the only practical solution to this world-wide problem.

Others argue that missions should not tackle institutional work, such as schools and hospitals, but leave these to the Government. In our area, and in many, many others, this would merely mean that thousands of children would have no schooling, and thousands of patients would die each year, as the Government just has not enough skilled and trained servants, nor a sufficiently stable economy, to begin to shoulder the work of this vast responsibility, willing though they may be.

In January 1957, we had another triennial field conference, this time with a difference—our African church elders were to take part with us. The conference was to be bi-lingual. Bangala and Swahili were to be used for the joint meetings of Africans and Europeans; but other meetings would be held separately to discuss specifically church (African) or Mission (European) matters, bringing together the findings at the next joint meeting. Dr Harris and I both presented medical reports, and then the southern group of churches added an urgent plea concerning their need for a medical service in the south, particularly requesting a general surgical service. After much prayer and discussion it was suggested that Dr Harris should come south from Malingwia to join me at Nebobongo. There he would train me in surgery, and then I would leave him at Nebo, and go south myself to start again a similar work for the churches there.

After the conference had ended, Florence Stebbing went on furlough. John and Elsie Harris joined me at Nebobongo for a brief week, with Joy and Cyril Taylor and their two little boys. Then they all left for their different stations, and I was alone. It was a strange feeling—but I loved it! For one thing, it was a tremendous challenge. Could one cope with the multitudinous tasks alone, and keep all the services going smoothly? By the Lord's strength and enabling, yes! And with it all, I found full scope for such determination and vision and administrative ability as I might have. But I do not doubt that it made me selfish. I had no need to consult with others, nor to consider their desires or feelings. I had no time-table to keep except my own. I had no need to be careful not to over-drive others. I could work at the pace I preferred. My African team worked willingly with me, each in his own department pulling his weight and doing his job, so that the whole machine rolled smoothly on. I felt a great glow of pleasure and pride. But with it there was an uncomfortable pricking of conscience that this was to my glory and not necessarily His. I was proud of them, each one of the big family, and they were mine—my nurses, my workmen, my hospital, my vision. And He had to teach me that they were His.

Ruth Dyer, another woman missionary, joined me for two months to do language study as she was moving from the northern to the southern area of our field, and also to be my companion. We were very happy together, and she helped me tremendously in preparing for the arrival of Dr Harris and his family. There was sandpapering and revarnishing of furniture, doors and windows, painting woodwork, supervising the workmen in distempering the big house. We did each room in a different pastel shade, using methylene blue, mercurochrome, malachtite green and flavine from the dispensary to stir into the baths of whitewash! They looked first-rate, the colours giving it a really professional touch. The Harrises were expected on Tuesday, 2nd May. We killed a chicken and prepared a feast. They didn't come. Ruth left me that week. I thought we must have got the week wrong, so next Tuesday we killed another chicken and prepared another feast. Still they didn't come. The next Tuesday I felt I couldn't go on killing precious chickens, so we did nothing—and they came!

On 16th May 1957, just as dusk was falling, they drove in. I was in the hospital with an emergency case—a man had been carried in with a horribly torn foot. As light was falling, and it was nearly supper-time, and I was tired (we can always make lots of excuses!) I hadn't lit the pressure lamps in the hospital, but was working in the half-light on the verandah outside, in most unhygienic conditions, and in a most unmedical manner. The first thing I knew of their arrival was when Dr Harris walked up behind me. I felt my pride fizzle out of me. I was caught doing everything just as one shouldn't do it!

8
Slipping Back

Next day Dr Harris and I walked round the whole site together as I showed him all aspects of the work. At midday we went to his home for family dinner, and I saw that, except beneath the pictures, all our beautiful colours had completely disappeared, bleached out by the sun. And I had a slight premonition that this might be a picture of myself. After lunch we gathered together for prayer and discussion, and to seek for a happy division of labour. In the evening we had fellowship with the church elders and laid before them our suggestions. Thus I officially handed over the leadership of the hospital to Dr Harris.

How hardly it came to me! Little had I realized how utterly Nebobongo made up my life, how each workman, each nurse, each child had curled themselves into my heart as part of my family. And now, officially, they were no longer mine. For the next year I fought out this fight, and through it found myself in depths of despair, seeing myself as a failure, useless, realizing that I had built the work around myself, and my personality, and my vision, instead of on Him. *Mine* was written on everything, instead of *His*. And how deeply it hurt, as, gently and lovingly, He had to prise my hands off His treasured possession.

There seemed to be endless frustrations. I had grown to love the liberty of leadership, the joy of working a thing out and seeing it through and making a go of it. But now I was once more just a junior missionary, and my ideas did not always make sense to those working with me. Through the past eighteen months I had learnt a good deal about administration—in my own way! But book-keeping and office work were certainly not my strong points. What the fourteen different books said should be in the fourteen different accounts corresponded to what could be found in the fourteen carefully labeled porridge-oats tins. But how I achieved this was not always so clear! Those who took over from me had somewhat more accurate views and more accurate methods, and doubtless suffered many headaches in sorting out and clarifying many mysterious entries. But it was not by any means easy to accept the very definite change in emphasis regarding financial affairs. I had felt so clearly led through the years in what I called a 'Muller' practice[1] As God gave a vision I would seek from Him the tenth part of the needed finance to see the project through, and then launch out in faith, trusting Him for the rest to come in as it was needed. Now I had to toe the line, so to speak, to a very different method of working, though doubtless it was the more usually acceptable. Now we asked the Lord to provide all that was necessary for a project before commencing work on it.

No doubt I was something of a visionary, and all my hard work and labours were working to one end, the fulfilment of a very clear vision of what I felt was Congo's greatest need, particularly in our north-eastern Province. I wanted to see bush clinics every fifteen to twenty miles, looked after by well-trained African dressers, where preventive medicine, child welfare clinics, ante-natal clinics and school-children clinics could form the prominent part of the work, along with the early diagnosis and prompt treatment of all the current endemic diseases, tuberculosis, malnutrition, leprosy, intestinal worms, etc. This could be followed by immediate transference to the centre for any not responding promptly to treatment. I longed to be freed from the central work, so that I could set up and organize, and then regularly visit, clinics such as these. I felt that they would need a fort-nightly oversight at the start. The people of an area would be told what day and time the doctor was expected and could gather at church centres where the local catechist or evangelist would buy up the opportunity with the ministry of the Word of God. I personally had little interest in the hospital routine work, feeling that there were several Government and Red Cross hospitals in the area which these clinics could use, especially for surgery. So the nurses' training school at Nebobongo had developed with this special emphasis, the preparing of young men to carry the responsibilities of bush clinics, both as evangelists and as medical dressers.

Now, however, a change came, and I was not willing to recognize the vision of another if it did not happen to coincide with my own. And what a continual cause of friction in church and Mission this attitude can be! Many in the Mission, and this certainly included the majority on the committee, felt that an established central work with proper surgical facilities was of greater importance than a string of 'inefficient clinics'. If I must travel, they said, why not tour the Mission stations, and help the other European nurses who were struggling to keep small hospitals and maternities going throughout our area with very little outside medical help or encouragement? Under pressure I agreed to do a six-monthly tour of the stations, involving a five hundred miles' circle to the south and a similar circle to the north, in a huge figure of eight. But our vehicle was old and not really road worthy; the roads were shocking, and the first tour coincided with the height of the wet season. When eventually I got home I felt utterly exhausted and depressed and discouraged. We had had endless difficulties with the car; two nights had been spent on the roadside; the response had been poor with only very small clinics at each place; the financial outlay had been very considerable, and I felt it just was not worth it. But the real cause of my depression was simply that I could not put my heart into backing up the vision of others when I felt it ran contrary to my own. I had certainly not learnt the grace sufficient for every need, nor the joy of being spent for Him in just any way that He might direct.

Back at Nebobongo the hospital was being developed, particularly on the surgical side, and much attention was being paid to the efficient training of the nurses ('male ward orderlies' is probably a more accurate description of our lads!) in ward care and technique. I continued with the school teaching, but now I had to learn to work with others. I found I couldn't have the lads just when I wanted them; they might well be involved in a ward-round, or even in theatre. Nor could I keep them late in school as I often did in the past, for other folk had their time-tables to arrange as well. In my heart I fought against these changes. Dr Harris would invite me to carry my share of the work in the hospital and to join him in the theatre, as had been planned at the field conference, so that I could learn surgery with him before going south. God overruled and undertook for us, but there is no denying that it was a stormy year! So many times my spirit rebelled. I was quick and impulsive, where my colleague was slow and methodical. Our African fellow-workers were quick to spot the lack of cooperation and failure in agreement on many matters, and some would have played us off the one against the other.

The sense of frustration and of failure grew. The devil made accusations on every level. My free, happy, outgoing love to the Africans was turned against me in my heart as I began to feel that I loved them more than my own white fellow-workers. I loved to go and spend a weekend with Pastor Ndugu in the bush, sharing his home and meals just as though I was one of the family, and found that I enjoyed it more than being invited to another missionary's home. My heart accused me on the level of Christian living. I was so often irritable, and there were even occasions when temper flared up inside me as I felt that a faithful African fellow-worker had been misjudged or wrongly treated. My heart seemed so hard. I was so often critical and proud in my outlook. Along with this my communion with the Lord shrivelled, prayer became a formality, Bible reading a burden. I longed for liberation and peace and joy.

This sense of frustration need never have occurred had we been more willing to recognize each other's gifts. Life would have been easier if we had all realized that one approach may be needed for a pioneer work starting almost from scratch but that other methods may be required as the work becomes established and less makeshift. Surely we all know that God has His pioneers; but He also has His consolidators. And it might have been easier for both of us if we had not tried to mix our differing gifts, but had each been given separate opportunities for their fulfilment.

Be that as it may, in my own eyes I felt again that I was a failure, empty, cold, unreal. It seemed I was putting on an act, with mixed motives, and deep in my heart cold doubt began to rear its head. I faced again the old taunting of the devil. Are you really saved? Could you be so hard and critical, could you lose your temper, could you be so jealous of another, if the Lord Jesus was really dwelling in you? You preach it all, but you don't live it. It isn't real! With my white fellow-workers I felt keenly frustrated. The root cause was misunderstanding. I felt they were critical and had misjudged much of the work just on the reports of others without coming to see it first hand. Equally I felt a growing barrier with my African friends, since I feared to share with them in the freedom of previous years, sensing that my somewhat unconventional approach only served to increase 'white' antagonism. And so I felt alienated almost from God Himself. There seemed to be no contact, just a sad yearning and loneliness.

One morning, I was taking morning prayers with our Nebobongo family, reading from Philippians 3:1-11. I chalked a large red cross on the blackboard, and listed on the left all the things man counted dear unto himself—public opinion, popularity, worldly wealth, security, etc.

Above this I wrote the word 'dung'. To the right I placed the words, 'That I may know Him.' Suddenly the Holy Spirit came down on the congregation, and with much crying many made their way to the front and got right with God. The move started amongst the pupil midwives, but spread rapidly to the student nurses and workmen. My heart cried out to God. How could I be used in this manner to bring others to the foot of the cross, to repentance, to joy of salvation, and all the time my own heart was so cold and untouched? I turned to the African elders and blurted out the depths of my own needs. Then I rushed from the church. Back in my own home I threw myself on the ground in a desperate, frantic plea before God for His mercy and grace to be extended to myself also.

The work of God continued in the church for several hours, amidst strong tears and joyous singing. Pastor Ndugu was passing through Nebobongo on his bicycle on his way to Ibambi, and hearing the noise, went to the church to see what was happening. There the church elders told him what had occurred and described how I had left the church. He came to see me. Quietly he sat beside me and listened to my broken, somewhat incoherent outburst. Then he left and continued on his way to Ibambi. That afternoon he returned, went to see Dr Harris and then came across to see me. He had Mr Scholes's permission to take me away to his home village for a week or so. He just told me to pack a haversack and get my bicycle, and together we cycled the sixteen miles to his village. There he gave me a room in his house—and there followed seven days of prayer and fasting. At first the heavens seemed as brass, the Bible cold and meaningless. By Sunday evening I felt I could bear no more of it. If the Lord did not meet with me I would accept that I was a castaway. I would continue my ministry to the African church as a teacher for the nurses, I would continue to teach the Word of God which I never for a moment doubted to be the absolute and certain truth, but I would not accept a missionary's allowance. I joined the Pastor and his wife round the fire, out in the verandah, as the others of the village scattered to their homes at about 10 p.m. We sat in silence, a silence you could feel, almost hear. As they earnestly prayed, slowly the Spirit of God reached through into my heart and broke down the barriers of pride, the frigid restraint, and revealed so much of self. He helped me to unburden my heart, to reveal all the rottenness and sense of failure, the fears and criticisms, the pride and selfishness.

Then, so gently and quietly, Pastor Ndugu took up my words, point by point, and led me to look away from myself to the Christ of Calvary. He dealt with the need of restitution on certain points, the need of apologizing and asking forgiveness on certain others, and a great calm came.

Four amazing days followed, spent in the presence of the Lord. It is hard to describe or put on paper the preciousness of that week, spent alone, utterly given over to the influence of the Holy Spirit speaking through the pages of Holy Scripture. My mind seemed to be more crystal-clear than I had ever known. I felt no need of sleep; I had no consciousness of hunger, nor of any bodily pain or discomfort. There was a tremendous, overwhelming sense of His presence, a deep awe and wonder; I felt caught up, as it were. Even time seemed to pass with no reality. I met Him. There was little or no emotional involvement. But there was a great sense of eternal reality, of light, of truth.

I remember cycling back to Nebobongo early Monday morning to be in time for a new week in school and wondering how to share with my African friends what the Lord had done for me. When I arrived, there were three senior student nurses on the verandah. They came over to take my bicycle and haversack, and at once began praising the Lord and shaking my hand as they saw the light of happiness in my eyes! I didn't have to say anything. Then they told me that for four years, ever since 1953 when the Lord first started to pour out revival blessing on the church, they had been praying daily for me that I would let the Lord work in my heart as He had in theirs. What faithful, loving friends surrounded me.

This was not the end of the battle—by no means! It might almost be called preparation for the next round. During the next few months the devil sought every means of causing dissension and discouragement as he so often does when we seek to make a new beginning with God. On every side, I felt his attacks. I felt I was almost too tired to continue to accept the pressure of medical responsibility, and at times I felt that I would gladly have continued as a missionary if it could be without the title of doctor. I could never get away from myself or my responsibilities. Wherever I went I was still the doctor and a crowd of patients would gather. A weekend off duty simply was not possible, and yet it was becoming very necessary after five years' steady work. I was tired of sharing my home with one and another, and the lack of privacy that this involved. And yet I felt deeply convicted by my attitude, knowing how readily others had shared their homes with me. I still felt misunderstood and criticized (possibly where nothing was intended) concerning my manner of living and eating, my friendship and unity with the Africans, my passionate desire for the setting up of the mobile village ministry, and other issues.

Added to all this, news from my dear mother and family was not happy at this time, and my heart ached to be back in England, possibly to give my mother a home, and to care for her and love her. No doubt sheer physical weariness at the end of five years of intensive work added to the struggle. I was also very hard at work trying to complete a textbook for the nurses' school in Swahili before going on furlough—typing out the manuscript, correcting proofs, preparing stencils, duplicating some hundred copies of each page, and then putting them together for our Mission press to bind.

I had eventually received permission to commence village clinics. Now that Dr Harris was also at Nebobongo to carry responsibility for the hospital and station work I had opened forty clinics covering a four-hundred-mile circular tour. Alternate weeks I spent on the station, teaching nurses' and primary school, and helping in hospital and maternity work. The weeks in between I spent out in the district visiting these forty clinics, seeing up to 2,500 patients a week, preaching the gospel, healing the sick, training catechists in the simple use of twelve medicines left in their care at each of these centres. Much though I loved this programme, as others had foreseen and warned, it was tremendously tiring and exacting and should never have been commenced at the end of one's term of service.

During the last months before furlough Susan came into my life and home. She was a foster-child of Pastor Ndugu, a girl about sixteen years old. Owing to the fact that she had been expelled for persistently breaking school rules, she had only had about four years of primary school teaching. Following this she lived for several years with her foster-parents in the village, rebellious and hard. But at last she had responded to the claims of the Lord on her life, and came to Nebobongo to train as a midwife. But within three months, she had been found to have the dreaded marks of leprosy. It nearly broke her heart and we had a hard battle to hold on to her for the Lord. At last He won, and she agreed to come and live with me and to help in the home, whilst attending classes with the other pupils, but sitting apart. We became very close friends and I shall never forget the wonderful early morning hours, spent round the fire with cups of coffee, studying the Word and praying together. We worked together through the first three books of the Bible, preparing notes in Swahili for a future commentary for the church. At this time also I was invited again to take morning prayers on the station, and it was a great joy to study and search out, and then present, the great truths of Scripture through the Letter to the Colossians, an hour a day for three months.

Then in June 1958, my brother and his wife and son prepared to visit me, as they were travelling home to England for a year's leave after nine years in South Africa. Great preparations were made to receive them! Susan and I travelled all one night to Stanleyville to meet them at the airfield. They were unfortunately delayed, and after waiting forty-eight hours for them, I set out on the return journey the following evening. Many advised me to wait till morning, but I was impatient. I drove all night and at 5 a.m. we left the road as I fell asleep at the wheel. By God's grace we were not killed, although the van was wrecked. After several hours of shock I was helped by kind friends who took me back home and cared for me.

That Sunday, there were farewell services at Nebobongo as I was to leave for furlough within ten days. Pastor Ndugu preached amongst others and I shall not easily forget his gentle, gracious rebuke. He preached on Haggai 1:5, 6. 'Consider your ways. Ye have sown much, and bring in little; ye eat, but ye have not enough; ye drink, but ye are not filled with drink; ye clothe you, but there is none warm; and he that earneth wages earneth wages to put it into a bag with holes.' I know that he was not preaching at me, but nevertheless I felt it nearly summed up my five years in Congo, especially my ministry at Nebobongo. There had been endless hours of sowing, yet what was there to show for it? I thought of all the love and advice and godly wisdom that had surrounded me, yet how had I benefited from it? Had it not run out as money through holes in the pocket?

My brother and family came the next Monday, and we had a marvellous three or four days together, using Philip Ndugu's car to show them all round our area. Everywhere we went they were given a tremendous welcome. They left on their way home to England on the Friday morning, and the following week I also left by air for my first furlough.

I had a month at home with my mother before entering the Tropical Hospital for treatment for chronic amoebic dysentery, and later for an appendectomy. I was very ill during the initial treatment. Due to this illness, and the heavy sedation I was being given, plus the great weariness after five years of missionary service, I allowed myself again to become depressed. I still had not learnt how closely linked are physical and spiritual health. This all-too-simple ruse of Satan to call reaction failure seemed to catch me out each time in seasons of strain and weariness.

Whilst in hospital I received a letter from my sister Diana. She was a nun in an Anglican enclosed order, a contemplative community. She had had special permission to write to me when they heard how ill I was, and sent, under constraint of the Holy Spirit, a few verses from Hosea, chapter 2, verses 14 to 16. 'Therefore, behold, I will allure her and bring her into the wilderness, and speak comfortably unto her. And I will give her her vineyards from thence, and the valley of Achor for a door of hope: and she will sing there, as in the days of her youth, and as in the day when she came up out of the land of Egypt. And it shall be at that day, saith the Lord, that thou shalt call me Ishi; and shalt call me no more Baali.' These were not verses that would normally be chosen to send to someone sick in hospital, but without doubt they were the verses the Lord had chosen for me, to wake me from a state of lethargy, and to deliver me from this frequent accusation of the devil about being a castaway. 'The valley of Achor for a door of hope.' It was a great promise looking forward to future triumph. In the valley of Achor Joshua had dealt drastically with Achan's sin, the disobedience which had brought defeat on the children of Israel as they pressed forward into Canaan following the victory at Jericho. The cause of their defeat was put out of the camp and faith in God for future victory was restored. So God's judgments become the gateway through which we enter into His promises and go on to possess our own inheritance in Him.

Immediately following my five weeks in hospital I embarked on a series of deputation meetings covering a large area of the British Isles. It lasted for twelve packed weeks, and I loved every moment of it! We were so busy I had not time for introspection! I was extremely nervous at every meeting, and felt a great burden to find the Lord's mind and message each day. But He blessed abundantly. I spoke mainly about the Revival, but often told also my own testimony, how hardness of heart and pride had held me back from entering into the full blessing for four long years, but how eventually, through the ministry of Africans, He broke my pride and dealt with me also. Many people were challenged during those weeks of meetings, and several testified that their lives had been completely changed as they met anew with the Lord. I was wonderfully happy; but once again, my personality being what it was, I found success and popularity going to my head. All the time I had to watch and pray that my rejoicing should be only in Him.

The following Christmas, at a Graduates' Fellowship Conference at Swanwick, through the prayerful interest of a doctor friend, I was put in touch with the Mildmay Mission Hospital in Bethnal Green, East London, and in February started there as a Houseman and Casualty Officer. It was strange being back in an English hospital, and not a little terrifying. Almost immediately we were in the throes of an influenza epidemic. All hospital beds were taken over for the acute chest cases and many elderly people died. We seemed to be on duty almost twenty-four hours at a stretch, and I found I was working longer and more tiring hours even than in Congo! Time for quiet and prayer in the early morning was almost non-existent. I was often too tired, and fell asleep when I tried to pray. How common an experience amongst Christian Housemen! It is well for us to remember that God understands and that a quiet time of a particular length and pattern is not a kind of magic formula, the one essential mark of the keen Christian. Rather it is the spiritual attitude of heart and mind that counts and sustains at such periods. I loved the work, and threw myself whole-heartedly into every part of it, including ward services and prayers for the out-patients down in Casualty. I made every effort to be absolutely conscientious in my work for each of the different consultants who visited the hospital and was pleased when they seemed satisfied. Once again I was driven forward by the desire to be a success.

This was a time when I began to look back and to compare the work I was doing at Mildmay with that in the Congo. Also I began to receive a monthly cheque for the very first time in my life! This brought a sense of security. I could buy things for my mother and her home; I could plan for us to go on holiday together. I was also putting aside for my return to the Congo, and sending monthly gifts to help them at Nebobongo. But the work at Nebobongo and its importance began to change colour, so to speak. I recalled the things that had occurred out there, the criticisms that had been made, the failures in relationships, the many frustrations in the work. Previously I had been willing for the Lord to show me that I was at fault. I wanted Him to deal with me, to empty me of myself in order that He might mould me into the likeness of Jesus and fill me with Himself. Now it no longer seemed like that. Why was *I* always in the wrong? Why did *I* always have to give in over everything that occurred? Why hadn't the Mission put money at *my* disposal for the medical work? Why hadn't the menfolk at other stations been more willing to help me at Nebobongo with buildings and repairs, with sanitation and feeding problems, with the upkeep of the car and the oversight of workmen? Why in fact had they put upon me, a woman doctor, jobs which ought to be done by men? And so the devil worked his subtle business and seeds of bitterness, jealousy and envy were sown. And with it all came a growing sense of insecurity for the future and a realization of great loneliness.

Suddenly I saw the answer clearly, and apparently the way to claim the answer. With this new sense of urgency I argued myself into believing that God owed it to me to work it all out my way. I too had the right to marry, to have a husband, someone I could lean on, someone to care for me, to protect me, to be always there as friend and counsellor, to take the responsibility, even to repair the broken furniture! Surely He could not ask me to go back again to Congo single. Perhaps for the first term of service it had been reasonable to expect this of me. There had been jobs to do that perhaps I should not have been so free for had I been married. But now, surely, it was different.

Temptation followed temptation. The devil put the thoughts and desires and growing hunger first. Then along came someone apparently eminently suited (so I thought!). Though he was a true Christian, I soon found out that he had no call to overseas missionary service. So I sought to be released from the Mission, feeling that he would never ask me to marry him whilst he knew I was committed to returning to the Congo. How subtle the adversary is! This new attack began as a desire to have someone by me in Congo. But if this was not possible, Congo would now have to be sacrificed, that I might have him for myself. We were thrown into each other's company for six long months, and I passionately desired that the Lord would give me the fulfilment of all I longed for. We had prayer and Bible reading together of an evening. We went out to services or to open-air testimony together on Sundays. He was always kindly and gracious. He never encouraged me; I only wished he would! I cut myself off from the Mission at this time, sensing that they would disapprove and knowing all the arguments they could use too well! I bought new clothes, and had my hair permed, and set myself to win him.

End Notes

1 Named, of course, after George Muller of Bristol, the founder of Muller's orphanage.

9
Fresh Vision And Triumph

My somewhat obvious *un*-spiritual state at this time led many to pray for me. Some of my friends persuaded me to go away for a long weekend to Herne Bay Court. Arriving on Friday evening, tired and depressed, I went to the final meeting of the previous house-party, with little heart or interest. As my eyes were already closing, heavy with sleep, from weeks of over-tension and mental unrest, the preacher announced as his text Hosea 2:14-16, '... the valley of Achor for a door of hope.'

I do not know what he said; I do not know who he was. I only know that every nerve felt raw and alive. These were the verses my sister had sent me nine months earlier when I had been ill in hospital. I went to my room that evening, fearful, afraid to meet God, knowing what He wanted to say to me but no longer wanting to listen. I wanted things my way now. I didn't want to be made hungry again after God; I didn't want His promise of love and comfort. I felt I had been following a will-o'-the-wisp for long enough, and I was a failure. This kind of life wasn't for me, and I didn't want to be cajoled into trying again.

I could not silence His love. The Hounds of Heaven were bearing down on me. I longed for Him with one breath. I longed for husband and home and the comfort and security this would offer with the next. I struggled till tears—burning, gasping tears—ran down my face. I struggled till exhausted. I fell asleep—*He* was there! I forced myself awake; I even leapt out of bed and splashed my face with cold water. I threw the window open. A gentle May breeze in the still moonlight calmed me. I slept again, and again *He* was there, gentle, loving—stern, demanding—beautiful, worthy. The sense of His presence faded as I sank into deep, troubled sleep. Morning light only brought back a bitter sense of battle. Why should He ask me to relinquish this that I most wanted?

I went back to London on Monday, knowing He would win—indeed had won—but nevertheless not wanting to give in, not wanting His victory, yet terrified to lose Him or to drive Him away.

What a mess! How clever the devil is! I did all I could to close my ears, to refuse to listen. At the same time, I longed for deliverance, for a deliverance which the next moment I didn't want! How contrary can we be?

One morning, several weeks later, I was struck in my morning reading by Galatians 1:16, 'When it pleased God...to reveal his Son in me....' I couldn't shake off the thought. 'Can't you see? Can't you see?' a voice seemed to whisper to me. 'Christ dwells in you. It is Him you are bent on destroying, not yourself. He *is* you. Christ in you, the hope of glory.' I felt baffled, uncertain, unable to bear the revelation, yet this was the truth I had searched for all these years. The simple naked fact of truth—*His Son in me*. Not just *for* me, but *in* me.

Next week I went to Keswick. Others had made this possible for me, arranged a locum and booked for me to stay in the IVF women's camp. The one from whom I so passionately desired human security and love and strength went too. I went to almost all the meetings. I had determined that the Lord should speak to me, that I would hear and that I would obey whatever the cost. And then I left Him to do it. I can remember the tormenting thought that perhaps I had gone too far. Yet however much I had rebelled and kicked, He *knew* that I loved Him, that I was bound to Him for ever and longed deep down to serve Him. In my extremity I had no-one else to whom I could turn. O God, don't leave me, don't cast me off!

On Tuesday evening I attended the meeting in the large tent, physically exhausted after having climbed painfully to the top of Scafell Pike during the day. The address was based on 2 Kings 2:1-11. Elisha's journey with Elijah, and the speaker applied it to our life's journey in retrospect. They began at Gilgal, the place of original committal (do you remember meeting Me on that evening of New Year's Day, 1945?). They passed through Bethel, the place of Jacob's vision where he erected his altar of surrender (do you remember meeting Me in the hospital that day in March 1950?), and came to Jericho, the scene of Joshua's initial victory (do you remember that day in October 1955 when I took you from Ibambi to Nebobongo?). Then Elijah offers young Elisha again the opportunity of remaining with the school of the sons of the prophets. 'Tarry here; you do not need to go any further.' But he refuses to leave Elijah. 'And they two went on' down to Jordan, down into the place of death, the place of separation from self and self-interest.

I was wide awake now, urgently listening, desperate to go on with the Lord even though it meant death to self. 'Ask what I shall do for thee', Elijah tells Elisha. And the quiet voice of the Master seemed to echo the question in my own heart.

I stayed to the after-meeting, awed, fearful, yet knowing that I must answer that voice and receive again from Him the reply. A quiet, unobtrusive counsellor came and sat by me. At last, in tears, I asked the fearful question. Could He forgive deliberate, wilful sin? Could He restore and recommission one who had chosen her own way, and I a missionary on furlough? The whole rotten story of the last few months was at last out, and with joy I knew that He had forgiven me. I told the Lord I was willing for anything He would say to me, and to do anything He asked of me, unconditionally.

I think I knew at once that I was forgiven, but I could not feel that He could 'lightly' forget. I was not sure that He would re-commission, or that He would be willing to use me further in His service. I felt that I had entered a 'second-best' experience, but my fight was over. I felt very exhausted but deeply relieved to know that He was again in charge. The next evening, after an amazing address on temptation, my friend and I went out together and agreed to give up meeting one another. There was a deep wound in my heart, but it was the only way for any future peace. The following day, while I was still at Keswick, I received a telegram, calling me to Newport for an interview at the St Woolos Hospital in connection with a House-surgeon's job there for which I had applied. I had a deep inner conviction that God was definitely at the helm.

As the wound slowly began to heal I realized that a new calm had taken possession. The intenseness of life, the acute awareness of every situation, the passionate longings and yearnings all seemed to have been replaced by a quiet acceptance. There was a sense of resignation, perhaps; a consciousness that I had no rights—no right to quote terms, no right to expect grace, no right even to feel, to feel saved, or happy, or at peace. I accepted utterly that, by the immense immeasurable grace of God and according to His predetermined counsel, Christ was in me and that He should now live out His life and purpose as He saw fit.

I wrote at once to Mission Headquarters, thanking them for having granted me a year's leave of absence, thanking them for their sympathetic prayers during recent months, and asking them to consider my reapplication for full membership at the next quarterly staff meeting, and also to consider an application to return to the Congo in May 1960.

My six months at Mildmay having ended, I went at once to Newport and took up my duties as House-surgeon. There was no applicant for the post of Houseman to the obstetrical unit, so I helped out there as well, and had three weeks' invaluable experience, including doing my first Caesarian operation under supervision! Then the Lord arranged another opportunity for me. The boilers in the theatre sterilizing unit had to be repaired and the theatres were to be closed for three weeks. During this time the surgical staff were going to take their annual holiday. This included the medical superintendent who was also in charge of the obstetrical unit. I was invited by the board to help out for that three weeks as an acting registrar. So I had the opportunity to learn something of the running and administration of a large British hospital, and of work in all the departments, which was to be directly related to the tasks that lay ahead, especially those of training African personnel in administration in the future Independent Congo.

The months at Newport were tremendously happy and busy ones. We worked closely as a team with ward and theatre sisters and nurses, and had plenty of night emergency calls. I had the joy of spending Christmas at hospital, and what a day it was! Dinner on the ward with staff and patients was almost a seven-course meal! We visited and chatted with everybody. The theatre staff, knowing my connection with Congo, had decorated the long corridor as a jungle track with palm fronds and elephants as a welcome to their jungle doctor! The ward service, for me the crowning joy of the day, seemed to be greatly appreciated by patients, relatives and staff alike. At the end of the service, Sister presented me with a cheque for £50 from both patients and staff to buy a general anaesthetic machine for the Nebobongo hospital. I was deeply moved by this symbol of their deep love and affection.

After Christmas we put on our 'variety show'. Hardly perhaps, the kind of task one would associate with a missionary on furlough, but strangely successful, and viewed as yet another avenue for showing the relevance of the Christian gospel to our everyday life. Each ward, each department, all the different groups of staff, including carpenters and electricians, took part, each saying thank you to the others for their part as a team in making the wheels of the hospital run smoothly. Even the Consultants joined in the grand finale which represented the crowning of the chief bard of the year at the Eisteddfod! It was a great (if amateurish) success to crown weeks of tireless preparation.

There followed three months of holiday and various meetings, including a happy week amongst the students at the Missionary Training College at Glasgow, and two weeks with friends in Northern Ireland. At the WEC quarterly staff meeting my request to be re-admitted as a member was granted and immediately an application was made for reservations on the Castle Line ship sailing on 20th May from London to Mombasa. This was followed by the usual bustle of shopping, listing, packing, labelling, visits to shipping agents and photographers, visas and permits, and at last we were ready to go.

It was not so easy leaving mother and home this second time, especially as rumours were beginning to circulate of anticipated trouble at the declaration of Congo's Independence in just about six weeks' time. I remember my last Sunday evening at Christ Church, Bromley, when I gave a short testimony and asked their prayers for the coming term of service. 'Is anything too hard for the Lord?'—even the unrest, political upheaval, communist infiltration and influence? It might be that our days would be short; it could be that our work would be taken from us. Suffering and persecution possibly awaited us in the Congolese church. But with their prayers we could steadfastly answer, 'There is nothing too hard for Thee.'

With me on the journey out was Elaine de Rusett, an Australian nurse coming to join me at Nebobongo, and young Bill McChesney, a 24-year-old American. I remembered so clearly my first voyage and the goodness of the senior missionaries to me in fellowship and in language study. I therefore felt a great responsibility not to fail the two new recruits who were with me. Each morning, after breakfast, we met together in our two-berth cabin, for prayer and Bible study. We read together through the book of Nehemiah, and day by day I talked to them about one of the stations of the Congo field, introducing them to the workers and the background development, the present work and situation and needs, and as far as I could, the Africans at each place. During each day I encouraged them to give some time to language study and helped them all I could. One day on board, after I had apparently been 'mothering' them, a dear elderly lady came up to me and asked if Bill and Elaine were my two delightful children? That cured me, much to their delight! I myself benefited considerably, of course, from going steadily through the Swahili again and revising my knowledge of both grammar and vocabulary. In the afternoon, I had the joy of helping another group of friends on the boat with their Swahili language study. They were going to Kenya in Government service. There was plenty of time for quiet, for prayer and study, for meditation, for letter-writing, and reading books.

At Genoa we had three days in the port whilst cargo was being loaded. We wandered over the town together. I can still see clearly a great storage shed down by the docks with a huge notice in Italian forbidding trespassers. Bill sauntered up to the door with his usual charming, disarming smile, and wandered in to look round. I was horrified and pleaded with him to come out. The last thing I wanted was to run into trouble in a foreign land where we were not known and did not know the language. Bill looked at my troubled face and grinned impishly. 'What's up? "The world belongs to all of us, so make yourself at home".' 'Bill,' I said, 'can't you read the notice?' 'No; me no read Italiano.' What a lad! Always full of fun, yet always so gracious and courteous. We walked the whole circle of the town, along the hilltops, following the ruined fortifications and walls, collecting wild flowers which he would send to his mother. She was not to see him again. Just over four years later he was martyred at Wamba during the Simba rebellion.

On arrival at Mombasa we were forcibly reminded of the difficult days that lay ahead. The day previously, while still at sea, I had received a cablegram asking me to consider seriously the advisability of staying in Nairobi until after the Declaration of Independence in Congo, so that we could see how things would go. The sender, a relative of one of our missionaries, pleaded with me to think twice before taking these two new recruits into such obvious danger. At Mombasa the customs officials and immigration officers would not stamp our passports nor give us leave to get off the ship, until we had pledged our return fares to England. They told us that, with still a fortnight to go before the Declaration of Independence, white refugees were already pouring into Kenya and Uganda from Congo. They advised us strongly to continue the round journey and to go home! They pointed out forcibly that they could not accommodate all these refugees in their countries, and therefore could not take the deliberate responsibility of adding three more to their problems. We pledged our return fares and left the ship.

As we went down the gangway, carrying suitcases and briefcases, an African porter came straight up to Bill, the only man in our group, and took his baggage, leaving us women to struggle with ours. Bill laughed, and felt he had at last reached a country that did things the right way round! Then he reached out and gave us a hand.

The shipping agent, Mrs Passmore, had us cleared through customs in no time, and everything was soon on to the train. So began our long journey up country through Kenya and Uganda. I was wise to some of the problems this time, especially in regard to the necessity of ordering a 'night-sack' with blankets from the guard. On my first journey no-one had told me how bitterly cold it could feel after sunset, as we climbed 5,000 feet up to Nairobi away from the stifling heat of sea-level, and I had frozen all night! At Kikuyu station, as the train shunted to a stop, there was my college friend, Sylvia, with a vast dog, come to meet us! It was quite exciting to meet up in the middle of Africa for just a ten-minute chat on a railway platform. She was teaching then at the Kikuyu Girls' High School.

On again, to Kampala, where we had to 'fill in time' for several hours waiting for our connection to take us on to the head of the rail-road. This final stretch of the journey took us through the most glorious mountainous country, up and up towards the Congo-Uganda border. I felt heavy with the responsibility of taking these two with me towards the dangers that everyone threatened, although of course both of them had made their own decisions before the Lord. But I was earnestly hoping that one of the senior missionaries would meet us at Kasese and, having read the cablegram I had received on the ship, make the actual final decision. What a joy as we piled out of the train, to see Frank Cripps waiting with the Mission truck! In no time we were loaded up, and piled in, Elaine and Bill travelling with Frank Bates, a young Australian missionary who had also come to meet us, and myself with Frank Cripps whose special responsibility was the Mission press and the training of Congolese printers. Soon we were over the border and through customs without the slightest difficulty. A little further on a halt was called at the roadside to sing the doxology and to thank God for having safely brought us thus far, into the promised land, surely 'for such a time as this' (Esther 4:14).

10
Treasures Of Darkness

What a welcome home! Did one ever fear that perhaps one wasn't really wanted? All along the route in, as we passed each out-church and village clearing where I had worked and preached, we were greeted by crowds of school children, together with the evangelist, catechist and their wives, all waving and cheering. Then at Ibambi, what joy it was to see again the Bible school students, printshop workers, school children, nurses, all singing and happy and shaking hands. Finally we reached Nebobongo itself to be met with big hugs and kisses of welcome home, and their 'special' hymn, 'Stand up, stand up, for Jesus, ye soldiers of the cross', learnt for the occasion. It was a thrilling day indeed—walking all round the station with John and Elsie Harris and their two small children, David and Lois, to see all the improvements and new buildings and permanent roofs, and then down to the village to greet all our dear Africans and fellow-workers.

John and Elsie were very tired. They had been out seven years, hard years with many changes involving two different language areas, and they had both had spells of sickness. They were ready for furlough and glad to hand over the responsibility. So I was back into harness once more, and how good it felt! There was need to walk carefully, to 'feel' the new climate of opinion with Independence only two weeks away. I listened in to all I could, nurses, patients, village men from over the way, and also radio reports from Stanleyville and Leopoldville. There were rumours, stories, vague threats, unrest and uncertainty.

One evening that week there was a meeting of our station elders and the male nurses in the dispensary. After a while they sent for us whites, all four of us. They were polite, but were obviously leading up to something. Eventually Joseph Bumukumu brought it out. 'We want to appoint an African leader', he said. 'Everywhere else has done it. At the Red Cross Hospital Dr Kadoner has handed over authority to a senior male orderly, Gwo-gwo, and he has become the new director. We want you to hand over to John Mangadima.' We waited, tense, a little uncertain, praying hard for wisdom. Then John Mangadima himself spoke, and saved a difficult situation. 'I don't mind being in charge of the nurses and the general administrative work. But I'm not a doctor and we can't do without our doctors, and I couldn't ever be over them.' All round there was a gentle 'letting-out' of held breath. They were content; we had not refused their request, but they themselves had made their choice that they wanted us to stay. We were quite clear that there was to be a new emphasis of authority, but we were equally sure that He would steer us through the initial rapids.

So 30th June came. For us it was a day of prayer and praise, with a football match in the afternoon—and a sense of waiting. Mayaribu, the headman of the nearest village, came to visit us, with six other senior village men from the immediate vicinity. They came wearing colourful, native straw hats and flowers, each carrying a little bouquet of flowers and some eggs. We went out on to the verandah to greet them, and Mayaribu made a little speech of welcome saying that they, the head-men of the region, invited us, their 'strangers', to stay with them in their new Independence. We were thus publicly 'accepted'. It was a moving moment, and we responded accordingly.

In the following days all work continued as usual in the hospital and maternity compound, the only difference being the oft-heard cry '*Uhuru!*'—Freedom! Liberty! Everyone seemed to be carrying a bouquet of flowers and wearing native hats and loin-cloths like their forefathers in place of the European clothing which was more usual in our area. Slowly the initial fear and tension relaxed, and somewhat amazedly, we accepted that Independence had come without demonstration or lawlessness.

Suddenly a different note was sounded. There was mutiny in the army at Leopoldville, which led to the rapid evacuation of Belgians and their families following wickedness and the raping of white women. Panic filled the air. Overnight, the whole picture changed. On Thursday, 15th July, two Mission cars passed our station going north. Later in the afternoon they returned with others, and called us all to go to a meeting that evening at Ibambi. Two of our senior missionaries had arrived that day at Nebobongo for medical care. Together the six of us, soberly and wondering, made our way to the centre. We began to gather in, until eventually there must have been over twenty of us. Everyone had different stories to tell, things seen, things heard, things feared.

It was very hard to think levelly in such an atmosphere of anxiety. Truckloads of soldiers had gone through that very day, singing in local tribal languages of what they would do to us on their return. Within an hour some fifteen of the missionaries had signed a list to say they wanted to go over the border, at least temporarily, to see whether things would settle down. Soon the great evacuation had begun. Throughout the night they packed and sorted and left, car after car. So it was that next day, tired and puzzled, I found myself back at Nebobongo alone. Alone, that is, so far as white companionship was concerned. It was a strange feeling. Even my car had gone to help carry those who felt they should leave. And yet there was a quiet peace, knowing that He had brought me to Congo for such a time as this. We tidied up the two missionaries' houses, packing away everything as neatly as possible, and then had a meeting in the church to discuss our immediate future. I found I was surrounded by a love and sense of security and protection that I had never known before. A deep new bond had been forged, and I knew that it was indeed He who had told me to stay with them at this moment of their great need.

Together we decided that the church elders should be formed into an executive committee responsible for all station affairs, spiritual and material. Agoya was appointed President, Mangadima as secretary, and Basuana was made responsible for the youth. The three together were to act as treasurer. I was unanimously asked to remain with them as advisor and friend in all matters. We had a wonderful time of prayer and praise.

That evening, a truck full of soldiers passed. During the night, alone in that large house, each time a rat scurried over the bamboo ceilings I started up in fear. At about 2 a.m. I got up, and knelt in prayer, and asked the Lord to liberate me from this dreadful fearfulness, and if He would, to send me someone to sleep in the house with me. I hadn't even got back into bed when there was a knock at the back door. I was terrified! This was it! They'd come for me. I could hardly force myself to ask who was there. 'We are', they answered, 'Mama Taadi and Mama Damaris.' I flung the door open, and burst into tears as I drew them into the house. 'The Lord woke us from sleep (in different houses, on opposite sides of the compound) and told us to come and sleep in your house so that you wouldn't be alone in these dangerous days.' I hugged them, made them up a couple of beds, made us each a cup of

Ovaltine; we read *Daily Light* together and then settled down again for the rest of the night.

Next day the Lord sent two other white ladies to join me, missionaries from another WEC station forty miles to the north. It was agreed that we should stay together for the first period of Independence until we saw how things would be. It was a joy to welcome them. I remember that first evening discussing at prayers together the recent puzzling events leading up to the evacuation of half the Mission and the fact that the final straw had been the threat of rape to white women by the mutineering army. Surely the Lord had died on Calvary for *this* as much as any other sin? It wasn't *our* sin or shame. We could remain pure before the Lord with His purity no matter what happened. Fifty years ago missionaries risked their lives from malaria or wild animals. Today it might be a different price they had to pay, a different danger to face; but surely He was still the same wonderful Lord who was worthy of any sacrifice made?

We had a month together, dividing up the work and responsibilities between us and doing everything alongside the Africans, helping them daily to carry more and more of the responsibilities. Many times they would say, 'What shall we do if you also have to leave us?' One weekend soldiers did visit us. I was away at Pastor Ndugu's village at the time. They made no trouble. We heard of troubles in other areas; rumours in fact abounded. But we saw little or nothing to trouble us. We often went up to Ibambi to discuss plans with the missionaries there. On one of these visits we heard of the decision which was eventually taken for two of our menfolk to go to the Ugandan border to collect those who had evacuated, those, that is, that now wanted to return. So on Friday, 20th August 1960, just four weeks from their departure, we prepared a huge meal for seventeen at Nebobongo, to welcome them home again. As they drove in we ran out to greet them looking especially for our nurse, whom we were so anxious to have come back to help us in the maternity compound, the hospital, and the leprosy camp. What a deep blow of disappointment it was to find there was no nurse in the party for Nebobongo! Yet here too, doubtless, the Lord was working, as it forced my hand to put more and more responsibility on the African nurses and midwives.

Elaine de Rusett joined me for two happy weeks, to glean all she could of Congolese dispensary ways and tropical drugs and dosages before going 250 miles northwest to our furthermost station to help them. Then again I had four weeks alone, my two lady friends having returned to their own station.This was a very busy period indeed, a foretaste of what lay ahead. In our immediate area of 200 miles radius, where there had previously been seventeen doctors and surgeons, we were now reduced to three, one a leprologist, one a pathologist and myself. We were faced with the difficulty of emergency surgery, none of us being trained or practised in such. Patients came to us from terrific distances, some having been carried through the forest for several days slung in a blanket on a pole between the shoulders of two carriers, and their condition on arrival was often too awful for description. Sometimes we worked round the clock. Weariness became habitual. To hear a truck drive up ceased to cause the fearful dread of soldiers but brought instead an equal horror as to what new emergency was being brought in. God enabled me through those weeks, even though a severe mental battle raged, to learn to trust Him for each needed victory.

Trouble was reported a hundred miles south. As a result three missionaries were brought north and came to live at Nebobongo—one of them being Florence Stebbing, with whom I had worked for the previous five years! She took over at once the oversight of the maternity work and leprosarium, but there, too, she had many difficulties. Since Independence an African midwife, Naomi, had been placed in charge. She was apparently doing very well, and appeared to be teachable. But she did not like having to work alongside a European again, and created much unpleasantness for Miss Stebbing. They were certainly not easy days. We longed to help our African colleagues, and to trust them, and to give them the authority they coveted. Yet we had to see to the maintenance of medical discipline—hygiene, cleanliness, locking up and signing for dangerous drugs—all of which they were beginning to think were merely 'white obsessions'.

An urgent call came from the young Congolese Government that I would go to help them at the hospital at Wamba, sixty miles east across the Nepoko river. So I started to work two days a week at Wamba, doing ward-rounds and operations and clinics for Africans and Europeans. It involved leaving home at 5.30 a.m. to be at the hospital by 8 a.m. Sometimes we did not finish until after 8 o'clock at night which meant not getting home until 10.30 p.m. Weariness increased. The work was not satisfying at Wamba, as I had no authority over the nursing staff and knew full well that the treatment I ordered was frequently not given. Discipline was almost unknown amongst them, and certainly none had the slightest understanding of a professional conscience towards the patients and towards the accurate administration of drugs.

On Tuesday, 13th February 1961, I set off for Wamba as usual, accompanied by John Mangadima, who was going to assist me at the day's operative list. Six miles from Wamba we were flagged to a halt at one of the out churches, and warned to return. 'There is great trouble in Wamba. All the whites are being tied up. Go home.' We argued that as medicals this was not possible. We had a responsibility to our patients. Whilst we discussed the matter, the crowd of casual passengers that had been travelling to Wamba by my van disappeared with all their goods! Mangadima and I continued alone. I had urged him also to remain and wait for me at the church. 'Never', he exclaimed. 'If it is safe for you to go, I go with you.' Just before Wamba we were stopped by wild rough soldiers at a barrier. Menacingly they commanded me out of the car. John stopped their wicked intentions by saying, 'Do not touch her! She is "one of us", our doctor', using a word in the local tongue meaning 'blood of our blood'; and they desisted. They took us into town to the Government offices. Here, as their doctor, I was promptly promised free passage, despite the curfew imposed on all other Europeans. Even as they spoke, two Belgian planters were brought in and roughly thrown into an inner courtyard. Fearfully, we went on to the hospital, where we heard the reason for it all. That morning, the report of the murder of Patrice Lumumba had arrived. Not a single nurse had remained at the hospital and there was nothing we could do. We went to our Mission station a quarter of a mile from the Government post where there were four missionaries working, and discussed with them the present dangerous situation. Then we set out to return home. At the large junction of three roads six miles out there were barriers across all the roads and numerous soldiers were inspecting the cars and trucks lined up on all sides, searching for hidden Europeans. We pulled in, turned off the engine, and settled down for a long wait. Suddenly we were waved forward. We drew out, and as we approached, the barriers were taken down, and each soldier came to attention and smartly saluted us—and we sailed through! God had gone before us and caused someone among the soldiers to recognize my car. Presumably they had received instructions from the Wamba Government to treat 'their doctor' with respect.

It was not always so easy. Two of our senior lady missionaries working in the southern area of our Province were grievously ill-treated and humiliated by the women's group of the Lumumba party. These women were quite as wicked and ferocious as the most brutal of the soldiers. Miss Kingdon at Wamba was threatened many times. I was stopped one day in Wamba High Street, as I set out home after a day of operating, because one of my indicator lights had not worked. Forced from the car at gun-point and driven into the police courtroom, I was held there at attention for over two hours.

We never knew what they might do next. One night about this time thieves broke into my house. Apparently they had drugged (or attempted to poison) me. But my dog had eaten most of my supper as I was not hungry, and she died next day. They stripped the house of curtains, cloths, jumpers, cutlery, foodstuffs, even my glasses and watch from the very room where I was asleep in bed. It left a horrid fear for weeks, making sleep very difficult.

Heart-break followed. One Sunday evening, Miss Stebbing and I were having prayers together. We heard a noise from the maternity compound and listened intently. Was this the noise of the outpoured Holy Spirit, of revival blessing? Yet something did not ring true in our hearts, and with a lantern we set out to investigate. We met Mama Taadi and Mama Damaris coming up from the village, also attracted by the noise and with the same thoughts in their hearts. Together we walked across. We found our four senior midwives and several pupils, dressed in their native clothes instead of hospital uniform, having a meeting in the compound, singing and beating an empty forty-gallon drum, and dancing. Before I had time to investigate further, Mama Taadi called me aside and asked the two of us to go back home. We did and prayed earnestly for wisdom and guidance.

Two hours later, the two Bible women joined us and told us the sad story. The crowd, with the midwives, had been singing in the native tongue songs of filth and mockery, to our hymn tunes, deliberately imitating many of the expressions of the times of the revival. They were joking about and jeering at God and all that is holy to us. In the wards, in the midwives' homes, in various parts of their compound, more than ten men from surrounding villages were surprised, and sent off. We spent the night in prayer, our hearts heavy with grief, a deep sense of failure and disappointment mingled with righteous indignation and horror at the wickedness that had been deliberately perpetrated by those whom we trusted, those in charge, those who had been preaching the gospel in the wards and clinics each day.

We spent the next day in prayer and fasting, and sent out into the area for the parents of all the midwives and pupils, and for the Church Council for the area. On Tuesday we all met together, and eventually it was unanimously decided that the maternity compound must be closed and all the girls dismissed. We must make a fresh start. The girls appeared to be amused, certainly in no wise subdued nor troubled. They went off, laughing and joking. Was it bravado? Was it a cloak, a bluff? How we longed that this might be so. Every girl was told clearly in the hearing of her parents, that if she was repentant and attended regularly at her local church, we would consider her readmission to the training school the following September term. They left; and within five months we heard that more than half of them were expecting babies. I thought my heart would break. How had I failed them? Where had we gone wrong? 'Independence' meant only this to so many, the removal of all restraints, throwing over all discipline, living as they liked, as unto themselves.

That same evening, as I drove to Wamba to take two pupils back to their parents, I arrived at the Mission station there just in time to assist at one of our missionaries' confinements, her first little one, a lovely girl! It certainly was a precious end to a tragic day, though it served to highlight the cunning of the devil in taking one of God's most precious gifts and debasing it into lust.

By this time, we were beginning to know many shortages. Village shops had none of the essentials that we wanted, powdered milk, salt, matches, sugar, flour. Even petrol and paraffin were very hard to get. Many Europeans had taken their cars off the road. For six weeks we had had no letters from home, which also meant no allowances. We did not know what it all meant, except that our Province was being boycotted by the rest of the Congo to make us toe the line. I was one of the very few still travelling to and fro, and therefore became the post-man for our own local mail, calling in at all the plantations and shops and the Roman Catholic compounds on my way to and from Wamba. We had a good Administrator, and his assistant was also very friendly and kindly to us. One day I took all our Intermediate Campaigner Clan, boys and girls, about twenty-four of them, all in uniform and carrying flags, to greet the Administrator at the Wamba territorial headquarters. As we arrived, we found that it was an important public occasion, with a party political harangue from one of the Ministers up from Stanleyville. My young folk stood at ease, in ranks, by the central flagstaff, in full sunshine, for two hours, listening to an impassioned political speech in a language that hardly any of us could understand! Making our way forward afterwards, I was led up the steps to be introduced to the Minister as 'their doctor', and in turn I was able to introduce the youngsters. They sang to him, and saluted, and drilled. Then he gave a further twenty minutes' speech on their behalf! He spoke very highly of them, and stressed the need of putting God first if Congo was to advance, and the need for all young people to learn discipline and obedience and hard work if they wanted to help their country forward. It was a great day!

The first anniversary of Independence Day was approaching. Schools had to be closed beforehand, as many people feared an outbreak of trouble. The church planned a day of conference for prayer and praise at Ibambi. Our Campaigner Clans at Nebobongo set off at 5.30 a.m. to march the seven miles to Ibambi, before the sun got too hot. There were about ninety of us, all in uniform and with flags flying, singing every step of the way—for those who could keep enough breath going! The church was well packed with over 2,500 of our local Christians attending. During the day, I did not feel too well, and by evening, when it was time to set off on the march home, I was very glad indeed to be offered a lift in a car. On Saturday we had a sports day arranged by the Boy Campaigners to which they had invited young men from the local plantations and the fat factory, and also the regional chieftain. It was a very hot and tiring day, which I thought accounted for my headache and feeling of fever. By Sunday, I realized that I was not well, but managed to struggle through the day's services, including the wonderful Communion Service in the evening when four of the Europeans from Ibambi joined us. On Monday I stayed in bed—and that was the beginning of a long illness.

Through that first week I remained at Nebobongo. Suzanne and Elena, two African nurses, slept in the home with me and did all they could to look after me. I tried to help with seeing hospital charts daily and giving any advice I could but the fever stayed high, and interludes of delirium and great depression alternated. Treatment seemed to be ineffective. The following week I was moved to Ibambi, to relieve Elaine and Florence, who already had all they could manage. At Ibambi I was nursed by Miss Muriel Harman.[1] I suffered another week of swinging temperatures and ever-increasing weakness, constant vomiting and severe headaches, before eventually the illness began to respond to treatment, and at last, after five weeks, the fever ended. I was very thin and appallingly weak. Just as I began to get up and sit in a chair, I developed jaundice and seemed to be as ill again as the previous week. This dragged on for another ten days. I felt embarrassed at being a burden to everyone, and so on 13th August I asked to be allowed to go back to Nebobongo, and slowly to resume my work. The two missionaries there had had a heavy time during those six weeks. However, the weakness just dogged me and made me virtually unable to do anything. Ten days later I felt I could go on no longer; I was just too weak to do anything. I vomited everything I tried to eat; the pain never let up. I felt the end was very near, and asked my two co-workers to call the church elders.

Even as I asked, they arrived at the back-door saying that the Lord had constrained them to come to anoint me in the name of the Lord. They prayed for me, anointing me and believing for His touch of healing. To me it was an act of obedience according to James 5:14, but I did not ask for healing. In a few hours the vomiting ceased, the pain eased, and I fell into a restful sleep. Next day, others had arranged for me to go away to Egbita, to the two lady friends who had stayed with me at Nebobongo the previous year, and a car came to collect me and take me to them. There was still an overwhelming weariness and weakness, but certainly less pain. And from that day, I slowly recovered. I spent six wonderful weeks at Egbita, being utterly spoilt and nursed back to health. Towards the end of my stay I spent hours each day preparing lecture notes in French for the coming school year for the nurses. It was very moving to realize how much the believing prayers of our Africans had played in my recovery, how they were growing towards maturity and making decisions for us, instead of our always making them for them.

When I got home for the next school year, early in October, my work at the Government hospital at Wamba had finished, for they now had regular visits from a UNO doctor. There were five doctors in the area, two of them excellent surgeons, and the terrible strains began to let up. But the shortages increased, and what goods there were we could purchase only at black-market prices. Blankets that I used to buy for the patients at 17s 6d were now over £3. Bowls and buckets could not be obtained. Penicillin was unheard of. We were down to our last thermometer. So in May 1952 I went the long 250-mile journey to Stanleyville with two Africans to see what we could do. We visited the Labour Exchange to discuss the possibility of getting permission for the local chiefs' men to build us new wards at the chiefs' expense. We visited the Treasury to discuss the possibility of the nurses receiving Government salaries. We visited the hospital and the Minister of Health to discuss our need of drugs and equipment. We visited UNO Headquarters and discussed everything and everyone! All this in an attempt to try and persuade someone to be interested in a little bush clearing called Nebobongo, and all on foot, dusty mile after dusty mile, as the car was being repaired in a garage. Most visits reached a satisfactory issue only after about five tries. Persistence and grace were essential! At last we had lots of promises, some letters, and a truck (borrowed from the Government!) full of blankets, bowls, buckets, thermometers and drugs, and we were all set to go home. While filling up our van at a local pump, I had my briefcase seized from the front seat of my car, with passport, driving licence, identity card, and all my papers.

The British Consul, Mr McGurk, could not have done more for me. He knew all the right people to see, and the right things to do and say, and within ten days I had a new passport (flown up from Leopoldville, with cabled permission from England), new car papers and permits, new medical certificates all signed, and almost all at someone else's most generous expense. Truly people were deeply kind to me, not least the delightful BMS family I stayed with, Mr and Mrs Saunders and their young son—who gave up his bedroom to me for my prolonged four-week visit.

At last, very encouraged, we reached Nebobongo to receive a grand welcome home. The boys' examinations followed. Then came the Independence Day celebrations. Two days later, a little lad, Timothy, the son of one of our church evangelists, was taken desperately ill. I had him in my home so as to be able to give him the very best possible attention, including night nursing care—and the next day we realized he had smallpox. We had eight cases in all. Timothy died the following Saturday. The father and I buried the child at midnight, alone in drizzling rain, to avoid every possible chance of infection. All the contacts were isolated in my home. It was a deeply anxious ten days. We vaccinated, in all, some 80,000 people in the area. There were some fantastic reactions to vaccine, ulcers right down to the bone, awful sloughing, high fevers, and three more patients died. At last, it was over. There were no further cases. The whole station had been bound over in strict isolation and quarantine. They responded wonderfully. One letter had gone out, the first day, duly stoved and disinfected, to seek prayer from home. When she received it my mother had rung the convent where my sister lived and the community bore us up all through that week, day and night, and God stayed the hand of the epidemic.

Very exhausted, never having properly recovered from the illness of the previous year, I was given permission to go away for six weeks for a complete break, out of the tropical steamy heat of Congo, out of the political unrest and constant threats and fear. I had a wonderful rest and returned very much refreshed. When I arrived back in Paulis by plane I was met and driven home to Nebobongo. There I received such a welcome you would have thought I had been away for a year, not just six weeks!

Storm-clouds were now gathering in the church. Before Independence all Europeans were invited to all church meetings and were on all committees. Now things were changing. There were tensions. There was a growing consciousness that the Africans did not wholly trust us whites, afraid that we were not really willing to give them absolute equality, absolute authority. They wanted to have their Independence in the church just as others had it in political matters. They wanted Africans to be in charge in every department, including the handling of the finances. The problems were very similar to those of adolescents all over the world. The desire to stand on one's own feet, and not be eternally tied to mother's apron-strings is only natural. So the missionaries were no longer invited to church meetings. Sometimes they were not represented on councils or committees. Decisions were made in the church with no reference to the Europeans or their opinions.

Affairs seemed to come to a head at Christmas 1962 over church finance. There was a good deal of heat in the church meetings and not a little bitterness. Above all there was this tragic lack of confidence between Africans and Europeans. One day two of the pastors and two schoolmasters came in for coffee, obviously very full, as it were, of the recent troubles. I stood a book on the table between us and asked them if they from their side photographed the book, and at the same moment I took a picture from my side, and then the two films were processed, would they say that my camera lied because it saw the opposite side of the book with a row of black faces behind it, so different from their photograph of the front of the book with a white face behind it. They saw the point, and we had prayer together and yearned that He would help us all through this difficult period of growing-pains.

Then came an unfortunate occurrence. In the summer, we had a young man named Gabriel Mangeyi brought to the hospital with tuberculosis. We knew him well, as he had been a student nurse at Nebobongo years before, but had been dismissed for adultery. He was now married to a woman well known as a harlot. His mother came with him to nurse him, but I forbad the wife to come to the hospital, trying to protect the twenty or more student male nurses from her evil influence. However, she came, and after three nights, Gabriel's mother came to tell me that this woman had sinned with the son of my evangelist Agoya.

The case was taken to the church, amidst much heart anguish. Throughout it all Stephen, their son, repeatedly denied the accusation of Gabriel's mother. But the council decided that Agoya and Taadi would have to leave us to take over a small village church, so that their wayward son could go with them to be under their direct discipline. For various reasons, however, action on their decision had to be postponed. Taadi was ill, and also expecting another little one. Also the church had no evangelist whom they could send immediately to replace Agoya. So several months passed without the sentence being implemented.

Thus it was that Agoya and his family were still at Nebobongo when we heard that Gabriel had been brought to repentance at a church conference and had confessed that the whole story had been a lie, to 'get even' with Agoya who had been responsible for his dismissal years earlier. My heart lurched badly. I felt I never wanted to see Gabriel, his wife or mother again after such evil.

On Boxing Day this mother came to see me at Nebobongo to say that she wanted my forgiveness. 'What for?' I asked. 'I don't know', she replied; 'but the church says I cannot make my Christmas Communion while I have anything in my heart against you.' I felt anger well up in my heart. What deceit! To say she didn't know what she had done or for what she sought forgiveness. She went on her knees to me—and in a moment, I struck her, pulling her to her feet and demanding that she never kneel to me, but only to the Lord. Stunned she left me, and miserably I turned and entered the house. I had lost my temper; I had struck an African. After an hour's fighting with myself, I went out, got into the van, and set off for Ibambi to take the matter to the church council. On the way, I overtook the woman walking back to Ibambi and gave her a lift. It was not the easiest of journeys!

Arrived at Ibambi, I went straight to the house where the African church elders were meeting, told them exactly what had happened, and asked them to mediate between us. They were amazed. Apparently this was the first time that a European had taken a case to the Africans and not to the other missionaries. They heard the case, African fashion, and eventually we both sought forgiveness and shook hands. Next day the two pastors came to see me at Nebobongo. Very humbly they confessed that it was jealousy that had caused them to insist that Agoya and Taadi should leave Nebobongo because I thought so much of them. Now they wanted our forgiveness and to assure them and myself that the church had agreed that they both should stay with me. And so that day yet deeper and closer links were forged between my heart and theirs as they acknowledged that I was indeed one of themselves. Humbly I realized that God was blessing us through it all, and teaching us to walk together in close fellowship without the barriers of pride and race.

National events were moving fast. Thieving was rife. It was hard, if not impossible, to get justice. Jealousies and suspicions were on the increase. Every man was afraid of his neighbour lest he lose his job through false accusations, and no man lightly agreed to help a European lest he lose his job through being thought to fraternize or encourage neo-colonialism. John and Del Gunningham, fellow-missionaries from the north-west of our Province, joined us for her confinement, and he did a wonderful job putting a new permanent roof on the other missionaries' house on the station. Whilst they were with us we had a visit from the Inspector of Medical Schools from Leopoldville quite unexpectedly, and Del did wonders in catering for everyone! Then the local chiefs sent us men to build new wards, an out-patients' block, and a new primary school for the children. The station was a noisy hive of activity for many weeks. The building programme was not without incident, grumbling and strikes, but we managed to steer through without too bad a break, and eventually everything was completed.

Christmas 1963 came and went without undue incident. But early in 1964 we began to hear rumours and odd scraps of news of troubles down in the south of Congo, including rioting, looting, and burning of villages. Unrest in our area increased. Shortages were more acute, prices were spiralling, and wages kept going up and up. Tensions between Africans and Europeans were no longer hidden.

As before, this was reflected in the church. The devil seemed to be fighting hard to destroy the work of years. Misunderstandings were rife; seeds of bitterness were sown in many hearts; feelings of distrust grew between different groups. Yet through it all God most graciously continued to bless the ministry of the gospel and many souls were added to the church. Through the four years since Independence we had taken a chapter a day from Scripture in our morning Bible School at Nebobongo, starting from Genesis, with a synopsis and analysis of each book as we commenced and finished it. The elders had followed right through the course, with detailed notes, forming each one his own commentary in Swahili. And now we were nearing the end. On Saturdays we had had classes for studying the doctrines of the Christian faith and always these were amazingly well attended. The choir was an active integral part of our church life, and the eighty members sang a Swahili translation of Handel's 'Unto us a Child is born' from *The Messiah* at the Easter conference—with no orchestral accompaniment other than the birds. They had learnt it to a tuning fork, line by line, in tonic solfa!

During the year, various projects began to come to fruition after years of praying. A branch of the Evangelical Alliance had been formed, uniting all the six Protestant Missionary Societies working in the north-east Congo. This was the corner-stone of the foundation of an Inter-Mission educational programme for creating one united full-grade secondary school, to prepare our Mission-trained youngsters for University entrance so that we might have keen spiritual men in the future government of Congo. There was also an Inter-Mission Medical programme for creating one central hospital, sufficiently well built and equipped to be passed by the Government as a training school for African paramedical and nursing personnel. These were thrilling days, and I was very privileged to represent our Mission at several of these Inter-Mission conferences discussing these programmes.

Then in July 1964, we had our triennial field conference, attended by all the missionaries and by two representatives from each African church council in the area. About twenty-four of us and nearly sixty of them met for a week of prayer and fellowship, and to discuss placing of personnel and projects for the coming three years. It was a blessed week, and many of us felt that God was very specially present in our midst, breaking down barriers, bringing us back to each other in a fuller unity and trust, and dispersing us afterwards with a renewed vision and purpose.

As we looked back during the months of travail that followed, we were always so grateful to God that He allowed us that week of united fellowship. We did not then know that it would be the last time that many of us would ever meet in that manner. Within six months, four of our missionaries were to be murdered, and all of us driven from the country. But our last memories were to be of the joy and happiness and unity of church and Mission together.

End Notes

1 Miss Harman, a senior missionary nurse, had spent over thirty years in the Congo. She had come to Ibambi four months previously, following the outbreak of troubles in the south of our Province. Later in the rebellion of 1964, she was killed by machine-gun fire after several weeks of harrowing experiences at the hands of the rebel soldiers.

11
Nearly Exhausted[1]

Throughout the years since Independence there had been a strange spiritual battle in my own heart. Often an apparent darkness and loneliness hedged me in, yet always there was the complete certainty of being in the centre of His will; often I lacked any consciousness of His presence and knew no burden in prayer, yet always there was quiet confidence of being a 'vessel only'. I had a growing hunger after Him, and a deepening realization of the wonderful process of identification with Christ for the Africans I was trying to win. 'Christ in you, the hope of glory' was the phrase often in my mind. He was working out His love for them through me. Every act of service was a manifestation of His love.

The church of Jesus Christ in Congo seemed to be going through a process of adolescence, and there were many growing pains. For fifty years the missionaries had been working in the area, preaching the gospel and training the early church, much as a parent does a child, with a somewhat similar relationship, one of paternalism. Now the child, fully grown, becoming yearly more educated and sophisticated, learning of other lands through radio and travelling, was demanding her independence, unwilling for the close parental discipline any longer, fighting to break free, determined to show that she could stand by herself.

There were many tensions. Some missionaries felt that the church was ungrateful for the years of sacrificial love, and that they were no longer wanted. Yet they were sure that the church was not yet ready for them to leave. The Africans felt that the missionaries did not trust them, that they always wanted to 'boss', to be in charge, to tell them what to do and how to do it. The problem was particularly acute in the matter of the church collections and other general administrative decisions. The Africans broke loose. They held their own meetings, dispersed their own finances, and asked advice of no-one. The 'parent' was hurt. Mistakes were made; finances were in a muddle; debts were incurred. The Africans were proud and would not concede that anything was wrong. They were afraid they might incur the 'told-you-so' attitude. The missionaries began to withhold their offerings, feeling that the funds to which they had been contributing were being mismanaged. The troubles increased and, as I have already indicated, some difficult years ensued.

On top of all this, possibly due to the great strain through which all were passing, there were misunderstandings amongst the missionaries themselves. I myself was criticized for siding with Africans against the missionaries, whereas one's aim was to seek Him in each situation and to see Him glorified in each life. There was consequent loneliness, linked with overwork and weariness. At such times I recalled again all He had suffered for me on the cross of Calvary; now it was my privilege to share the suffering for those I was trying to reach. He was made sin for me; how closely was I willing to be identified with Him? with them? Was I prepared to face the cost?

Our Mission motto was deeply burnt into my heart: 'If Jesus Christ be God and died for me, then no sacrifice can be too great for me to make for Him.' This was my firm belief, and I prayed God that I might be found worthy.

On 7th August 1964 came the outbreak of the rebellion in the north-east province. We were caught absolutely unawares, not having the slightest thought of all that might be involved. I was setting off in the Mission truck to Kampala in Uganda, a thousand miles east, to collect two tons of medical goods and supplies, food and petrol, when the news that Stanleyville had fallen to the hands of the rebels reached us. We waited to see what this would involve. No-one was very perturbed. We had had troubles and riots for the last four years.

Eight days later, on Saturday, 15th August, the soldiers reached us. A truck-load drove into the hospital compound bringing with them a wounded civilian. That was the start of five months of occupation. They were brutal and coarse, rough and domineering. Their language was threatening and obscene. All of us were cowed. We did exactly what they demanded, mostly without argument. We gave them what they asked for without debating the price. Africans carried·flowers and shouted the slogans of the day as an act of obedience to the new powers. Rumours poured round us. We heard of murders, brutalities, beatings, stealings, looting and burning. We did not wish to be involved so we obeyed. We heard that the rebel army had taken first Wamba, and then Paulis, with very little resistance. Some said that the streets ran with blood, that they had to walk with care not to step on a corpse. All the previous leaders, all those who had been in Government pay, were being systematically liquidated. They were searched out, evilly treated, and ultimately brutally murdered. Cars and trucks in the area were commandeered. To hear a vehicle on the road was synonymous with the approach of the army. Whenever they came to the village they brought a terrible sense of fear, a presence of evil and wickedness. And they were for ever passing, passing. Would they enter? What ought we to do?

Thus began the war of nerves. We had rebels amongst the patients, especially in the men's ward, and I felt they could well be spying on us. Care was necessary in every word we spoke. The soldiers came to visit friends day and night, but one never knew when they drove on to the compound for what they had come. Many times they told us in those first weeks that this war had nothing to do with us Europeans. It was a party-political, civil war. They had nothing against us as whites, and especially as Protestant missionaries. They wanted us to stay and continue with our task. When the New Order was established, they would recognize our good work officially and do all they could to obtain the supplies we needed. But in almost the same breath they would threaten us that, if we meddled with politics, if we interfered with their method of administering justice, if we helped any 'wanted' man to hide in the hospital, then we should be treated as traitors and shot. And the hospital would be burnt to the ground. It was not easy to keep calm in such an atmosphere.

Suffering? Yes; it began early on. The mental suffering of uncertainty, not knowing quite what they would do, nor when. At Nebobongo we were virtually cut off from the rest of the Mission since we were not allowed to travel. And we were completely cut off from the outside world, for there was no mail or radio communication with anyone outside the Province. There was no way of letting anyone know how we were. At first we all thought it would speedily be over, one way or the other, and that we should be allowed to continue our work under the former or latter Government. Then things began to drag. We saw truck-loads of young teenagers passing along the road and were told that they were conscripts going to the front to fight. We never saw any coming back. We saw a van go by full of European nuns and priests. Later it returned. Where had it been and why? We feared for them and what they were being made to suffer. We heard that the local chief had been caught, bound and beaten; then he was taken to the people's tribunal at Wamba, found guilty, flayed alive and eaten. No wonder we did not sleep well. No wonder we were not hungry.

Suffering? Yes; in fear for our own people. One of our girl nurses was assaulted. Two of the women were taken from the maternity compound, rudely flung on to a truck and driven off. They threatened to take two of our little girls to 'serve' the soldiers. Primary school children were being rounded up in other areas as army conscripts. Would they come and do the same here? They inspected our homes, searching for transistor radios and tape-recorders, threatening death should they find any. I had none; but would they go and search the other home where both the missionaries had them? They demanded food, and clothing, and spectacles. I gave what I had. Then came the time when there was nothing to give, and they raised their rifles to strike me as a liar—and I feared for the physical pain. A male nurse, away on holiday, made his way back to us through the forest, telling of being hunted for ten days, his father having been murdered, his home burnt and looted, and his mother dying of heart failure. We were one with them, identified with them in their suffering, and our hearts bled with theirs.

Suffering? Yes; the day when they turned against us whites. News was seeping through that the National Army was employing white troops, mercenary soldiers from South Africa and other lands, and that the rebel army was being turned back. Rebel soldiers were being killed despite the witchcraft and the promises made at their initiation rights. It must be that the white man was using a more powerful witchcraft, possibly emanating from the white people in the area. Therefore we were to be bound and herded together, possibly shot. They were brutal and drunken. They cursed and swore, they struck and kicked, they used the butt-end of rifles and rubber truncheons. We were roughly taken, thrown in prisons, humiliated, threatened. We were driven forty miles north to be shot—but God intervened and we were driven home again! The whole church had been praying ceaselessly for our deliverance. We were four weeks under house-arrest, four weeks filled with petty interferences and pilferings, endless threatenings and uncertainties. The Christians rallied round wonderfully to help us and out of their poverty poured on us gifts of chickens and eggs, rice and peanuts. Each time a truck-load of soldiers arrived they were always there beside us, to protect us and encourage us.

Suffering? Yes; impossible though it seemed, the situation got worse. We were taken away from our dear Africans and placed under close guard, under prison conditions, in the Roman Catholic convent at Wamba. We saw the nuns wickedly treated, beaten and humiliated. We were completely at their mercy, and yet strangely God moved upon them to protect us, and also to feed us. Rumours fed our fears, and each long day led into a long night of waiting, hoping, expectant for deliverance the following dawn, but only to meet with disappointment—and to start again. We heard that our stations had been utterly ransacked and destroyed, and we longed for news of our Africans. Were they suffering for having befriended us? We felt we were always being watched and had to take extra care of all that was said and done.

Then came Christmas Day, and with it the next move. The soldiers began taking us group by group, in a small open van, a hundred miles east. The idea, apparently, was to keep us with the retreating army as front-line hostages. The group I was with was taken on the Sunday, but after traveling only seventy-five miles, we were put off at a house in the jungle—nineteen defenceless women and children surrounded by some seventy-five men, soldiers and others, all filled with hatred and evil intentions towards us. Food was scarce; water almost unprocurable. Danger was imminent; fear was in the very air we breathed. Wickedness surrounded us on all sides; it seemed inevitable that we should be killed. And in my heart was an amazing peace, a realization that I was being highly privileged to be identified with Him in a new way, in the way of Calvary.

I witnessed the outpouring of hatred against the white man. I became very conscious of the extent to which we had earned this. If I was willing to be identified as a European with the sin of the white people against the African in the past fifty or more years—the injustices, the cruelties, the hardships, cheap labour with flogging, black women-folk and illegitimate children, bribery and corruption in courts and administration—then perhaps, in some small way, I was privileged to be part of the extirpation of that sin. We whites had to be identified with it, to bear its penalty, to suffer for it, that Africa might be rid of it, to start again freed of it. This was our hope; this was what made it worth while. Somehow He was working out His purposes for our Congo; somehow He would bring ultimate blessing out of the terror of

124

all this suffering; for He alone could make even the wrath of man to praise Him.

Now the end seemed very near. We were expecting death at any moment. The guards were becoming more and more restive. A sense of oppression was closing in on us. Suddenly there was a distant noise. Was it friend or foe? Everyone stiffened and listened intently. We were bundled into an inner room, flung on the ground, kicked and beaten. Then the guards retired, locking the door. We heard the distant noise growing; it was machine-gun firing! Hope soared, could it be our deliverers? They mustn't pass us by; they must see a white face somehow; we must show them we were there. Would our guards fire on us through the window? Nothing seemed to matter any longer except the thought of deliverance. I threw myself forward towards the window. There were jeeps, trucks, men, noise, shouting, firing. Someone was kicking at the door. Women were crying, children were sobbing. The door gave, and a white man burst through to us. The room seemed to fill with white soldiers.

'It's all over; don't cry, mother. Yes, yes, we'll take you all. No hurry; take your time. We can't take any luggage, I'm afraid, as we're a bit full up.'

So their chatter soothed through our tumultuous thoughts. We were safe! It was all over. We were still alive. The terrible nightmare was over.

End Notes

1 The fuller story of this chapter, as told in the diary kept throughout the five months of the rebellion, has been published under the title *Doctor Among Congo Rebels* (Lutterworth Press and Christian Literature Crusade, Fort Washington).

12
Gloriously Worth It!

Home! It was less than three days from the moment of deliverance, but it was hard to believe it. The mercenary soldiers had been kindness itself. That Wednesday evening we were taken to their barracks in the Paulis brewery, all ten of us Protestant missionaries together, united at last with our two menfolk. They carried up jugs of hot water for us to have the first proper wash for many weeks. They served us a lovely hot meal which we could eat in peace, not fearfully glancing round in case of trouble. They brought us mattresses and blankets to sleep in comfort on the floor of their large sitting-room. Next day, they showed us all over the site, chatted with us, photographed us, and at last waved us farewell as we left in a great American transport plane along with 125 other refugees.

At Leopoldville we were given a tremendous and moving welcome by the missionaries there who had been anxiously praying for us and waiting for us over the months. On New Year's Day everyone helped us—to get clothes, to arrange passports and papers, to book seats on a flight to Amsterdam. That evening we were again in the air, flying towards Europe—from 90° to snow! At each stop on the route friends known and unknown seemed to vie with each other in giving help and showing consideration, especially at Amsterdam where we changed planes for the final flight for London.

Through a battery of television and newspaper cameras, to the customs sheds, and straight to a telephone booth. Excitedly I put in a reverse charge call—I hadn't a penny in the world—and there was dear Mother's voice. What a moment!

That evening I was home. The long five months of nightmare were over. But it was not immediately easy to wake up and realize that we were still alive. We had lived facing and expecting death for too long to accept easily the fact of life again. Family, friends, newspaper reporters, church, letters, flowers—it was an overwhelming welcome, as to one back from the dead. At hospital, where we went for general medical check-ups as soon as an appointment could be made, we were all given every kindliness and consideration, and were each recommended to take a fairly long spell of quiet convalescence. For me it was nearly ten weeks before I really snapped out of the stupor and daze, back to reality, and began to realize once more that life had present-tense claims and that there was still plenty to be done!

After a lovely four-week holiday with my mother and sister down in Cornwall, mainly sleeping, eating, reading and resting, I felt reorientated, for He enabled me to look back on it all and to see it was a great privilege, offered to me from His nail-pierced hands, gloriously worth while in His perfect economy. There followed six months of deputation touring, which took me all over the British Isles and twice to the continent, speaking at some two hundred meetings, telling of the great and all-sufficient grace of Jesus Christ, and urging people to accept the burden of believing prayer for our Congolese church.

We knew nothing of their needs at that time. Had they suffered reprisals for our deliverance? We longed over them, travailing again that Christ might be formed in them. It was a glorious tour. My desire was to present a positive message of His redeeming love, of the greatness of Calvary, the privilege of suffering with Him, the realization in a new way of His pre-eminence. As I told the story of His dealings with me to His praise and glory, my heart became fully comforted and in tune to accept all the suffering as from Him. The wounds were healed. The mental shock was alleviated. Slowly He filled me again with a great joy and wonder at His precious goodness.

Then in August a thrilling day arrived, bringing our first letters from our Nebobongo family. The National Army had at last reached them and delivered them from the long ten months of rebel occupation. The first, dated 6th June, was filled with praise to God for His goodness to them and to us in keeping us all safe. They told of all the rumours they had heard of our fate, of their fears for our safety, and of their great joy for us when they received our letters from the hands of the delivering soldiers of the National Army as they arrived on 5th June. These had taken five months to travel forty-five miles!

A group of the faithfuls had stayed at each of our stations, guarding the property as best they could and watching and praying daily to see how the Lord would overrule. In April, however, the rebel soldiers had made Ibambi their headquarters, taking over all the houses and everything they could find, hoisting their flag, and ordering the remaining

Africans to serve them as house-boys. Some managed to get away, with nothing but the clothes they wore and their Bibles in their hands. They lost everything just as we had. 'We are now as we were when you first came to Congo fifty years ago', they wrote. The rebels had declared that on 15th June they would kill all the evangelists. But on 5th June the delivering National Army walked in! Everyone had fled to the jungle for fear at the approach of the army and troops, but were soon persuaded to come back to the station. What a day of praise followed! The great church at Ibambi was filled to overflowing as crowd after crowd gave thanks to God for their deliverance. 'All the church monies have been taken; all the chairs, tables, *etc.,* destroyed. But we have one piece of wealth left—our salvation. How we thank and praise God that He sent you to us to give us the only true wealth, that no man can take from us, that cannot be destroyed, the truth as it is in Scripture, our Lord and Saviour Jesus Christ. Hallelujah!'

Letters began getting through to us, week by week, and all were similarly full of praise and joy, and ended with a plea to us to return to help them and to have fellowship with them again as soon as it was safe and possible to do so. Our hearts were stirred. There were no grumbles, no bitterness just praise. And the sense of their need was overwhelming. Two and a half million Congolese in the north-east province without one single doctor, black or white, with no secondary school teachers, their shops empty, no grain for planting, without clothes, food or medicine. At once, we put in our applications to go back just as soon as it was considered reasonable by the powers that be. I continued deputation with renewed vigour and refreshed vision, telling of their need for our prayers, and for further personnel for the tremendous task of re-establishing all the church services they were so sorely in need of—spiritual, medical, educational. Two months in a post-graduate course followed, preparing one's mind for the task ahead, and letters went to and fro. A new programme was slowly emerging in our hearts to meet the new day of opportunity as well as the urgent needs of the hour.

Our Africans, both the local Christians and those in local government, want us back to work alongside them, as brothers and fellow-labourers. But it will be, it must be, a new relationship, that of adults of maturity. No-one who has been through such sufferings can come out the same as before. I believe we have been welded into one as never before. The tensions and suspicions between African and European have been destroyed; and we must see to it that they are never restored.

At Christmas 1965 we had a wonderful family reunion, the first for seventeen years! My brother and his wife, my three sisters and their husbands, together with seven nieces and nephews were all gathered together, and it certainly was a great day. It was just one more climax to this amazing year, as each one could look back and praise God for His infinite goodness and preserving care in so many different ways. It was also the occasion for saying farewell, as I set my face to prepare for returning to the land of my adoption. Making lists, shopping, packing, labelling; visits to shipping agents, consular offices, and to doctor and dentist; arrangements with bank manager and with income tax offices. Then came the final meetings and farewells, the letters and reporters. But above all, there was the joy of planning for, and purchase and construction of a fully equipped mobile hospital. This is a long-wheel-base Land Rover, with its overweight springs and four-wheel drive to stand up to our impossible roads, fitted and equipped with a small laboratory, pharmacy, dispensary and everything needed for major emergency surgery, and convertible into a caravan at nights, with electric light and air-conditioning! A long-cherished dream is at last seeing the light of day, provided by the generosity of Christians, stirred to give to help the Congolese in their need, through the many deputation meetings. Surely He has seen fit to give it to us 'for such a day as this'.

11th of March 1966. What a day of joy; the day we sail for Congo, back to our beloved African fellow-workers, to take up the task again that He has committed to our hands. We go back at a time of unprecedented needs. In our northeastern Province, with its two and a half million Congolese, there is a strong, virile, active church, with her own pastors and elders. But they ask us to join them to help in the vast task of education, primary, secondary, technical, medical and theological, at a time when they have only a handful of Africans trained for teaching in senior primary schools, a hundred or so for junior primary, but none for the senior schools. There is the essential need of aid for their medical programme, for they have no doctors, less than a handful of fully qualified nurses, and only a hundred or so assistant nurses, scattered in badly damaged, poorly equipped, rural dispensaries, with no medicines, no supervision, and the constant threat of the outbreak of serious epidemics. They look to us also for help in organizing youth work and training the new generation to take its place in the world with respect and not shame, with courage and not constant fear, with honour in the place of bribery and corruption. They need men and women to help with the printing of good literature, with its writing, translation and distribution; to help with the establishment of a theological college for the training of pastors to lead the young church, men who will take their place as teachers in the different area Bible schools for training their own evangelists. Possibilities abound on every side. The doors are wide open. The invitation has been issued to all who have seen the vision, and heard the call of the risen Lord, to those who know the joy of the mystery, 'Christ in you, the hope of glory.' Surely indeed in the coming years, we are going to see 'the valley of Achor' become 'a door of hope'.

Epilogue

I have used some of the three weeks which it takes from London to Mombasa to put the finishing touches to this story of God's dealings with me. As I have read the chapters again it is clear that certain landmarks stand out very clearly. There are lessons which I had to learn and warnings which I still need to heed.

First, I would put the realization that in myself I was a failure. I was unable to reach the standard I myself had set, let alone God's. Try as I would, I met only frustration in this longing to achieve, to be worthy. I'm sure that, for me, this first lesson had to be thoroughly learnt so that, when I did come to acknowledge God as my Lord and Master, I might not succumb again to the temptation to feel that I could succeed or achieve anything ultimately worth while in my own strength.

Secondly, I had to learn that, of myself, I could be ashamed of sin and hate its consequences, but that I could not actually hate the sin itself. On the contrary I found pleasure in it. I despised myself for enjoying what I knew I ought to hate, but I continued to enjoy it nevertheless. Like Paul, who describes what seems to have been a somewhat similar experience in Romans 7, my position was, 'I do not do the good I want, but the evil I do not want is what I do.' Now hatred of sin is a gift of the Holy Spirit. After trying hard to make myself hate what I knew I enjoyed, and nearly despairing in the effort, I came at last to the limit by asking God 'to make me willing to be made willing to hate what He hated', and He graciously did for me what I asked.

Then I had to learn that there are some glorious views *en route*, as well as many pleasant valleys, that do not necessarily help in the upward climb. Certain experiences came and entered my life. They could have grown big and all-important, but when measured against the course of the journey they were found to be non-essential to the main progress. Again, other incidents were eventually found to be of passing interest only. But they might have seriously hampered the journey if carried along as an important item. I gladly accepted and entered into each experience as God graciously bestowed it, but I had to learn to cling to Him, my Guide, and not to the various feelings stirred by the passing views.

Then those wise words of Elizabeth at Mission Headquarters in my training days have remained with me through the following years as a beacon on the path. 'If you're doing it for me (or for any man) you may as well go home.... You're doing it for the Lord and *He* saw the first time you cleaned it....' The day all our midwives had to be dismissed and the maternity compound closed—I asked myself, How had I failed them? Where had we gone wrong? Recriminations, accusations crowded into my mind. What will the Mission say? or the church? This was fear of man. 'You are doing this work for *Me*, and I have seen all you have poured in, of heart and soul; I know.' So He breathed peace into my striving heart—the same old message, but ever new.

Another deep truth I have learnt, and one we can all cling to, is that God is personally interested in each one of us as individuals and that He will engineer our circumstances and daily lives so that He can thereby make us like Jesus. This takes the sting out of much that could otherwise hurt. He allows various accidents and happenings to occur, things which will affect us deeply, perhaps, only so that, through them, we may be drawn closer to Himself.

There were the times of deep humiliation, coupled with a sense of insufficiency, both as a doctor and as a missionary. Here, too, these negative experiences were allowed to reveal positive truth. Only as I found my own insufficiency did I realize His sufficiency. Such ability as I had to lead, to organize, to administer, all tended to strengthen my personal ego and pride. This was true also of my popularity with the Africans and the respect I received from the Government. My pride was big enough already! It was a stalwart prop on which I leant for self-encouragement to continue and to stick the job. God had to take the prop away, and I did not like it—until I found that He was there, willing to fill my every need and to give all the encouragement I desired! Even my inverted pride in my inabilities had to be dealt with. I said I could *not* operate. I had not been trained and I was scared stiff. I just wasn't willing to trust the Lord to work this out. I did not want Him to make me willing to operate; I wanted to go on not wanting to! But when during the first six months of Independence He allowed every surgeon in the area to leave, I just *had* to operate. Then He showed that He was able to undertake for this need also as I was willing to be made willing. My pride in my inability had been as great a prop in my self-preservation as my pride in my abilities was to my self-realization. Both had to be taken away that I might learn that Christ wanted the pre-eminence in every department of my life.

In the Introduction (for those who paused to read it) I mentioned the great importance of distinguishing between the slight going down from a peak experience in order to set out across the valley to climb yet another higher peak, and the real going down of returning to base. The former may appear to be a stretch of the journey in shadows, but the latter would have been acknowledgement of defeat and failure. For many years, I did not discern this difference, and thereby suffered many long heartaches unnecessarily, listening to the devil's accusations instead of the Spirit's counsel.

Another clear truth that has come out so forcibly into the sunlight through the last few chapters is that God has no second-best. This is very often a contradiction of terms. If I am in God's will for me, it is His very best for me. God is eternal present tense. If I step out of His will, then I deliberately choose my own path and I have nothing of His best. When I confess my error, seek His loving forgiveness, and return to His will, then at once He restores me. It is always present to Him, so at the moment of restoration I am in His present will for me. Once repentance is real, and forgiveness sought, the past is past, and has no longer an interpretation in the present. The present may well be different from the 'might-have-been', it may well be affected by the consequences of previous disobedience and sin which can leave their mark on both character and circumstance, but nevertheless, it is the best in the immediate now. I have found this to be a most liberating and glorious truth. If it were not so, who among us would not live his life in an atmosphere of continual regret?

The night I was first taken captive by the rebel soldiers He worked that liberation for me in the midst of all the horror and anguish! I saw it in a verse in Peter's Epistle: 'For what glory is it, if, when ye be buffeted for your faults, ye shall take it patiently? but if, when ye do well, and suffer for it, ye take it patiently, this is acceptable with God' (I Peter 2:20). In that moment, I *knew* utterly and unquestioningly, whatever the past might have held of failures, that I was in the *second* half of the verse. God allowed the circumstances to be such that even I, so often a veritable 'doubting Thomas', could not argue. Therefore He showed me, with a gentle smile, a smile of reproof, perhaps, that I had taken so long to learn, a smile of deep love that I truly wanted to learn, that I was 'acceptable with God'—and this could only mean that I was in the centre of His will. Certainly this could be no 'second-best'.

The last months of 1964 brought to a culmination so much of all He had been teaching me through the years. The suffering just seemed to highlight His love. I have summarized in my own heart the specific lessons of my months in captivity to help me not to lose anything of their wonder and their worth.

1. *Participation in His suffering is necessary* to each one if we are to fulfill His will in this world;

2. *The pre-eminence of His Son is essential* that we may know in very truth His all-sufficiency at all times;

3. *Praise through His sacrifice is possible* even in the midst of danger and horror, as we rejoice in His working out His purposes.

Above all, I have learnt a little of the tremendous privilege of walking with Him, of being identified with Him. Christ not only bore my sin; He was made sin for me. He identified Himself utterly with us sinners that He might redeem us. Now if He should seek a body, a vessel, in whom to live, that He might identify Himself with the deepest needs and hungers of Congolese hearts, was I willing to be this vessel? More than willing! I entered into the great privilege of bearing about the One who had paid the supreme cost.

'Brethren, I count not myself to have apprehended: but this one thing I do, forgetting those things which are behind, and reaching forth unto those things which are before, I press toward the mark for the prize of the high calling of God in Christ Jesus' (Philippians 3:13,14).

Book Two

He Gave Us A Valley

**Part Two
of
An Autobiography
by
Helen Roseveare**

Contents

Apologies

Very few names are used throughout this book. This is not because I think I achieved all this alone. It is not because I am unaware how deeply indebted I am to the many who made up the team throughout the years. I have not wanted to involve any in the responsibility for my mistakes, my thought processes and sometimes faulty deductions. The blame is mine: the hard work was ours: the glory is God's alone.

Brief Historical Résumé

1925 Born at Haileybury, Herts, England.

1931-1944 Primary and secondary school education.

1945 Converted while a medical student at Newnham College, Cambridge.

1953 Sailed to Africa under the auspices of the Worldwide Evangelization Crusade (WEC) to the Belgian Congo. Eighteen months establishing medical services at Ibambi, NE Congo.

1955 Moved 7 miles, to establish WEC medical centre at Nebobongo, comprising:

> 100-bed hospital and maternity services; leprosy-care centre and children's home; 48 rural health clinics in immediate vicinity; training school for national para-medical workers, that is male and female assistant nurses and midwives.

1958 Two years of furlough with further medical training in UK.

1960 Independence: formation of the Republic of Congo.

1964 Rebellion+Simba uprising (civil war): five months' captivity.

1965 Rescued by National Army: one year's furlough in UK.

1966 Returned to Africa under the auspices of WEC to Congo/Zaire, to give seven years' service in an inter-mission (comprising five missions and churches) medical project, at the Evangelical Medical Centre of Nyan-kunde, NE Zaire, to establish:

> 250-bed hospital/maternity complex and leprosy-care centre; training college for national para-medical workers; several regional hospitals and dispensaries; radio-advisory link-up throughout the medical services; a 'Flying Doctor Service' through the Missionary Aviation Fellowship, to all regional hospitals; a central supply depot for drugs and equipment.

1973 Home to UK after twenty years of African service.

Was It All Worth While?

'But all these things that I once thought very worthwhile—now I've thrown them all away so that I can put my trust and hope in Christ alone. Yes, everything else is worthless when compared with the priceless gain of knowing Christ Jesus my Lord. I have put aside all else, counting it worth less than nothing, in order that I can have Christ, and become one with him, no longer counting on being saved by being good enough or by obeying God's laws, but by trusting Christ to save me; for God's way of making us right with himself depends on faith — counting on Christ alone. Now I have given up everything else — I have found it to be the only way really to know Christ and to experience the mighty power that brought him back to life again, and to find out what it means to suffer and to die with him.'
Philippians 3: 7-10 *(The Living Bible)*.

1
Laying Foundations

We chugged steadily across Lake Albert in the small steamer. The mosquitoes were ferocious, and yet unable to imprison me within the butter-muslin walls that surrounded the low bunk in my insufferably hot cabin. I leant on the bulwarks, gazing across the dark ripples, piercing through the night to get my first glimpse of the mountains of what was then the Belgian Congo.

A deep excitement surged through me as the earliest grey of dawn touched the peaks. Was it really possible, after all the years of training and planning and expecting, that at last the true adventure was to begin? I was twenty-eight, with a university degree in general medicine and surgery, from a good, happy home background, stepping out into a new beginning. It was 14 March 1953.

Eight years before, in my first year at university, I had met some Christian students whose quality of life had so challenged me that I was forced to face up to the demands of Christianity. After three months of listening and questioning and watching, various circumstances led to my spending a week at a houseparty in London during the Christmas vacation. I turned up at Mount Hermon College to join a gathering of keen Christian girls and young women, training as officers for young people's camps and houseparties the following summer. I just didn't fit: I didn't talk their language. I couldn't understand their spiritual jargon — but I could understand their happiness and friendliness.

I soon found that I enjoyed the orderly Bible study sessions, and I started to read avidly through Paul's letter to the Christians at Rome. The truth began to penetrate my thick skull — it was true! It was no myth. It was no out-dated fairy-tale. This God was real, and true, and vital. He cared. He cared for me personally and wanted — fantastic realization!— my friendship. By the end of the week I had capitulated to the clear facts, the obvious reasonableness and the exciting challenge of the gospel. God loved me enough to die for me: would I say thank you? I would and I did. God loved me enough to have a job for me to do in His service: would I sign on? I would and I did. Perhaps it all

Map of the NE region of Congo/Zaire

Key

— roads

---- rough division between mission areas

† church/mission centres

● towns

AIM Africa Inland Mission, marking 17 of their church centres, called in Zaire CECA.

AOG Assemblies of God Mission, marking four of their churches, called in Zaire CADZ.

CBFMS Conservative Baptists of North America (not shown on map, working further to the south), called in Zaire CEBK.

EM Emmanuel Mission (Brethren group), showing three assemblies, called in Zaire CAFEZa.

UFM Unevangelized Fields Mission, showing eight of their churches, called in Zaire CEHZ.

WEC Worldwide Evangelization Crusade, showing 13 church centres, called in Zaire CECCA.

seemed a bit of a gamble at the start. I knew so little; but I knew I wanted peace of heart and purpose for living — and no-one else had offered me both. No other religion or political group even hinted at a way of deliverance from sin, a fresh start with a clean slate, a new indwelling power to enable me to achieve the goal. A Christian leader at the houseparty wrote a verse in my newly-bought Bible: 'That I may know Christ, and the power of his resurrection, and the fellowship of his sufferings' (Philippians 3:10). I went to read the verse in its setting that evening, and was tremendously challenged at Paul's dramatic way of stating what I was beginning to feel:

'But what things were gain to me, those I counted loss for Christ. Yea doubtless, and I count all things but loss for the excellency of the knowledge of Christ Jesus my Lord: for whom I have suffered the loss of all things, and do count them but dung, that I may win Christ, and be found in him, not having mine own righteousness, which is of the law, but that which is through the faith of Christ, the righteousness which is of God by faith: that I may know him, and the power of his resurrection, and the fellowship of his sufferings, being made conformable unto his death; if by any means I might attain unto the resurrection of the dead' (Philippians 3: 7-11).

A terrific gamble! What if it didn't pay off? What if it was all an illusion, unreal and untrue? Wasn't it almost too fantastic to believe anyway? Wouldn't one be dubbed a religious fanatic?

Despite the crowding in of such thoughts, I was amazed at myself. Within minutes of a great personal transaction between myself and God, whereby I simply thanked Him for dying for me, believed Him for His forgiveness, and accepted His invitation to serve Him, I had already an ability to laugh at these apparently-specious arguments to put me off. I knew with an unshakable assurance that God was real, that His salvation was true, that I was accepted by Him into His family and His service. God's orderly array of facts in the Bible, plus the consistent witness of the unhypocritical, outright good lives of my new friends, plus now the new ingredient of the persuasiveness of His Spirit in my heart, won the day for me. A great sense of thrill, mingled with a growing sense of privilege, took possession of me.

It took six and a half years to get my medical degree, six months in missionary training centre, six months in Belgium studying French and tropical medicine — and at last, the five week boat and train journey to

East Africa and across half of the great continent to the border of Congo.

Then started eleven extraordinary years of hard work and happiness, mingled with heart-breaks and disillusionments, heights of apparent success alternating with sloughs of despair; yet the net result of all this, judged by the world's standards, was not particularly impressive.

By August 1964 a small 14-acre plot of land in the great Ituri forest of the Congo basin had been turned into a 100-bed hospital and maternity complex with all the necessary ancillary buildings and services. Many of the actual buildings were already there before ever I arrived: many of our team of workmen had been trained by previous missionaries. Subtracting the inherited start from the visible finish, it might seem that we had done very little in those eleven years.

I suppose one hundred patients underwent surgery each year, some of whom would otherwise have died; one hundred young men and women were trained as hospital orderlies and assistant midwives, all of whom would otherwise have remained in relative ignorance; many thousands of babies were born, who would have been born anyway, but with a 50% increase in the chance of survival; many tens of thousands of sick were treated, scores of whom would certainly have died without our help. But there were moments when I was tempted to ask if this was enough to warrant the enormous outlay of energy and strength.

Individually, and as a team, the medical group involved in the project had learnt a lot over the years. But would that accumulated knowledge justify the expenditure involved and make the whole thing worth while?

The first of many missionary-lessons were taught and learnt right at the start in 1953 at Ibambi. Starting with nothing but an upturned tea-chest, a camp table and a stool, a primus stove and a saucepan, I discovered what it was to be fenced in with difficulties. With no helper, black or white, so much that should have been done to maintain medical standards just proved impossible. Good training told me that a patient with a high fever and chills, painful eyes and profuse sweating was probably suffering from malaria. Treatment in those early days was quinine in a suitable dose according to the weight of the patient, but only after the diagnosis had been confirmed in the laboratory, by seeing the parasite in a blood-smear in the microscope. This microscopic procedure, even in an adequately equipped laboratory, would take a well-trained technician at least five minutes. With fifty or more patients daily showing symptoms of malaria, this would have added over four hours to the day's work. With no electricity, these four hours would have to be worked into the programme during daylight. Yet besides these fifty malarial patients, there were probably fifty others with chest complaints, fifty more with abdominal pain and diarrhoea, and countless more with ulcers and sores. Chest patients needed ten minutes each for history-taking, examination and diagnosis, even without laboratory examination of sputum or radiological examination of lungs. Yet they probably received a cursory glance. Each abdominal sufferer needed careful stool examination besides all other routines, possibly some fifteen minutes each . . . .

The day simply wasn't long enough. And so malarial symptoms prompted treatment with quinine, with a quick estimate of weight and no laboratory confirmation. I actually asked God to give me a gift of discernment so that I could pick out the one or two really sick patients with pneumonia or tuberculosis from the line of people with coughs and colds. Similarly, one built up through experience an almost uncanny sense which sorted out the roundworm sufferers from the hookworms, and the amoebic dysentery sufferers from those with bacillary infection — and God overruled.

When I began to realize that over 200 patients were being treated daily, and record cards showed that probably 75% or more were responding immediately to the initial treatment given, I began to see that it was not necessarily a lowering of standards to treat malarial symptoms without laboratory confirmation: rather it was a necessary adaptation to circumstances, with a change of method to achieve the same goal, and with somewhat more realistic hopes of success. These same 200 patients daily, having received something that aided their physical pain to subside, were then much more open to listen to the preaching of the gospel.

Then the first students came. What a motley crew they were! Yokana and Mangadima both from seventh or eighth standard (the equivalent of first or second year at an English secondary school); Mapuno and Bakiogomu and two other lads probably from fourth-grade primary schools, and non-achievers at that; and then Elizabeth Naganimi with no formal education at all, but a bright, keen spirit and a desire to learn and serve. So my second round of difficulties started. I was not a trained teacher; I had no course material; I was going to try to lecture in a mixture of two 'foreign' languages, French and Swahili, neither of which was the first language of student or teacher; and lastly, I was not myself a nurse, and therefore did not know the subject-matter that I hoped to teach!

Again God came to my rescue, and slowly we learnt to overcome this second hurdle. For the first eighteen months of our new training school we wended our way day by day, with moment-by-moment improvisations to meet each immediate need. God taught me to teach as the need arose. There were huge and hideous ulcers every day in the clinic, so I taught how to cleanse them, curette them, treat them and bandage them. A patient came in with burning fever, and so we launched into a lecture on how to use, read and understand a thermometer. In the ward, a post-natal mother developed a high temperature, so we taught the dangers and causes of infection, and how we could prevent as well as treat them. A baby was brought in with bronchopneumonia, and I demonstrated the use of the stethoscope and how to arrive at a diagnosis. An endless stream of patients, with a seemingly limitless supply of abdominal symptoms, provided us with material to discover the use of the microscope and to learn to recognize every possible species of intestinal parasite.

Students and lecturer learnt together and language very soon ceased to bother us. We created our own course material (aided eventually by the notes of a senior missionary health officer) and went at our own pace. The day of reckoning lay ahead, when we went together for the State final examinations. I for one was intensely nervous, and feared the ditch beyond the hurdle would be our undoing. But the students, in blissful ignorance of what was involved, confident that they knew what I had taught them, and assuming that this must be sufficient, went through with their heads high. By dint of interpreting French questions and Swahili answers, the examiners were eventually convinced that all but one of our group would do good rather than harm, if let loose in a rural dispensary; and we went home rejoicing with six Government-stamped and signed certificates, and six 'medical evangelists' were launched into our new medical service.

There were other difficulties too, on a more personal level, regarding my relationships with my fellow-missionaries. Early on these problems led to loneliness and a sense of insecurity, of not being wanted or welcomed or quite trusted by the fellowship. This, combined with the work-load and consequent inability to take a night off-duty, or to go away for a week-end, brought out in me an irritability and shortness of temper that often caused me considerable loss of sleep. I'd always had a hasty temper, but this had largely been under control for the previous eight years, since my conversion to Christ. Now the hot and angry word would burst out again, before I could control it, and to my shame. Patients who came to the dining-room window while we were at the midday meal would get a sharp word from me to 'go to the dispensary, and not bring your germs to our home' — and a sad look would come to the faces of senior missionaries, who treated every visitor to their home with kindliness and respect.

Evangelist Danga, in charge of the catechists' training course and the workmen's programme at Ibambi, took me to task for this un-Christlike behaviour. 'Don't excuse yourself. Call sin sin, and temper temper. Then face up to the fact that your white skin makes you no different to the rest of us. You need His cleansing and forgiveness, His infilling and indwelling, the same as we do. If you can only show us Doctor Helen, you might as well go home: the people need to see Jesus.'

During my eighteen months at Ibambi I was enormously helped by Danga and the student catechists, by Bakimani and the Bible School students, and by Pastor Ndugu and teams of church elders from various areas of the Ibambi church, to put up two large wards and outbuildings around our dispensary. They taught me to use an axe; to choose the right tree to resist termites and rotting; to select good clean grass and durable fibres for thatching. I learnt how to plan the layout of the building with regard for the prevailing wind, the slope of the roof with regard for the tropical rainfall. I knew how to dig out lime from the right forest streams, and to make whitewash for the walls, not only for its aesthetic look but for its disinfectant value. Together they taught me in the evenings, around the fires, to slice well-dried bamboo and to bind it correctly to make strong, resilient beds, and to weave palm-fronds for roofing and grasses for mats.

Then in 1955, following the graduation day of our first class of students, the medical team was asked to move from Ibambi to Nebobongo, seven miles north. We were asked to take over the care of the maternity and leprosy centres, with the associated orphanage, that

Edith Moules had started fifteen years before. Here there were 14 acres of land, sloping down one way or another from a half-mile-long central strip of plateau. Available for immediate use were two brick-built, thatched bungalows for missionaries, similar buildings for maternity care and midwives to the north, and for orphans and widows to the south. A large, unfinished dispensary building half a mile to the west was almost all that was left of the previous thriving colony for the care of leprosy patients, nearly one thousand of whom had been transferred to a Government camp eight miles to the north, or else returned to their forest villages.

So we moved and restarted our medical centre, this time with the outpatients' clinic in the sitting-room, the pharmacy in the dining-room, and the night nurses' room in the guest-room of my new bungalow home. We became instantly aware of our urgent need of other arrangements! The smell and the noise by day, the disturbed hours and the ease of theft by night, made life almost intolerable. New buildings were a must. But how? There was no Bible School with its students, no catechists' school with its workmen, and we did not even have our own church pastor with his team of elders. So who would put up our needed buildings?

I often felt very frustrated by the church arrangements, by which Nebobongo was only an outpost from Ibambi and not a church in its own right. This greatly aggravated the difficulties with regard to buildings. For anything we needed, or for permission to do anything we planned, we had first to apply to Ibambi, which involved a cycle-ride of seven miles of switchback road in all weathers. This became a constant irritant. The danger of a hot, unguarded retort when asked to do a medical trip to some distant outlying place for one of the missionaries, when I felt (possibly unjustly) that they were unwilling to see our need of help at the medical centre, became more and more real.

We were such a small, insignificant team, yet we were asked to carry such a huge and important burden. At first there were only Florence Stebbing and myself as the missionaries involved, with Agoya our evangelist and his wife Taadi, a group of para-medical auxiliary students and of pupil midwives, and a handful of men, discharged from treatment in the leprosy care centre during the previous years. None of us had talents or training as builders, plumbers, electricians or mechanics. We learnt by trial and error to make bricks and to fire a kiln: I went to Ibambi to copy in diagram-form their beehive kiln, and then to a local rubber plantation where the Belgian agent had a large, six-firing-hole wet-brick kiln. We discussed the various possibilities, the amounts of firewood necessary for each type, the ease of construction, and, in addition, how to fill in the Government forms needed to authorize the construction as well as to pay the taxes for the firing.

Later again, between clinics and classes, we learnt painfully and slowly the difference between cement and concrete, and how to make each to a consistent quality; how to lay foundations and footings, do corners and bonding, set doors and windows; how to prepare roofing timber and to hoist the triangles and fix the trusses; how to square the corners of the asbestos sheeting and bore the holes for fastening it with nails; how to fix a ridge so that the building did not leak, and the guttering to take advantage of the rainfall.

But it all took time and money; it involved sore hands and blisters; it needed tact and wisdom in handling unskilled labour on nominal wages. And sometimes it was truly hard to see if it was really worth the effort. Through it all, the unskilled labour became at least semi-qualified, to the standard to which the teacher had been able to be taught! This did something for general self-respect and morale, but it also did something in regard to desire and demand for higher wages!

During these years there was the continual problem of responsibilities beyond my training. If the ease with which I responded to the missionary call to service overseas was due in part to my own inherent dread of professional criticism and competition, and the realization that in the heart of the Ituri forest this was unlikely to exist, now there was the horror of responsibility. True, in the medical missionary's life there is unlikely to be much pressure in the rat-race for promotion. On arrival at Nebobongo I became immediately, in the eyes of the national population and the missionary personnel, if not in my own estimation, the senior consultant surgeon, physician, pediatrician and obstetrician. But there was no comrade, no colleague, with whom to discuss cases or to share problems. Always I had to make the decisions of life and death by myself: and I knew only too well how inadequate was my training for this vast responsibility.

In particular, the burden of care for white colleagues weighed on me. Not that I ever wished to treat white any differently from black: far from it! But my African patients did not know enough to be critical.

They trusted me unquestioningly and loved me unreservedly. They knew instinctively that by God's grace I would do for them the very best in my limited power, and that this was better for them than no care, or even than witch-doctor care. European patients, however, knew what they wanted, and what they expected: they had home standards with which to compare our frail and insignificant service.

Then these same Europeans stopped coming to me. Missionaries and tradesmen alike started to make the long, tiresome journey north-east to Dr Kleinsmidt, or the even longer journey south to Dr Becker. And I allowed jealousy to creep in and increase my frustration. How perverse can one be? I feared them when they came, and was hurt when they didn't come! I felt vaguely humiliated by my failure to provide the service that they wanted: and I felt even more wrapped up in a medical loneliness and weariness.

Then in all this whirlwind of activity — construction of new and repair of old buildings; teaching of students and preparing their course material; caring for patients, surgical, medical and obstetric; leading the spiritual as well as the physical life of our family of workmen, students, pupils and children; organizing and supervising some forty-eight rural clinics; ordering and preparing our drugs and medical stores; supervising the work in the small laboratory and down in the leprosy-care centre — in all this the Lord graciously visited our Nebobongo work with revival.

For four years the revival fires had been burning brightly in all the surrounding area, from some 700 or 800 miles south to 100 miles north, from 200 miles west to 100 miles east. Possibly about 100,000 forest villagers had been touched by the fervency of the Christian church in those days. Church services were alive and exciting: no longer slow, monotonous hymns and short, uninteresting sermons. Now everyone sang from their hearts with their faces alight with joy: everyone listened to the preaching of the Word with interest and expectancy. Lives were changed, and ordinary folk lived out what they believed in. Hypocrisy and insincerity were hardly known any longer, especially among the older members of the congregations.

In an ever-changing congregation like ours at Nebobongo, where patients came and went and the student body changed every two years, we needed continuous waves of revival to keep us alight. Joseph Adzanese from the Ibambi Bible School, with his wife Mary, and another couple came to spend ten days with us. Much prayer had been made before and during the convention, and the Lord graciously worked in our hearts. Pupil midwives were first touched: sins were confessed, hearts were cleansed and then filled with joy. Next the blessing spread to the workmen and their families; and finally to the paramedical auxiliary students.

Through the ministry of that convention, and a further ten day visit to Pastor Ndugu's village, twenty miles away to the east, I also was deeply blessed by the fires of the Holy Spirit. In particular the Lord revealed to me the sin of criticism of others, pride in my own achievements, failure to trust Him in my own inabilities, almost glorying in my frustrations. He showed me again the dangers of over-busyness, much doing, tireless activity, if it wasn't backed up by prayer. How easily it would all lead to spiritual bankruptcy, and work for work's sake, with no goal of spiritual fruit. In a prolonged period of time apart, alone with God, He filled me again with an intense joy and the deep peace of His abiding presence.

Shortly afterwards I went home to England for furlough and much-needed rest and refreshment, and a period of further medical and surgical practice so as to be better able to cope with the tasks of the future.

Back to Nebobongo in June 1960, as the great day of Congo's Independence dawned. John Mangadima was appointed as Administrative Director of our medical centre, in accordance with the practice of the hour. John had been one of the first group of students who arrived for training in July 1953 and qualified in October 1955. Since then, he had followed two years of training at the Bible School at Ibambi, where he qualified at the close of 1957 as an evangelist and Bible teacher. He returned to Nebobongo at the beginning of 1958 and worked alongside Dr John Harris, another missionary doctor who was in charge at Nebobongo during my period of furlough. Mangadima was proving himself a very able medical auxiliary, a conscientious surgical assistant, a keen and willing administrator: but more important still, from my point of view, a real companion and friend.

Four troubled years of strains and tensions shook the new, young Republic, during which time we sought to consolidate the work of the medical service and to prepare national workers, such as John, for the task of leadership and responsibility. For this, above all else, we required Government recognition for our training programme, and legal certificates in the hands of our qualified workers.

Ever since the inception of the training school for paramedical workers at Nebobongo, we had been applying for this recognition. It was true that, before Independence, our applications had been made with no very great fervour. It had not seemed so essential then, and we had known that the all-Roman Catholic Government was hardly likely to favour a Protestant medical service with official recognition. Through the years of the colonial era, our students had been able to sit their final examinations alongside other students in the region, drawn from similar schools run by the Roman Catholics. The priests had not demurred, as my services as a lady doctor were available to help the nuns in the area as required.

But following Independence our African colleagues started to put pressure on us to make the school 'official'. This was not just as a status symbol, but also because of a growing fear that only para-medical workers with authentic diplomas would ultimately be accepted into the nationalized medical service. Perhaps I was slow. My French was poor; my efforts were spasmodic; my conviction of the rightness of the move was half-hearted. Whatever the reasoning, the recognition had not come. Then a letter came, implying that all un-recognized schools, para-medical as much as secondary, would be closed down. To be accredited was suddenly an urgent necessity.

Fresh letters were written, new forms filled out, different applications put in. Nothing happened! No response was received. John Mangadima pleaded with me to try again. I was fearful of annoying the authorities by my impatience: I was fearful of grieving my team by my apparent indifference. Eventually I re-applied.

One day, as I was using ten spare minutes during the lunch break to clean out the carburetor of our van, a smart car drove up to my front door. There was Dr de Gott, the local government doctor from Paulis (now Isiro), and with him two strangers, whom he introduced to me as I hastily wiped my hands. They were Dr Trieste, a government inspector from Kinshasa, and Mr Jenkins, a male nurse with the World Health Organization, together responsible for the medical and paramedical teaching programmes throughout the country.

I was shattered. My always-scanty knowledge of the French language seemed to desert me altogether. I was tongue-tied at the awfulness of the situation. This was our legal inspection. On the next hour depended all we had worked for during the last ten years.

Tears stung my eyes. It all seemed so unfair. Why could they not have warned us, sent us word, allowed us time to present ourselves in the best light possible? The telegram to warn us of the date of their arrival arrived two days later, and presumably they never knew that we were completely unprepared.

Dr Trieste almost ignored me, talking rapidly to Dr de Gott about plans they had for developing the three Red Cross hospitals in our area, Pawa, Babondi and Medje. They had just come from Pawa, with its superb ultra-modern buildings and equipment, and excellent laboratory facilities. They were going on from us to see the other two, and also Bafwabaka, the large Roman Catholic centre. They had merely stopped at Nebobongo on their way through, to save petrol. The very way they talked showed that they had never even considered recognizing us.

Their patronizing tone put me on my mettle. We put on the very best show possible. As they went round, I refused to be cowed or defensive, and staff and students responded wonderfully. They spoke up in answer to questions and challenges far better than I dared to hope. I launched out into French explanations, amazed at my own audacity.

True, we did not then get the recognition we so much coveted, but we were not just written off. We were given two to three years to improve our buildings and to increase our patient/student ratio. In fact the report was remarkably conciliatory, and even complimentary in parts; but as the inspectors were leaving on that traumatic afternoon, I sensed a complete lack of sympathy between the central Government inspector and the local jungle situation.

We did not get recognition. We did not have legal diplomas. There seemed nothing more we could do at the time. What frustration to realize that John Mangadima, capable and mature enough to step into my position, had no official papers to legalize such a move. Legally, he was an 'assistant nurse', as his general education had reached only a certain level. Practically, he was an able houseman to me in surgical and medical services, and a capable assistant in administration and organization.

Not only was I frustrated in my own keen longing to see a national take the lead, but so also was John. He was frustrated in that he had not sufficient outlet for his keen ability, not sufficient stimulus for his acute mind, and particularly not sufficient general knowledge to appreciate that all this was due not to the white man's superiority and unwillingness to hand over, but rather to circumstances of place and timing of birth quite beyond our control. His natural nationalism made him often appear proud; his frustrated leadership ability made him often appear bossy and even offensive to others in the team.

Then suddenly in August 1964 we found ourselves plunged into the horrors of the Simba uprising. The brutality and coarseness of those evil men almost overwhelmed me. Through ten months at Nebobongo they wrought havoc, destroying property, stealing possessions, inflicting cruelties, instilling fear. Shops emptied of all stores. All work ceased and the economy crumbled. Good men were murdered, many others tortured and mutilated. All sense of order and discipline disappeared and anarchy took over. We foreigners were rounded up and taken off to prison, from where we were eventually rescued by the National Army and flown to our various homes. The nationals were hounded and threatened, their homes often burnt and all their possessions looted. Schools were all closed, and even small school children rounded up to serve as 'Simba reserves', many being killed in battle. Hospitals and dispensaries tried to stagger on, till all supplies were exhausted: and then they too closed down and medical workers, like all others, slipped away into hiding in the great Ituri forest.

Many times in the first ten weeks John, like others, stood by me, and would gladly have given his life if he could have protected me. One day, a car-load of apparently friendly rebel soldiers drove up to my house. John went with me as we crossed the courtyard to them from the school. They asked to be given berets, such as they had seen other rebels wearing. These others had declared that they received them at Nebobongo, but in fact they had stolen them a few days previously from the store of Youth Club uniforms in my home. There were none left, and I said so. Immediately one of them accused me of lying and of refusing to give them what they wanted. He raised his rifle to strike me with the butt-end — and John threw himself between us and took the blow. Eventually we calmed them down with a quip of humour, offering them each a bowl of loganberries and condensed milk and saying that, in English, these were also called 'berries' — and the situation passed.

Another night seventeen wild youths, armed with spears, clubs and crowbars, swarmed into school, demanding our vehicle, the keys and the driver. After much haggling I was eventually forced to drive them to

Wamba, 70 miles east, in darkness and rain with no lights or windscreen wipers. Two miles up the road we pulled in at a plantation-factory, to ask for petrol and motor-oil. When a local mechanic brought these, he was then asked to repair the lights and self-starter. I meanwhile stood alone in the dark, conscious that death was very near. I had earlier deliberately disconnected lights, starter and wipers, an act that, when discovered, would be considered blatant sabotage and worthy of instant death. At that moment I became conscious that I was not alone. Turning my head, I found John once again standing beside me, and Joel, a first year student, with him.

The lights shone out. Shortly afterwards the engine revved up. In a moment of startled silence as the engine cut out, the rebel lieutenant asked if it had been an act of sabotage. 'Assuredly', the mechanic replied: and seventeen enraged youths turned on the three of us, now clearly visible in the full glare of the headlights. The three of us tensed to take the assault, expecting to be instantly in the Lord's presence, when, suddenly, all seventeen were checked, poised in full charge, unable to move a muscle. God had stepped in. It was as though we were surrounded by an invisible barrier of heavenly glory, which blinded our assailants as the midday sun might have done.

'Go on! Kill us — it doesn't matter. We shall go to be with Jesus which is far better. But one day, God will demand our blood at your hands.'

Suddenly, inexplicably, as though they had forgotten our existence, they swung round, loosed from the grip of the paralyzing power. Laughing and jeering they piled into the van, forcing the mechanic to drive them away into the night.

And the three of us were left there in the dark and the rain, alone and cold, but alive. As we walked home in awestruck silence my heart was deeply moved that these two had stood by me, ready to die if need be, rather than let me face the ordeal alone.

The same happened on the day I finally left Nebobongo. I had been captured several days previously, taken away at night with only the clothes I stood up in. We had been driven to Isiro to be shot, and then had been reprieved, brought back and since held under house-arrest. A senior officer of the rebel troops had visited us and agreed that it was best for the three women missionaries from Nebobongo to stay with those at Ibambi. Then someone had casually remarked that I had not been given time the previous week to 'pack my suitcase' — in the midst of assault and wickedness!

So the rebels had arranged to escort me to Nebobongo to collect whatever I needed to return and live at Ibambi. On arrival, they gave me an hour . . . .

The Nebobongo church council gathered at once in my home, and we read from the Bible and had prayer together. Then I handed to one the keys of the office and showed him the books and all the money in hand. Together we agreed to divide it all at once, and to give it out to each member of the 'family', rather than leave it to be stolen by the rebels. I had listed all my 'property' — portable typewriter, ancient bicycle, pressure lamp — and written a letter transferring ownership of each item to one and another member of the team. I talked to Mangadima about drugs and equipment, medical and surgical procedures, and handed him the whole responsibility for the medical service, as acting director in my absence.

Their total silence, tear-filled eyes, pathetic nodding acquiescence in everything I did and said, told its own story. Hearts were being torn open. Each was reeling under the sense of impossible and unwanted burdens of responsibility, and the realization that the one they loved and respected and relied on was actually leaving.

The rebels came back and ordered me to the lorry— plus the hurriedly-stuffed suitcase. And my little adopted daughter Fibi, just ten years old, clung to me, sobbing pathetically.

'Mummy! Mummy! Take me with you! Don't leave me behind again! Please, please, Mummy, take me too!'

My heart ached with a great twisting pain. I hardly dared to look at the child as she clung to my skirt and I pressed her to me. I kissed her tight curls, as my eyes were blinded with tears—and heard a quiet voice beside me:

'Doctor, when Jesus was on the cross, He turned to John and asked him to look after His mother. I'll take your little girl in the same way'— and he gathered Fibi up in his arms and carried her away to his own home. In the moment of my urgent emotional crisis, John had been able to swallow his own grief and the poignancy of his own loneliness and need, and rising above it, to think only of my need.

Then, after we had been driven away, John quietly took over the direction of the medical centre, showing great wisdom as well as courage. Rebel soldiers were everywhere: some were in the wards as patients, one young man with compound fractures of thigh and leg in the surgical ward, and another with severe schistosomiasis in the medical ward. Everything the nurses did was watched and reported. Entering the pharmacy stock-room daily became hazardous, as rebel gangsters always followed, and it needed endless tact and skill to steer them out without their looting the shelves. There seemed little possibility of obtaining any further supplies, and John realized the urgency of preserving all that remained and using it sparingly and without waste: and most certainly, they could not afford loss by looting.

Late one night, silently, alone, alert and watchful, John slipped over to the store and set to work. He divided everything into ten piles — penicillin, aspirins, anti-malarial drugs, vermifuges, sulphonamides and vitamins; syringes and needles, thermometers and bandages, powders and creams. He parceled up each pile into cartons and plastic bags, listing each article as he did so. Then, glancing cautiously round the deserted courtyard and listening intently for the sound of anyone else awake and prowling, he slipped out with one load, one tenth of all he had.

In the early hours of the morning he woke a village workman and handed him the precious packages. 'Go out now, from the back, in the dark, and bury these somewhere. Tell no-one; don't look inside. Then if rebels demand to know anything, you can honestly say you know nothing. One day I shall ask you for them, but till then, forget about them!'

John quietly repeated this procedure, going every twenty minutes to nine other different workmen. By 4.30 a.m. he had delivered all ten precious burdens, and no-one knew that another had also received a similar task. By daylight everything was buried and all traces covered — and John took a quick hour's sleep before the new day's activities burst upon him.

Through the fifteen ensuing months, roughly every six weeks or so, he visited those ten homes again, one by one, under cover of dark, and recovered his precious stores: and the hospital continued caring for the sick, rebel and civilian alike. Many must have marvelled, and possibly questioned, the apparent ability to continue treatment all that year, with never more than a week's supply of drugs visible! But John kept his secret locked in his heart till after the deliverance by the National Army, and our return with new stocks and supplies.

Other problems faced John and the evangelist Agoya. One was the presence in the nurses' training school of several students from distant parts, who did not know the local tribal languages. Every time rebels raided the hospital and nurses' homes there was danger of a beat-up, as all strangers were suspect of hostile activity. So they arranged for these students to leave and go to stay, two by two, in church homes in nearby villages, away from the main road. But there, another problem arose. Now, instead of the rebels suspecting them, it was the local population who rose against them, treating them as spies as they could not talk their language.

So they were all brought back to Nebobongo, and Agoya and John arranged to care for them themselves, in a hurriedly constructed dormitory not far from the medical centre, hidden in the local forest land: and there they remained in safety through six months of rebel activity.

At last the National Army arrived and drove out the rebel forces. Nebobongo became an official refugee camp, and troubles even worse than those of the rebel occupation broke upon them. Everyone hiding in the forest was commanded to come out to one of these official camps, so that the National Army could move into the forest to flush out and kill all the rebels. Our small village with facilities for about five hundred under normal conditions was suddenly overrun with several thousand starving refugees — and who was to control the mob?

John and Agoya, with other Nebobongo workmen, did all they could. Every refugee was allocated a 'spot' for sleeping. Church and class-rooms were used, as well as every home and cook-house, and even some of the hospital wards. People were packed in like sardines. Workmen patrolled the food gardens and the avenue of fruit trees, and gave out stores as they could, but nevertheless wholesale destruction and looting commenced on a scale far beyond that of the rebels.

Suddenly the leaders found that the students they had so carefully guarded throughout the rebellion had become the chief of the looters. My lovely home had become a battle-field: 'first come, first served' was the order of the day. The students stole drawers from the sideboard to make suitcases and took the very books from the shelves to make mattresses! Too late the leaders moved in to protect property — there was virtually nothing left to protect!

Then the day came when these same students packed up 'their' belongings to set off on the long trek of 300 miles or more to their homes. National soldiers heard they were setting off, and moved in rapidly. According to the new laws, none could 'walk', that is, travel from one region to another, without the Colonel's permission. The students were therefore taken to the Colonel. One was actually his nephew! Before signing road-passes for them, he demanded that each one should open his suitcase (the drawers of my cupboard closed with padlocks stolen from the pharmacy!).

There was a pause. Soldiers stiffened, alert to the students' hesitation. A menacing silence filled the air.

'Open up,' the Colonel commanded in a cold, quiet voice.

The suitcases were full of stolen property — my clothes and my cutlery, pharmacy drugs and hospital equipment. The punishment for stealing at that time was death.

At that precise moment John cycled up, driven by some inner sense of urgency, and took in at a glance the whole affair. The six students would be shot, including Samuel Yossa, the Colonel's nephew. There was no favouritism, no tribal link now, which could save those who used rebel tactics: they would be wiped out.

John stepped straight through the group and stood before Colonel Yossa.

'Sir,' he spoke with quiet respect, and yet with fearless authority. 'I am responsible for these young men. Let me die in their place.'

A stunned silence. All eyes seemed riveted on John, and then slowly moved to Colonel Yossa. The latter hardly knew John, nor all that was represented in the drama before his eyes, and he turned to his local adjutant for advice.

'This man is our doctor, sir. He is utterly trustworthy, amazingly capable, the medical director of the local hospital. These are students from their training school ....' His voice trailed away. The situation was beyond him. What could he advise? He'd never heard of anyone offering his life for others. He and most others were maddened by the criminal act of the students, especially after the way John had cared for them through the previous months. So far as he was concerned, they deserved death. But John . . .? It was impossible to comprehend.

The Colonel gazed steadily at John and marvelled. Yossa was a godly man, and he deeply admired the quiet courage and devotion of this young man before him.

'Take them away,' he said to John, 'and deal with them as you see fit. Don't let them come near us again.' And he dismissed them all.

John told the students to close their cases and go back to Nebobongo. He was tired and emotionally exhausted. He watched them go, with eyes full of sadness, unable to understand why they hadn't responded to all they had heard of the gospel. The Colonel touched him gently and John turned. The older man held out his hand and they shook hands, one gentleman with another, and the Colonel quietly said: 'God bless you, sir. And thank you.'

As John turned to leave, a soldier gave him six road-passes for the errant students, at a signal from the Colonel; and two days later, the students left Nebobongo to trudge homewards — sobered perhaps, yet rebellious and angry at heart, as their suitcases had been emptied and each filled with two days' food rations only.

From then on, from July 1965 until our arrival in April 1966, John and evangelist Agoya did all they could to reorganize life. There was much to discourage, and at times they were tempted to despair. Chaos and disorder were on all sides. Shattered buildings, roofs riddled with bullet-holes; not a glass window intact; doors and windows and their frames ripped out for firewood. My home was stinking with filth, as the 300 refugees housed there had feared to leave the building during the twelve hours from sunset to sunrise. The refugees had completed the destruction of the primary-school buildings, started by the rebels, smashing forms, desks and blackboards for beds and firewood. Nothing was safe from them.

The committee, organized by John and Agoya, counted up all their resources, everything they had been able to salvage. They brought the books up to date and prepared for a six month 'period of delay', knowing that they could make no contact with the outside world till far more had been achieved in the way of 'mopping-up' operations. The leaders found they had sufficient funds to allocate a very small token salary to each workman, with which they tried to encourage them to pull themselves together and start work again. Buildings were the prime concern. They checked up on each, evaluating the degree of damage and what would need to be done to make them, at least temporarily, usable. They balanced one against another, and so decided to rip down one to repair the next.

The work proved to be positive therapy against the depression caused by the senseless destruction of the rebellion, and against the disillusionment setting in from the apparent inability of the delivering National Army to do anything for their succour. As the people pulled together to do something of worth, their minds started to tick over and they were slowly persuaded that it was really possible to start all over again. The more they chatted and discussed the pros and cons, the more they came back again and again (so they told us later) to the phrase: 'If only they (*i.e.* the missionaries) come back . . ., and they realized how much we had meant to each other, black and white, just in the even tenor of our everyday lives.

They tackled my home first. The whole long south wall had to be pulled down, the roof shored up, and then all rebuilt, using bricks gathered from the other missionary dwelling which had been destroyed. New window and door frames had to be invented — and the local carpenter Bebesi mysteriously produced a saw, plane and other necessities, suspiciously encrusted with red earth! Up in the roof, a smashed packing case provided shutters for one window. And so on. Greek merchants had returned to Isiro, 40 miles north, and Aunzo, my cook, was authorized by the group to go and bargain for a roll of cloth, using the tithe of all their meagre monthly allocations — and from this, sheets were made for my bed, curtains put up at my bedroom window, and a cloth laid on the bamboo table that the leprosy patients had laboriously plaited for me.

Taadi, our evangelist's wife, gathered the women together and organized a veritable battery of activities, from a baby crèche to four classes for the primary school children, from digging, weeding and planting food-gardens to gathering in large quantities of firewood for hospital and homes. Somehow she scrounged one precious chicken from somewhere, and daily they watched it fattening for my welcome feast, for, they reasoned, 'She must come back to us soon!'

After the initial flooding with some 3,000 local refugees, these were allowed back to their own villages to start life again: then came the second wave of several hundreds of refugees from 60 to 100 miles in every direction, mostly from the south, desperately seeking food and clothing, housing and security. They were grouped according to tribes, the healthiest in each group being appointed leaders. Each group was assigned a small area down in the largely disused leprosy camp, where they were told to build a new row of dwellings, with cook-houses and toilets, and to cultivate a stretch of land behind each dwelling. Slowly a degree of self-respect and disciplined order was inculcated. There was ever-growing optimism and, I was later told, the frequently-expressed confidence: 'Surely our doctor will come soon!' For me, it was not quite as simple as that.

2
Am I Willing To Return?

We had been rescued from captivity on the last day of 1964 and flown home to England. The ordeal over, we had time to rest and recover. By January 1966 the civil war in the republic of Congo/Zaire was virtually at an end. National Army leaders and the major in charge of the mercenary troops were prepared to invite missionaries and traders back to the northeastern region to assist in the work of rehabilitation, so we were each faced with the question, 'Am I willing to return?'

That there was need for rehabilitation workers was undeniable; the task to be performed was reported as Herculean. Utter destruction and devastation had swept through the vast territory, leaving hundreds of burnt-out villages, derelict schools, plundered hospitals, destroyed shops and thousands of pathetic refugees, homeless and hungry.

Each of us had to weigh up the situation: the need was glaringly obvious, but so also was the almost total lack of material aid to meet that need. The lull in rebel activities was clearly reported, but so also was the sheer impossibility of flushing out every rebel soldier from the thousands of square miles of dense forest. The declared wish of the majority of the population for the return of their 'foreign' friends to help them start life again rang clearly in private letters and public broadcasts, but so also did the definite opposition of a minority group, who felt that the very presence of the foreign missionaries and traders had actually caused some of the worst atrocities of the rebellion.

I looked back as well as forward, as I tried to make the all important decision. So many memories kept interrupting any orderly line of reasoning, making it almost impossible to reach a sane conclusion. It certainly seemed a crazy thing to do, to go back and start again from the beginning, with nothing except the knowledge that a similar uprising, with similar incidents, could easily happen all over again.

As I tried to review the past thirteen years, the kaleidoscope of experiences that had led up to that final devastating experience became blurred. I could not think beyond the five months' captivity in the hands

163

of the Simba rebels, with their savage brutality and the wanton destruction of all that had seemed so real and worth while, the bestial, heart-breaking, ultimate cruelty of humiliation and rape, of fear and fierce physical pain. The vividness of this final frightful nightmare tended to blind me to all the joy and achievement of the previous eleven years.

I could not just cancel out, as though it had never been, the memory of that awful night of 29 October 1964. I had to learn to live with memory in an understood perspective: I had to learn to accept it as part of the whole before I could possibly face going back to the same place, the same work, the same companions. So I deliberately relived it ...

... the shattering hammering at the double doors of my bungalow home at Nebobongo in the early hours of the morning; the rough, hoarse voice demanding entry in the name of the rebel army; the fear-oh, that dreadful physical torture of fear, with the throat dried and almost closed, the heart strangled and almost stopped, unable to breathe, unable to think. The near panic of senseless unreality. All of 'me' twisted in an agony of terror — and then the calm quiet that seemed to take over like an outside force.

As I nervously clutched a flimsy housecoat over my night-dress, pulling back the bolts of the door, God had seemed very far away and I had felt very, very small and alone. They had swarmed in, rough, uncouth, jeering men in various oddly assorted garments, smelling of dirt and drink, demanding the man of the house. One separated himself from the rest, in army uniform, leather-belted with holster and cartridges, dark angry eyes, a sense of smouldering hate: clean-shaven, I remember with surprise, with a hard mouth and discoloured teeth. They searched the house; their greedy hands stole what they saw, and their greedy eyes sought me in the glare of their torches. One touched me, and I winced and drew myself inwards. They started to go, stumbling and drunken, laughing and wicked.

The lieutenant had called me back, down the short corridor to my bedroom. 'Go in and ...' Perhaps I didn't hear: perhaps the hammering in my ears of surging blood and fear made me think he said 'undress': he denied it later. I fled out into the dark night, stumbling in the mud, fighting down wild panic as I fell.

'My God, where are You now? Where is Your peace now? Where victory?'

The soldiers came. Naked beams of light stabbed the night, and I was alone. They found me, dragged me to my feet, struck me over head and shoulders, flung me on the ground, kicked me, dragged me to my feet only to strike me again — the sickening, searing pain of a broken tooth, a mouth full of sticky blood, my glasses gone. Beyond sense, numb with horror and unknown fear, driven, dragged, pushed back to my own house yelled at, insulted, cursed.

'My God, my God, why have You forgotten me, forsaken me?'— the wild cry of a tortured heart — alone, oh, how alone!

Suddenly Christ had been there. No vision, no voice, but His very real presence. A phrase came into my mind, 'led as a lamb to the slaughter', and I saw as it were the events in the garden of Gethsemane, the trial scene, the scourging of Christ, the long march out to Calvary bearing the cross, to the crucifixion. One outstanding fact seemed to dominate the whole: He made no resistance. For my sake, He went as a willing sacrifice. Then, as swiftly, He spoke into my heart: 'They're not fighting you: these blows, all this wickedness, is against Me. All I ask of you is the loan of your body. Will you share with Me one hour in My sufferings for these who need My love through you?'

Two such contradictory reactions possessed my heart in that instance. How could He ask me to *love* these wicked, evil brutes? And yet, how could He, almighty Creator God as He was, condescend to ask me to do Him a favour? Always I was on the asking end, telling Him my needs and expecting Him to give me all I needed: and here He was, presenting me with *His* need and offering me the inestimable privilege of satisfying that need — the loan of my body.

Even as these thoughts chased each other through my dulled mind, the horror of the night continued. I screamed in pain, humiliation, fear — above all, *fear* mingled with pain. Yet, at the same moment, an intense sensation of peace, a strange, deep joy, as He, God, took over from me. Such a mixture of emotions, perhaps it can make no sense to others, yet He was *real* — vital, vibrant, real.

My mind tumbled forward to that day six weeks later, in the convent prison in Wamba, when I had tried to comfort a beautiful young Italian nun, to restore her sanity after repeated raping. She too had given up home and loved ones to come out to Africa to serve God. Maybe I didn't often feel much sympathy for the Roman Catholic cause; maybe we'd had wordy battles on various occasions as we had struggled against each other; and yet, in our suffering, we were one.

165

This young nun had suffered till her mind was torn apart with distress. Her whole reason for living was gone: she had failed to keep her vow of chastity (so she reasoned, unreasonably) and so was eternally damned.

Now we groped towards each other, despite religious and language barriers, to seek the face of the God who is love, who is peace and power and truth, in the very midst of all that was hate and turmoil, our weakness and their falseness.

'Have you ever stopped to think that the Virgin Mary was called an adulteress by her own friends?'

She recoiled from me as though I'd struck her. Her eyes, dulled before with numb misery, sparked with anger in defence of the holy name that I had degraded.

'Stop!' I pleaded, before she could form a reply. 'Think! Be realistic! It's true. She was pregnant, yet not married. Joseph would say nothing. She just said that it was not his child. What could they all think? Of course they accused her, cold-shouldered her, left her alone and thought the worst of her.'

I paused to let the apparent shock sink into her fuddled mind. Her eyes pleaded for mercy. I was adding misery to misery. Was I just mocking her, trying to torture her, cashing in on her private suffering?

'Child' (she seemed so young, so vulnerable, so pathetic). 'Mary accepted all that with joy for you and me, that the Saviour might be born, the pure, holy Son of God, born of her, Mary, yet conceived by the Holy Ghost. She took the libellous taunts, she bore the stigma, in dignified silence, triumphing over it, because God was in her' — again a long pause, and she slowly let out her breath — 'for you and me.'

Slowly light began to enter the dark eyes. Could this be true?

'Can you take this sin of cruel man against your flesh for His sake, as Mary took the world's condemnation? You haven't sinned: God forbid! It isn't our sin. They've sinned against us, yes, but we are only *bodies* for the Saviour to indwell. You haven't lost your purity—rubbish! We never had any anyway: all our self-righteousness is as dirty rags in God's holy sight. But if we have Him who is all pure indwelling us, their wickedness can't touch Him or sully His purity.'

She began to talk, to unwind, to tell me of that awful night and the whole nightmare of humiliation. After suffering bitterly at the hands of the coarse soldiers, she had been singled out and taken to the Bishop's Palace. 'But surely he was brutally murdered? Why am I being brought here?' her tired mind had questioned.

The cruel, mocking face of the Colonel of the rebel forces would never leave her. In her Bishop's home, to add insult to injury, the Colonel had claimed her as his wife. All she had, all she held dear, all she understood, was destroyed, shattered, trodden underfoot.

'Why me? Why twice? Why couldn't it have been another?'

Dare one offer her the obvious solace? 'You protected another. Perhaps because you were taken twice, another was not taken once.'

Even in offering this obvious 'comfort', my own heart shrank in horror at the implication, and yet peace and strength came with the wording of the comfort. The God of peace had breathed those words, and they held peace for our hearts. We eyed each other: it was a solemn moment in the very presence of God and slowly both of us felt a great inflowing of immeasurable peace. We touched God, and healing poured into our hearts. That was the first week of December 1964.

I was brought face to face with my own reasoning, my proffered comfort, during the last three days of our captivity, after that bizarre Christmas of 1964, still imprisoned in the convent at Wamba. We had celebrated Christ's birthday despite our prison conditions, with praise and prayer, carols and a crib for our nine children: even with an enormous turkey for lunch! Then the rude interruption of our midday meal: 'Pack. You're being moved.' Curt, to the point.

As always, the fear— the unknown always seemed more evil than the known. Was it just a trap? The first load of nine nuns and four others . . . the second trip with eleven priests and our two protestant men . . . a third trip . . . . The waiting, the fierce hoping despite hope, the anxious uncertainty. Then our turn came, at 8.30 p.m. on Sunday night. Rough, crowded, cold, dangerous. That frightful moment when our apparent friend, the Commander of the rebel military police who had protected us during our five weeks' imprisonment in the Wamba convent, left us: and we lurched on into the night, with only an evil lieutenant in charge.

The stop — nowhere, but a house looming out of the darkness. The harsh order to get out . . . and the truck took off into the night, back towards our prison in Wamba. My eyes followed the disappearing roar, while my stomach knotted in a cold sense of despair, a certainty of unutterable evil.

We were ushered into the first room: a settee, a few chairs with no cushions, a table at the other end; windows seemed to be all round and rough guards seemed to be everywhere. We sat crouched on the cement floor, our backs to the wall, watching warily like trapped animals. Three or four younger guards, slightly better dressed, swaggered towards us and we shrank back. The first grabbed at a young woman missionary and Jessie Scholes, wife of our team leader, moved quickly to intercept him. There was an ugly moment as he raised his gun to strike her angrily for interference . . . and the younger woman leapt up, almost offering to go with him, rather than see Jessie struck or hurt.

'She's suffered before,' my coward heart encouraged me.

They dragged another to her feet and took her away. I shrank wretchedly behind the settee and watched her go, with misery and fear in my heart.

'What did you counsel that young nun? O.K. for another, eh, but not for you?' So some voice seemed to taunt me. Still I shrank and prayed to remain hidden from their wicked seeking eyes.

'They're looking round for more prey. Don't forget, everyone left in here, but for you, is so far untouched,' and there seemed to be only one young guard at that moment.

He took me, out into the dark.

Half an hour later I stumbled back into the front room, without looking at anyone, stumbling over dozing forms in the darkness, till I found the settee and threw myself down, wrapped in my own misery. My mind was agonizingly tired. I seemed to be only just holding on to sanity. We were waiting for death, almost all hope of deliverance gone. There didn't seem any point in resistance. Why couldn't they just kill us and be done with it? Why the suffering first? Who would be benefited by all this?

The others weren't back: my heart winced for them and I found solace in praying for them, for their minds, for an ability to accept. Perhaps because I was a doctor, or because my life hadn't been all white in the past, or just because I was me, I had been able to adjust mentally to some extent to this new method of attack against the missionary.

One of the other girls stumbled in . . . minutes ticked by on leaden feet. Another came back. My heart went out to her and my arms drew her down beside me. She sobbed helplessly. We didn't talk. I just held her close to me and loved her, till she quietened and dozed in utter exhaustion. How much her love to protect another had cost her. Oh, those brutes, those brutes, how dared they touch her?

I shook myself from reminiscing and tried to think soberly and constructively. Those five awful months of captivity in 1964 were only a passing episode. I needed to remember honestly the work from 1953 to 1964, and all that God had enabled us to achieve in His service; and then to discover if my part in this work in Congo/Zaire was finished, or if in fact He wanted me back there to help in the mammoth task of reconstruction.

Just what the task might involve was practically impossible to imagine from the comfortable affluence of an English home. Just how extensive had the destruction of the rebellion been? Greek traders, brought to prison in Wamba in December 1964, one month after we had been captured, had reported everything destroyed — buildings, equipment, school and hospital supplies: but we had hoped that they exaggerated. Then the first letters to come out of the war-torn region in August 1965 told us of the loss of all things, and we began to sense a little of what might be the truth.

Doubts gnawed in my heart. Did it really make any sense, starting all over again? The devastating destruction, the enormity of the task of reconstruction, the infinitesimal offering we would have to share: and then what? What had happened once could flare up all over again. What guarantee had we of any lasting peace? What assurance that we wouldn't be wasting our time, that newly-erected buildings wouldn't be pulled down, that newly-stocked hospital pharmacies wouldn't be ransacked?

Were we really wanted? How could one begin to assess this in realistic terms? I didn't want to force my services on the Africans if in truth they didn't want me, or would rather be without me. During the years since Independence was declared in June 1960, foreigners had frequently been shown that they were not welcome. Doubtless we deserved much of the treatment we got. For fifty years Africans waited, stood, were ignored and by-passed while Europeans were served immediately with courtesy and given a comfortable chair in pleasant surroundings if a slight delay was unavoidable. It wasn't really surprising that there was a backlog of African hurts to be worked off, by reversing the roles: 'I waited, so now you wait.' Unfortunately the white man had little of the patient forbearance and amazing long-suffering of his African partner, and would often retort or flare up, thereby giving the tormentor great satisfaction at realizing that the needle-prick had found its mark, and so perpetuating the process indefinitely: 'as white, so black.'

True, it was no use being over-influenced by the memory of the coarse shouting of one drunken soldier at a road-block: 'Go back, you dirty white colonialist! Aren't you the cause of all our trouble?' however unnerving it had been, that wild stormy night. Nor must I dwell too much on the treatment I had received at the immigration offices in 1961. A well-dressed, correctly-spoken officer had ignored me all day, leaving me standing outside on the veranda from 9 a.m. till 4 p.m. My passport lay on his table. He chose to see some twenty or so nationals, all but two of whom had arrived after me, and then told me to 'come back tomorrow'!

Yet these were straws in an anti-colonial wind.

There were of course other straws which blew differently. John Mangadima, as my surgical assistant and close friend, had gone with me, on 13 February 1961, the two-hour weekly journey to Wamba by car, for a day's work at the Government hospital. Just before reaching Wamba we had been flagged down and warned to go home.

'All is chaos. People are fleeing. All the foreigners are being held in prison.'

Puzzled, uncertain, fearful, yet knowing that we must go on to fulfill our medical responsibilities to the patients, over a hundred in number, who were waiting for us, we drove on towards the town. Halted and challenged (and mentally almost demoralized by fear) by a gang of rough soldiers at a makeshift road-block in the suburbs, we were eventually escorted to the authorities. Suddenly everything changed. Smiles, hand-shakes, pleasantness on all sides, and a piece of paper giving me freedom of movement as 'their doctor'. Probably no higher honour could have been offered me at that moment, but the conditions were hardly auspicious for recognizing honour. However, that day I was accepted, and wanted, as a doctor to serve them: that day the soldiers stood to attention and saluted as we drove past.

Unfortunately I had different treatment only four weeks later, from the same soldiers, the same authorities, in the same buildings. I was then held prisoner for four fearful hours, because my indicator lights had failed to show I was turning right off a roundabout. The car was brought to a halt by violent gesticulations and wild shoutings. I was ordered out in no uncertain manner and hounded into the police station, accused of no-one quite-knew-what, pushed around unceremoniously and threatened continuously. I was ultimately fined £20, which I did not have on me. Asking permission for a policeman to escort me to the home of our missionaries for assistance, I was shouted at and ordered not to prevaricate, told to 'pay up or else . . .'. Deciding that silence was the better part of valour, I just stood. Struck and jeered at for not knowing how to answer, becoming muddled with fear and uncertain in my comprehension of the local French, I just stood.

By then I had been as convinced that I was *not* wanted as, four weeks before, I had vaguely dared to hope that I was wanted. So Government officials, soldiers and police had made it pretty clear that, by and large, they no longer wanted the interfering presence of the foreigners.

But what about our own students and medical workers? Was there possibly a different attitude there? I longed to believe that, after the eleven years during which we had lived and worked together, some might be able to overcome the national distrust of the foreigner. Couldn't they believe that we honestly only wanted to help, with no ulterior motive, no paternalism, none of the 'neo-colonial imperialism' about which they were indoctrinated daily from eastern broadcasting stations?

I recalled a particular episode at our Nebobongo medical centre in 1962. John Mangadima, besides being my assistant and friend, was also a strong nationalist, for which I respected him. Sometimes this came over as an 'anti-white' spirit, as on the occasion when the wife of the national regional administrator spent three months in my home, due to difficulties during her first pregnancy. On one of her husband's rare visits to her, John approached him for his advice concerning the scale of wages that the missionaries paid to nurses and workmen. The administrator called a select meeting of local leaders of our medical centre in my sitting-room, and then asked me to attend. I was frankly nervous, as I had never known if we were wholly within the present law or not, nor whether our interpretation of the law would be acceptable to whoever was in power at any given moment. If the administrator had said that my scale was not acceptable, it could have landed me in enormous difficulties, such as back-paying all hospital employees for two years to

171

Government professional salary-scales, involving as much as £5,000: or a prison sentence to equivalent value, which in Congo at that time might have been for the duration of my life!

We met in strained silence, each avoiding looking at the other. I was scared, but I didn't want to show it. John was half-ashamed, half-belligerent. He loved me and respected me, and he didn't want to hurt me, but nevertheless he wanted to know the truth. He reasoned: 'Everyone knows that the white foreigners are not always straight: they can play with words to forward their own ends.' Not that he blamed us. He really believed that I meant well, but I was white. It wasn't my fault, he knew, but he couldn't ignore it. He felt responsible for the other members of the team who were more easily swayed by my words.

Damaris, the head midwife, was obviously grieved. She wished this confrontation had not occurred. She believed that I'd be hurt and would have done anything to protect me.

Taadi, the evangelist's wife, sat beside me, obviously horrified that anyone could dare to question my word. She believed in me implicitly, and yet she feared some sinister, unknown force.

Each one waited for the other to start. The only one at ease was the administrator. He signalled to John to 'state his case'. John was afraid now, the eyes wary, weighing his words carefully.

'Basically, is it right, under the excuse of a private contract, to pay salaries far below the Government minimum?'

Put like that, it sounded mean, and God knows that I never wanted to be mean. But it was this or nothing, and wasn't this better than nothing? There could be no hospital, no church medical service, if we had to pay Government minimum professional wages. We simply didn't possess the money.

'Show me your pay-book,' the administrator ordered John.

Grudgingly he passed it over. He and I were both afraid of being proved wrong, yet neither wanted to hurt the other. The air was tense.

'Really, you are fools,' commented the administrator to the world at large. 'In the world there are two groups of people: those who work for a salary in this life with no preparation for the future, and those who give no thought to the present but are well prepared for the future.' I almost gasped; who would have thought that a Government official could talk like this?

'You have the immense privilege of belonging to the second group:

I have the stupidity to belong to the first. And you want to change over?'

John looked decidedly uncomfortable; Taadi was beaming; Damaris smiled her gentle, sad, understanding smile; I breathed a little more easily. The administrator never did answer the actual question. I was to remain for ever in doubt as to whether I was legally right or wrong; but he changed the whole atmosphere and authorized us to continue to find our own solutions.

Had I been able to look into the future and see the tremendous problems of the same kind that lay ahead I might well have decided against returning to start again in 1966. Even without that foreknowledge, there were lurking doubts in my mind as to whether our students would really want us back or not. I knew full well that they desperately wanted classes, teaching, anything we could give them to get life going again. But they were students, educated men and women, not children, and they would be bound to weigh up the cost. Was the apparent price too much to pay? It would mean deliberately subjecting themselves again to what they could only call white domination and paternalism; once again having to say the eternal 'thank you' and to kow-tow to those who seemed always able to give.

I tried to look at the situation dispassionately, to see it with their eyes. I was asking them to trust and believe me, often contrary to their common sense; to believe in my poverty and therefore inability to pay Government wages, when they could see what to them was my blatant affluence. I owned and ran a car: they couldn't. I had curtains at my windows and mats on my floors: they didn't. If I fell sick, I went for medical aid, even if this involved a 500-mile journey by air: all they could afford was a second-hand bicycle. This was all undoubtedly true, however poor I might be in comparison to my counterpart in England, or, more to the point, my African counterpart in Zaire itself. It was true, even if I could comment that I chose carefully and prayerfully how to deploy what little money was at my disposal. My so-called self-sacrifice and generosity were of my own choosing and should not therefore be thought to merit a favourable acceptance and understanding on the students' part. Could I honestly envisage a situation in which I could so get alongside the student body, so listen to their viewpoint and their suggestions, that they would be equally willing to listen to mine, and in mutual trust we could beat out solutions to the many problems that lay

173

ahead? If I wanted to be sure that they trusted me, was I really sure in my own mind, firstly that I was wholly trustworthy, and secondly that I was willing to trust them equally?

As I tried to weigh it all up, it certainly seemed questionable whether we would receive a welcome on returning to serve in the Zaire of 1966, from Government officials, soldiers and police, qualified medical colleagues and co-workers, or from the student body. And yet....

The letters came....

Mangadima, now acting director of the church medical service in our area, wrote and told me of the well-nigh emptied shelves in the pharmacy, and of the endless queues of pathetic refugees and patients seeking medical care that the team were no longer able to supply. He told me that five of the team were working at Nebobongo and four others back at their outlying rural hospitals, so far as he knew, doing what they could with practically nothing. He mentioned that all were working for love of their own people, as no funds were available for salaries. He told me that eleven of the forty-eight students who had been in training when the rebellion disrupted classes had made their way back to Nebobongo, asking if he, John, could not teach them 'till our Doctor comes back'. He ended: 'We don't really expect you to come back after all you suffered from our people, but if God should persuade you to, we will never cease to thank Him, and to love you and care for you as never before.'

Damaris, head midwife at Nebobongo and now in charge of the maternity unit there and the small team of pupil-midwives, also wrote. She told how wonderfully, even miraculously, God had helped her during the months in the forest, both in caring for the orphan babies committed to her charge, protecting them from sickness and starvation, and also in helping women during their confinements in the forest and in the maternity-unit, with little equipment and no help but God's. She told also of the bullet-ridden roof and walls of the maternity-unit, of the smashed windows, of the looted beds and mattresses, of the stolen instruments and equipment. She ended: 'When you come back to us, Doctor, we shall have nothing to offer you but our love, but of that you shall have an unlimited supply!'

Colonel Yossa of the National Army, the uncle of one of our students, wrote to tell of the appalling needs of the people, thousands of

174

refugees needing medical care, thousands of young people needing training. 'If you will come, I personally will do all in my power to ensure your safety, and to assist you in procuring the necessary supplies with which to tackle the task to be done.'

Pastor Ndugu, the spiritual leader of our local church through the eleven years I had served at Ibambi and Nebobongo, a man I had learnt to love and respect, wrote: 'Can you consider returning to us? We need your love and understanding and fellowship; we need your courage and vision and determination; we need your knowledge and wisdom. We have little to give you in exchange, except our love and care, and the peace of God, in the knowledge that you are doing His will.'

Mike Hoare, the commander of the mercenary troops who delivered us from the rebels one year earlier, wrote to others: 'The needs of the people are so overwhelming, that we are prepared to accept responsibility for the safety of the missionaries if they wish to return to start the work of rehabilitation.'

A former student, Cornelius Balani, wrote: 'Don't blame us, Doctor, for all that has happened, but pity us for all we suffer. Come back, please! We are waiting for you expectantly. As God enables us, we will see it never happens again. Please don't remember as important the occasions of student unrest and disobedience: but remember rather the joy and gratitude of those whom you helped to succeed, and know that we others today need you to train us also to serve our people in the medical service.'

Bebesi, carpenter and mason, one of the senior workmen employed by the Nebobongo hospital, wrote briefly but succinctly: 'One wall of your home has been blown out and all the roof riddled with machine-gun firing. The other missionaries' home is far worse. So we are stripping it to repair yours. It will be ready for you in two months. I will make shutters for all the windows, as the glass has all gone. I will make you a new bed. You can pay us something when you come, if you want to: but we are happy to work for you without wages, as we love you and want you back.'

Note. The story of these first years, 1953-1966, as summarized in these first two chapters, is told much more fully in two books: *Give me this mountain* by Helen Roseveare (IVP, 1966) and *Daylight must come* by Alan Burgess (Michael Joseph, 1975).

3
Back In Harness

During the three-weeks' journey by boat to Mombasa in March 1966 there was ample time to evaluate my decision to return.

During the year at home, as we had spoken of our African brethren in their suffering, we had built up for ourselves an image of what we passionately wanted to believe. This image had become more real to us than the fading reality of our own sufferings. We accepted the biblical truth that 'in everything God works for good with those who love him', and then we allowed our imagination full play. We pictured the blessing our African co-workers were entering into, in direct proportion to the magnitude of their sufferings.

When their first letters had come, this imagery took even more definite shape and our hearts were thrilled. We glimpsed a preconceived vision and set about preparing for its fulfilment.

Why didn't someone shout at me: 'Pie in the sky!'?

It would have been a good thing if someone had taken me firmly to task, and forced me to listen to sense. Human nature just doesn't work like that. Intense sufferings and emotions do not always produce a total change of personalities.

I had to get down into the valley and look at things a little more realistically: to wake up to life's hard blows and not live in a little world of my own. God did get me to the place, during that sea-voyage to Africa, where I was willing to go back without expecting any dramatic change, willing to accept the difficulties and frustrations that are every-day occurrences in Africa. I should have to learn to see it all with their eyes and understand with their hearts. At home, some had thought we were rather wonderful or courageous or some such adjective, to be going back to Africa again. But our Zairian co-workers weren't likely to think like that: doubtless they were expecting us to return. They had also suffered. Had we not been together? I had had a year's holiday, and hundreds of Christians had given generously to replace all I had lost. Our African friends had just plodded on.

'Why didn't you come sooner?' Would that be their question?

Would I be hurt by their reasoning?

Then, too, for a year they had carried on alone: they had managed the finances, repaired the buildings, cared for the sick, been responsible in the pharmacy.

'Will she take it all back from us again?' Would I feel they were obstructing the fulfilment of my vision by their pride, or their obstinacy, or their unreasonableness?

They needed me to raise money for their wages; they needed me to provide the drugs and the equipment, the training and the transport; they needed me as a buffer between themselves and the Government, giving authority to their work.

'Will she do what we want her to do?'— with no question about my vision or my preference, my training or my conception of what I ought to be doing as a missionary. Was I going to resent their reasoning?

During the sea-voyage I became conscious of the old fears again. Why on earth was I going back? Large areas of our region were still in the hands of the rebels. Half a million Africans in the Isiro area had not seen a doctor for eighteen months. Communications were almost at a standstill, and shops were empty of all supplies.

My active imagination painted the scene of long hours and heavy responsibility, not enough drugs and poor co-operation from the Government, uncertainty and insecurity, and I began to think I was a bigger fool than even I had previously reckoned!

Five days in the intense, still heat of Mombasa hardly helped to encourage us! Everyone fights for themselves in a bustling African port or railway station, and noise is an integral part of getting the job done. No good 'thinking white' here. Gathering all our luggage together, re-labelling it for the 1,000-mile journey to the Zaire border, weighing in, clearing customs, loading on to delivery trolleys for port to rail-head, re-checking, paying — all with the rapid calculations needed from one currency to another, and from pound weights to kilograms — in the never-ending roar and rush, heat and haze — all this was a mammoth task, or so it seemed to me!

We faced what seemed like endless delay in unloading the vehicles, endless red-tape in clearing the ton of medical supplies in our van, endless bureaucracy involved in getting permission to drive the 1,000 miles across two African independent states to a third with all the customs formalities, and bearing British licence plates . . . and then on the fifth day I found that the van's battery was missing. My heart sank.

'Possibly the battery has been stowed in the rear of the van, back in England, along with the cab seats, spare wheel, windscreen wipers and other movable parts, to prevent stealing,' I murmured hopefully.

All right, I was allowed to open the vehicle and unload, in the presence of the bonding officer — and also in the presence of the blazing overhead tropical sun! Slowly and laboriously I shifted half a ton of equipment out of the van to the ground, sorted out the needed parts for the journey north-west, and then painstakingly reloaded. There was no battery. There was very nearly complete exhaustion.

The van was sealed and bonded. Four o'clock struck, and all the officials melted into the sticky air except for one agent, who set about to tow me and mine into a bond garage for the night. I climbed into the cab, behind the fast-shut windows, to join the eight hours of captured sunshine in a veritable oven, and I had to struggle to hold back the tears.

Eventually Jessie Scholes and I did escape from the stifling heat of Mombasa and started out on the long climb to the cool of Nairobi, 5,500 ft above sea level. Up again, to 8,000 ft; through the rift valley with its magnificent views; yet again up, to 9,000 ft, and then across undulating hills and down the long slope to Lake Victoria and Kampala in Uganda. More immigration and customs formalities, opening a bank account and doing essential shopping, servicing the van and registering with the British High Commission; and then we said goodbye to Ugandan civilization and set off on the last lap to Zaire.

It was hot and dry. The murram roads threw up clouds of red dust. All along the route smiling villagers and happy school children waved to us. Herds of wild elephants and wildebeest, wart-hogs and antelope grazed in the surrounding grasslands. So we reached Pakwach, 1,000 miles up-country from Mombasa. This was then the railway terminus, at the source of the Nile.

There to our joy were all our thirty-nine pieces of luggage, but we had no papers with which to claim them — that is, not the right pieces of paper! Three hours of typically African haggling and bargaining, spread over a two-hour midday siesta break, eventually secured their release from a highly-amused station-master, by an almost-demented lady-missionary doctor! Hiring a lorry from a local Indian trader was

178

child's play in comparison, and thus everything was transported to the Zaire border, still fifty miles ahead of us, up a tremendous escarpment of narrow, twisting rocky road with glorious views.

It was hard driving. At one place we ground to a halt, and I had to search for the book of instructions to discover how to get into low-ratio gears! At another awkward and narrow hairpin bend we encountered the local bus descending the mountainous route, loudly demanding that I reverse to the previous 'passing-point' — which I equally loudly refused to do, demanding my right of way as the ascending vehicle.

'No,' yelled the bus driver, 'I'm the biggest vehicle.'

'Doesn't matter,' I retorted; 'I've a trailer and can't reverse here.'

'I've forty passengers. You must let me through!'

'I'm a doctor: you must concede my right of way!'

Eventually, through sheer inability to reverse down that hill with the trailer, and with dogged pigheadedness, I won! So we continued on through billowing dust to the Ugandan border. Customs formalities were quickly and efficiently completed, and we set off on the eight-mile journey through no-man's land to the Zaire border.

Here we hit reality head-on. A young American was waiting for us. In fact, he had been patiently waiting for five days! He had the necessary documents to clear all our drugs and equipment, and the van itself, through customs, duty free — but there were no officers when we arrived! After a two-hour wait they rolled up, smell and gait revealing only too clearly where they had been. National Army soldiers accompanied them, carrying rifles, and we quickly realized that we were under a military regime.

It was a strange feeling, this long-anticipated home-coming, so unlike the carefully-rehearsed imagery. It was rough and raw, with coarse language and barely-concealed dislike, drunken and disorderly. It was terribly akin to the rebel occupation — and a tight knot constricted my stomach, and fear welled up in my heart.

'Why have I come back? I must be mad. . . .'

That first night, at the Christian village of Rethy, we were graciously welcomed by missionaries to their bare home, stripped by the rebel occupation. I slept badly and, in nightmare, re-lived the whole horror of those five months of captivity, waking in a sweating panic with one idea only, to get out as soon as I could. I was sure I had made a mistake in coming back. I had thought I'd truly forgotten the suffering. I had thought the fear had died. It hadn't.

I thought I would be wanted, welcomed. I'd built up my own image of what I expected the new relationship to be between national and foreigner, as a result of the suffering — and it just didn't fit.

As we drove from the mountains of Rethy down to the foothills, to Nyankunde, I tried to fix my thoughts on the task ahead of us. Here, at this small Christian village nestling among encircling hills, was the possibility of developing a medical centre and training school for national para-medical workers, and I had been invited to join the team. Dr Becker, a seventy-year-old veteran American surgeon, was already here with two or three European nurses, working in the small thirty-bed hospital that had escaped the ravages of the rebellion.

Dr Becker had worked for over thirty years in Congo, mostly 100 miles to the south at Oicha. Except for his far-superior talent and knowledge, his work there had been much as mine at Nebobongo, with surprisingly similar results, both as regards the painfully unsympathetic inspection by Dr Trieste in 1963, and the traumatic cruelty and disruption caused by the rebellion in 1964. He and his wife had not gone home for furlough, but merely across the border to continue their work in a similar hospital in the south-western region of Uganda. The moment that it was considered 'reasonably safe', they had returned to their labours in war-torn Congo.

I spent one evening with them at Nyankunde, on our way through to our own region. The church was willing to offer us, as a medical team, forty acres of land in the valley next to their own. Already available were two small wards, and two homes for doctors and nurses. In their own valley there was also a fairly small building that had been the outpatients' department, with laboratory, pharmacy and dressing-rooms, before the rebellion. The immediate suggestion was to develop the second valley with a 250-bed hospital and maternity complex, a large block for outpatient clinics and chapel, a building for doctors' consultation-rooms and special ancillary needs, a central laboratory, pharmacy and operative block. The old outpatients' clinic building could perhaps be used as the paramedical training school until new premises could be built.

We talked far into the night. The need was obvious: the means were non-existent. It would have to be team work. Would I ever fit in after years of 'running my own show'? On Saturday we drove on down from the mountain grasslands into the dense forest jungle and through to Isiro. During that long drive over some 300 miles of rough murram roads, mostly through thick, tropical rain forest, the packed-earth surface cut and criss-crossed with deep gullies from the torrential rains, there were long stretches without a sign of habitation. Then the scattered villages, poor and derelict seemed to contain only the old, and small children. The many barriers with National Army patrols to control any rebel movements were the only sign of young men. At each of these barriers, we were made very conscious that we were not welcome. The rough drunken soldiers seemed to feel the whole rebellion was, in some mysterious way, our fault.

We approached Isiro, our district town, at 10.00 pm., tired out. The busy, bustling high street with its gay and noisy shops was deserted and silent, roughly shuttered and desolate.

By now, almost in tears and twisted with fear, I was certain I had made a terrible mistake. Emotionally I just couldn't take it. I told my companions that I'd have to leave.

'O.K., fair enough. But you are our driver for the moment. Take us on the last fifty-mile stretch tomorrow, and we'll make arrangements to get you on the first army plane to fly out next week.' I'd rather face the shame of failure in the relative peace of England, than bask in England's acclaim for courage in the blatant revolution of Zaire. We were not wanted. No-one was calling us brave, or weaving haloes round our heads, or hoisting us up on pedestals. Far from it. We were unwanted: in the way: a nuisance. Hadn't they told us clearly enough to get out and go home, and leave them to cope for themselves without our endless interference?

Next day was Easter Sunday 1966. We drove into our village of Nebobongo, 1,500 miles from the east coast of Africa, at about 8.30 a.m. — and we were mobbed! It was just overwhelming. They were all in church, as we drove up the hill into the village, and they just poured out Taadi, Damaris, Riotina . . . I couldn't name them all, they came so fast. Then there was John Mangadima, and my twelve-year-old Fibi — we cried a little, among all the hugs and laughter. Nurses, midwives, workmen, house lads, wives, children — all hugs, kisses, handshakes, tears, laughter, hand-clapping, singing, praying, rejoicing.

The news had flown down to the leprosy camp, and the patients came up the hill on their stumps, singing and laughing, with bunches of hibiscus and frangipani gripped by their fingerless wrists. Tears ran freely at their abundant love.

On to Ibambi, at about 9.30 a.m., just as the 3,000 local Christians were coming out of morning service. It was quite indescribable. Pastor Ndugu and his wife Tamoma just hugged and kissed me till I felt I would break down altogether. We were nearly torn limb from limb. We shook hands and laughed and wept for a full hour, before being swept back into church for a service of praise and thanksgiving. One has to hear a choir of 3,000 singing from their hearts to believe it possible.

Three thousand faces were radiant, alight with an inner joy and peace.

However, I remember beginning to notice the marks of suffering, the scars on wrists and bodies: then the poverty. The men were in beaten-bark loin-cloths, the women in grass skirts, as they had been fifty years ago when the first missionaries arrived, but as I had never seen them before. There were practically no Bibles or hymn-books — everything had been stolen or destroyed. Some were unbelievably thin, all their ribs sticking out, from months of hunger and near starvation. The lovely church building was pock-marked in the roof, and walls, and floor, from the strafing of machine-gun fire. There was a look of tired strain in many eyes.

Then again, all was swallowed up in the tide of joy, in just being reunited, in knowing the two years of rebellion-suffering were over. The tears did much to wash away the ache and the fear, and eventually blotted out the nightmare and restored peace of heart and mind. Here we were wanted. There was no doubt of that!

They said they had not dared to believe we would ever come back: 'not after all you suffered', they said — and yet their suffering had been so much greater than ours, so long-drawn-out and hopeless. We had gone home from our sufferings and, surrounded by the love and generosity of Christian friends in the homelands, we had been re-equipped and refreshed. They had nowhere to go; this was home. They too lost all, but there were none to replace their loss and re-establish their way of life. Yet they were not morbid, or jealous, or filled with self-pity, just amazed that we were back!

To me, the sense of being wanted was almost stifling in its intensity. They loved us so greatly, I was almost ashamed at how little I deserved it. When we had left them during the captivity, we had distributed all our possessions among them, rather than see the rebels claim everything. We had hardly dared to expect ever to return. Now several Africans brought back to us these gifts to help us settle in again — table and chairs, crockery and cutlery, curtains and blankets — everything they had been able to hide from the devouring hate of the rebels.

In the week that followed, I visited several of the primary schools in the area and talked to children and teachers, and to our educational director. It was truly remarkable how they had carried on. Some groups were gathered in the open air under palm trees, the children doing their writing and sums in the dust of the ground with their fingers. Other groups had put up palm-frond shelters, and children were using bark-slabs as slates, with scrub-thorns as pencils. Masters were teaching all the subjects, including elementary geography, agriculture and hygiene, with no textbooks. 'All I can remember, I tell them, and they repeat it till they've got it by heart,' one young teacher told me.

Hardly anywhere did I see a blackboard or any chalk, desks or forms, exercise books or pencils. There was just *no* equipment. Yet as I entered a school-compound, the children would leap to their feet, give their little bow of courtesy with their arms crossed on their naked chests, and then beam at me with happiness. Everywhere they sang, often in four-part harmony. Everywhere they were thrilled to see and welcome a visitor. Nowhere did I hear grumbles or complaints at their poverty—yet the needs were so overwhelming, the task seemed completely impossible.

Sometimes the teachers would unburden their hearts to me. They felt their own Government had forgotten them, passed them by. Who would remind them? They had heard that all those teaching with the old pre-independence diploma would be required to give up teaching in a year or so, as only the newer, senior diplomas would be recognized. Who would upgrade them? Or who would replace them? The school buildings everywhere were in terrible disrepair, equipment largely stolen or destroyed, yet there were more children than ever before demanding teaching. Who would rebuild and re-equip the schools?

The educational director of all our primary schools was obviously at his wits' end, dejected and frustrated. Government demands seemed so unrealistic and unsympathetic. The new demands for senior diplomas would cause the inevitable closure of most of our schools. The law binding us to pay the minimum salaries would cause many to be redundant, at a moment when we needed everyone! He had hardly any money available, few qualified staff, no equipment, the buildings all in disrepair; yet the population had gone up by 50% in the previous six years and there were thousands and thousands of children clamouring for teaching. Where should he start? Which way should he turn? Which task should he tackle first?

'Couldn't you please help us?'

They urgently needed someone to train more schoolmasters, taking evening classes, organizing correspondence and vacation courses; to open a secondary school for the crowds of teenagers; to supervise the primary schools, to help sort out all the correspondence relating to Government-subsidized salaries — and *I could* help them. I even longed to help them. Yet . . . .

The medical needs were as great. There were hundreds of sick and no dispensaries, no nurses, no equipment. There were no drugs. The immense difficulties of transport and obtaining import licences were practically insurmountable. Yet I was there among them as their doctor, and they clamoured for help.

The first day after our return we drove our van, the Mobile Hospital Unit, plus trailer, up to Nebobongo, amid enormous enthusiasm. Road-barriers went down before us, happy, smiling guards saluted us: and the Nebo family turned out in force to greet us. How thrilled they were! It was exciting to show them everything — the folded-up stretcher support and the rolled canvas stretcher on wheels; the basin for scrubbing up; the six cans for our stock medicine; cupboards with fitted microscope, laboratory equipment, balance, pharmacy equipment with all the surgical equipment with autoclave and drums; and the forty fitted tins of drugs. The fan, the electric light, the tent extension, the window and fitted mosquito-netting — they looked at and studied and exclaimed over everything. We unpacked and sorted out, put on shelves and filled long-empty bottles from dispensary, maternity, wards and leprosarium, to a continual chorus of excited amazement.

Yet as I went across to do a ward-round, I knew only too well that it was as a drop in a bucket compared to realistic needs. The only thing not in short supply was the patients — thin as rakes, with bloated bellies and spindle legs with great weeping raw areas: tuberculous coughs seemed everywhere, glassy eyes staring out of emaciated sockets. Skin diseases, eye diseases, intestinal diseases. One little three-year-old with cerebral malaria; another with Kwashiokor, weighing only nine pounds. One little boy had an acute cancer of a knee with secondary chest complications. I wrote up treatments from the new stock of medicines just being unloaded from the van to the pharmacy, and knew that, when they ran out, there were no more — nothing but poverty everywhere. No-one had money to pay for treatment; no-one had money to pay a nurse's salary; no-one had money to repair or refurnish the wards. Nothing but poverty: nothing but poverty. The words beat a tattoo in my brain, even in my dreams — mixed with the endless bullet-holes.

I had been down to see the leprosarium, where another welcome party awaited me with flowers and banners. A tremendous effort had been made to repair the large dispensary, but every wall was 'pock-marked' from the machine-gun firing.

I went on a tour of inspection in the maternity block. Everywhere needed paint, but there was none available. Doors were spintered with bullets, and the walls even more pock-marked than in the leprosarium. A great effort had been made to make the roof rainproof, plugging each of the hundreds of bullet-holes. Walls were newly whitewashed, cement floor freshly scrubbed — but this only seemed to accentuate the innumerable bullet-holes. All the ten beds had been destroyed, and the mothers were lying on the floor on raffia mats. The delivery-room had been scrubbed spotless, and a vase of gaudy yellow-orange daisies nodded at me from the delivery table. Two soap boxes on crude legs, covered with butter muslin, housed two minute premature babies — and even here, the mosquito-netting was torn with bullet-holes.

The midwives' homes were clean and tidy, yet leaking badly, roofs strafed by machine-guns. There were no lines of clothes as in the old days, no books, no private possessions — they had lost everything and were bravely starting again.

Back in the hospital, we were called to the operating-room to see a woman who had been struck by a falling tree. I found everything scrubbed and ready for an emergency, a drum freshly sterilized that day with all they had left. There were no scissors, one packet of razor blades: only round-bodied needles and some out-dated cat-gut of rather large dimensions. Looking up as I was scrubbing my hands (in a new basin I had brought that day) I saw one panel of the ceiling had been blown to bits, and two others were pock-marked. Glancing round, every wall showed bullet-wounds, kindly covered with fresh whitewash, but glaring reminders of recent suffering.

The radiographic unit had apparently been totally destroyed: there was no sign of it. The anaesthetic machine had been badly damaged. And everywhere bullet-holes. Poverty and bullet-holes.

They were to be my diet for weeks to come as we fought to overcome both.

Then there were the refugees. They came in droves, endlessly. Mostly they came from the south, shuffling over 50 miles of rough mountainsides, up from the Ituri river basin, over the gold-mine range, and down into the Nepoko river valley. They were destitute and starved. Their pinched faces, bloated bellies, yellowing hair and raw, bleeding feet haunted me for weeks. They told us of hundreds more who never reached us, lying down and dying by the roadside as the final weakness and inability to go on overwhelmed them. And the others just moved on, driven by desperation, unable to mourn, unable even to care.

Day after day, week after week, they came. Who passed the word down the line, that Nebobongo had something to offer? No-one ever knows where hope is born, but their stubborn determination to live, to survive, fanned the flickering hope into a steady beacon of light — and the hundreds became thousands, who trudged relentlessly on. Desolate, hungry, naked, sick. Out of hiding, out of suffering, with nothing — no clothes, no food, no tools, no homes.

One month from our arrival back in Zaire, having soaked in a little of the appalling needs everywhere — for schools and teachers, for hospitals and nurses, for refugee centres and supplies — I made my way to Kinshasa, over 1,000 miles away, across the vast jungle basin of central Zaire to the western border of the continent. There, amongst other projects, the Protestant Relief Association managed to get 14 tons of supplies together for me: 60 bales of blankets and clothing, 150 cartons and sacks of dried milk, over 100 sacks of bulgur corn, half a ton of medicines including precious antibiotics, and umpteen sacks of bandages! I managed to buy some £400-worth of blackboard paint and chalk, exercise books and pencils, basic textbooks and maps for one hundred primary-school teachers. Besides which, some hoes, axes, knives and scythes were bought to tackle the great need of rehabilitation.

These were all loaded aboard barges and began the slow journey up-country to Kisangani, where the barges would be unloaded and the supplies transferred to lorries. Then there would be the long, 300-mile journey over fantastically difficult roads. They might conceivably reach Nebobongo in two or three months' time, if all went according to plan!

I flew home to Nebo to continue organizing the distribution of clothing and food that we had been allocated by the local relief organization, encouraged to know that these other 14 tons of supplies were on their way. Agoya and John Mangadima, along with other helpers, were tireless in their care for the hundreds of sick and the thousands of destitute. Immense patience was needed in keeping order along the vast crowds as twice a day they mobbed the 'distribution centre', the small courtyard outside Agoya's home. There, each received a measure of rice or bulgur, a measure of palm oil and one of salt, a bundle of greens and, once a day, some protein addition — dried fish, sardines, corned beef, peanuts or beans.

In the middle of our multitudinous tasks came a sudden, urgent request to go to Isiro to see Colonel Yossa, of the National Army. The week before I had met some Greek traders who had told me they were going to Wamba, where 6,000 refugees had just been liberated by the army. The Greeks had mentioned the destitute state of the refugees through malnutrition and sickness, and also the desolation of the small town, with roofless and windowless homes and broken-down, empty stores.

Now Colonel Yossa wanted to discuss with me the medical needs of these people. He told me that two young Belgian doctors had been in, with a team of national nurses and a supply of medicines, but . . . they were frustrated by the enormity of the task and the paucity of their means, and also by the bribery and corruption, the stealing and selling of supplies, even within the team.

The Colonel appealed to me to do something — anything to help. 'You missionaries have your own way, and you can succeed where we have failed.'

I wavered, and wondered. Could we tackle it?

'There are probably some twelve thousand — they all need you.' My heart lurched. It was sheer lunacy to touch anything so huge.

'Please think about it. We're not ready yet, as we must flush out the rebels from the surrounding jungle and make it safe for you first. But

I'll send for you when we're ready!'

Meanwhile, a hundred jobs clamoured for attention. We worked all one morning moving the pharmacy across from the badly-damaged hospital building with its leaking roof, to a room in my house. Every bottle and tin was scrubbed and relabelled, every drug was counted and listed, a long and messy job, but well worth while when finished. Another missionary spent hours sorting and checking three cartons of second-hand spectacles, labelling each lens and packing them in order. Some workmen were busily putting up four class-rooms for the primary school; another group were cutting poles in the forest for a new home for our evangelist Agoya and his family.

In between other occupations, I squeezed two hours each day to give revision classes to nurses and schoolmasters in Mathematics, French, General Sciences, Geography and Scripture. The aim was to prepare them for the entrance exams to special Government two-year courses, so that they could be upgraded to the new minimal standards.

Ward-rounds were of course a priority. We did all we could with what we had to help some of the tragedy that faced us. Every day, each ward seemed full of pathos, deeply-lined faces, emaciated bodies, skin strung taut across sharp bones, racking coughs, listless eyes. Some particular cases stand out clearly in memory, such as a thin, eight-year-old girl eaten up with a tropical ulcerative disease with great open, weeping sores; a ten-year-old boy with sarcoma of the knee; a four-year-old with cancrum oris, the whole upper gum and lip eaten away back to the nose with a black necrotic ulcer. Always there were pneumonias and cardiac failures, gross anaemias and tuberculosis, every stage of ascites and avitaminosis. The eye diseases had to be seen to be believed. And in the first two months, we finished our precious initial supply of anti-malarial and antibiotic drugs. Where and how to get more was still unanswerable.

Our leprosy patients demanded their share of love and care. During the first few weeks I managed to see them all, old and new, and do fairly thorough examinations and make out new report cards. We had nearly 400 new cases of leprosy in the four years from Independence to the Rebellion: but now, following the deliverance, we were flooded with almost another 400 new cases among the refugees.

I was given an overwhelming reception. Everywhere was spotlessly clean — pharmacy, treatment centre, examination room, waiting-hall, hospital ward — tables and cloths, report cards and medicine bottles. Outside, the courtyard was swept clean, and even flower-beds weeded and tended. The half-mile long road through their village was bordered with pineapples, and neat, well-cared-for food-gardens with peanuts, rice, manioc and plantains behind each small home. These people might be sick, with fingers and toes mutilated, their feet and hands often ulcerated and stumped, but they were happy and hard-working.

Throughout this period of two or three weeks, we kept hearing reports that the people at Wamba were in great need, with many, many dying of starvation and illness — and I wrote a note to Colonel Yossa to say that I would go for a week in mid July, if medicines could be procured. I suggested he should get an American army transport plane loaded with relief supplies from Kinshasa to Isiro, and we would see to fair distribution at Wamba.

I had to go to Kisangani on another urgent errand, but I talked there also of the urgent need at Wamba for relief work. Suddenly things started to happen. Bill Gilvear of Relief Agency talked it over with 'Big Bill', an American in charge of a private air-service, put at Zaire's disposal during that difficult period. I was bull-dozed into preparing a report of what I thought I could handle (clothing and blankets and food for 10,000, and medical supplies for treating at least one quarter of them). These were made out in six copies, in French and Swahili, stamped and signed, and flown to the American Embassy. I thereupon became terrified at what I had offered to do and, not for the first time, wondered why on earth I had become so involved.

Radio messages started snapping over the thousand miles from Kisangani to Kinshasa. Our request was reiterated and confirmed. Eventually it reached the President's ears. Everything seemed to be whirring into top-gear activity.

Then a message came that Kinshasa would provide drugs, but we must collect our own relief goods. So I set out on a crazy walk round Kisangani, from store to store, from Greek trader to Indian trader, from Protestant Relief warehouse to Catholic Relief warehouse: and slowly, by sheer stubborn determination, I coerced them into supplying me with over 10 tons of corn, oats, bulgur, wheat, milk, soya bean oil, plus clothing and blankets.

Then the 15-ton transport plane flew in from Kinshasa, and I hurried out on to the tarmac to check the bulk supply of drugs, only to find the plane was empty. 'The General of the National Army is sorry, but your order is too big.'

Another almost frenzied rush around town. The pilot gave me only two hours to collect what I could before he must take off, if he was to make Isiro in daylight. The Spanish doctor at the Government hospital gave me all he dared; the newly opening medical faculty of the University shared all they had with us; Dr Barlovitz, a private doctor in town, supplied a huge crate from his own clinic; both pharmacies in the high street fell to my impassioned pleas; and what with twelve more bales of clothes and blankets, two more tons of milk and soya bean oil, we filled that plane in those precious two hours!

I tried to get my breath back on the one-hour flight to Isiro, and started to plan for the task ahead. Lists of urgent needs flashed through my mind: camping equipment — beds, blankets, kitchenware, food, tableware, chairs, tables. Lists of people I could ask to help me — Colin and Ina Buckley from Isiro, Agnes Chansler from Ibambi, a junior nurse from Nebobongo, my cook and the Wamba pastor would all need to go.

When we reached Isiro, life really began to move fast. We faced deluging rain and miles of slippery mud. At one point on a steep, narrow hill, with deep water-gullies each side, two lorries were already stuck! I ploughed out in wellington boots, measured the gap, and weighed up the possibility of getting through, when the Egyptian driver of the second lorry offered to drive mine through in exchange for a lift into town — an offer I accepted gratefully!

Packed up, with trailer behind, we set off on the hundred miles to Wamba on the Saturday afternoon. As we crossed over an almost non-existent bridge into the Wamba territory, we were struck with the desolation — broken-down houses, unkempt gardens, deserted villages submerged in a wilderness of weeds.

Perhaps notes from my diary of the next seven days will give the best impression of that fantastic week.

Saturday 16 July. Arrived at the post at dusk, we went to report to the officer in charge. The first shops we passed, the transport house, the Government offices, the post office were all completely roofless and destroyed. The prison still stood in its sordid square. Along the one main road, all the gardens had been cleared and tidied: buildings were mostly inhabited by army, and in fair condition: till we reached the shops. One, two, three, four — the main shopping centre — utterly destroyed. What pathetic waste! We found the two white mercenary officers sitting with our Greek friends, Mr Mitsingas and Mr Dimitriou. We chatted amiably, and told them we wished to stay at the Mission for a week.

Up at the Mission, we went straight to Daisy Kingdon's home — in fairly good condition. It had been the 'Simba' headquarters and office, and was now being used as National Army government office. Various families in possession but they moved out for us. We swept and cleaned, and slowly moved in. Certainly rough living! None of the original furniture. Few odd tables and rickety chairs, and doorless, shelfless, cupboards, and *dirt!* Windows and doors largely without hinges or fixtures — but we soon had a pot of tea boiling and felt ready for anything.

Back again to see the Greek merchants and 'borrow' buckets, bowls, mugs, etc. for the work of distribution, and then to the Catholic Mission to invite them to take part with us in the distribution.

Sunday 17 July. Three church services and fellowship with some 500 church members. Prepared for tomorrow. A team of 50 helpers are all ready, each knowing their part. Chairs, tables, cards, date-stamps and ink-pads, bowls, buckets, mugs, spoons — all have been checked and distributed to the helpers. Bamboo 'fences' have been erected to guide the crowd where we want them. 200 vials of penicillin have been prepared, and 16 syringes and 144 needles sterilized. Between us nearly 5,000 report cards have been serially numbered.

Monday 18 July. A grand day! We heard them coming at 5.30 a.m. — and in no time some 400 were queueing up. All the helpers were soon in place, each with their necessary equipment. Primus stove burning, with saucepans of syringes and needles: bowls of Quaker oats with mugs for giving out: bottles of iron tablets: and so on. At eight o'clock we 'opened the doors', and in half an hour we had near anarchy! About a thousand people scrambled to get in first! At that moment, the mercenary lieutenant and three Congolese soldiers drove up in a jeep — and in ten minutes, perfect order!

By midday, we were through for today. 2,600 people had passed through, of whom 400 received medical cards, 70 of these being for severe malnutrition (almost 3% of those we saw). Ten of these malnutrition cases were deeply pathetic to see. One woman with six children — all emaciated, with swollen feet, sores, yellowing skin and hair. We gave what treatment we could, of supplementary protein and vitamins and also penicillin injections.

It is interesting that only 16% of the people were in acute need of medical aid: probably 50% were suffering from diarrhoea, mainly due to malnutrition, but doubtless also due to intestinal worms and dysentery. Ninety-four people had severe eye infections. We expect to see much more sickness tomorrow, now that the news will have spread around.

During the afternoon, a note came up from the African head-nurse at the Government hospital — a woman obviously needing a Caesarian section operation. I went down at 4.00 p.m. and we did it together — with the one and only blunt scalpel, four artery forceps, no sponge-holders, no gauze, no general anaesthetic — but all went well. We had no masks or gowns, just gloves: and no nail brushes. What poverty! But we had lots of faith and goodwill, and God helped us.

Tuesday 19 July. A thick, damp mist as light slowly broke through this morning, and the queue had started. By 9.00 a.m. there were about 2,000 to the left of the church porch, all with tickets from yesterday, and about the same number to the right, stretching as far as the eye could see, across the compound, all along the football field, out and across the main road, and down through the gardens opposite. And still they came! Everything was very orderly, with two soldiers to help us outside and fifty-six church elders helping with the distribution inside.

In all today, 5,176 people went through, representing 2,032 families. Of these, 1,015 received medical help, about 20%. The malnutrition cases were truly pathetic. Skin and bones, oedema and ulcers, thrush in their mouths and glazed eyes. We gave each of them milk, every two to three hours — they just *grabbed* it, and cried for more. They were starved and desperate.

At midday, two more truck-loads of supplies arrived — milk, oil, corn and clothing. In the afternoon, some essential shopping, plus pulling a molar tooth for the Greek trader! In the evening, we erected more barriers to direct the crowd for tomorrow's task of distributing clothes — trousers and a shirt for each man, a piece of cloth and a blanket for the children, and a dress for each woman.

Wednesday 20 July. What a day! We're all almost worn out! By 6.00 a.m. the battle was on, in a cold damp mist, a queue stretching away to the far boundary of the compound. When the doors were opened, the flood released! In seven hours, 4,630 had been through, including 650 sick, receiving penicillin, worm treatment, eye ointment, iron tablets and milk. Then we prepared for the 'first-timers': a vast and ever-increasing crowd. In four hours, we had let 2,238 people through, and treated a further 328 sick, bringing today's total to 6,868 people served with oats, corn, iron tablets and each receiving a garment, and 978 sick helped medically.

From 5.00 to 6.00 p.m. it *poured* with rain and I was soaked, walking up and down the line, keeping order, enforcing discipline, acting as a barrier against gate-crashers. Many 'Simbas' joined the lines, but I'm afraid I hauled them out. I just couldn't agree to giving them food and clothing after all the suffering they have inflicted on others. The last two hours, we had the car headlights on the queue: the extension light on the exit: and two pressure lamps and five storm lanterns in the hall.

On Thursday, all the population is expected to clean and weed the town and surrounding area. I've been to see the Congolese lieutenant this evening, to ask permission for our sixty assistants to have a day's holiday, and also for the 1,400 people on penicillin treatment to be allowed to come up for their injections. He agreed amicably.

Thursday 21 July. I suppose this amazing week will end one day! This morning we did some 600 injections, treated over 100 Kwashiokor children, tried to keep order among the thousands who hoped for food and clothing distribution, encouraged the soldiers with a good deal of humour to keep calm and not to throw their weight about!

This evening, we have given out full food rations to the 116 'helpers' and their wives and families — about 550 altogether: and clothes! What a tremendous job, fitting every little boy and girl, woman and man, with a suitable garment. It has taken a *long* time, but we had to do it after dark, to avoid attracting another vast crowd. Giving out clothes attracts more than even penicillin, and far more than food!

Friday 23 July. By 6.00 a.m. there were vast queues in every direction, and a great wave of unbelieving disappointment when I broke the news that we could serve no newcomers, only those with tickets in their hands. Once again at the door a green date-stamp on their medical cards, a purple date-stamp on their food cards: divided into four files, to receive a mug of Quaker oats and a mug of soya bean oil: passing by the medical workers for penicillin injections, eye ointment or bandages: handing in their tickets at the exit, where I collected all food cards, and any medical cards with five consecutive dates, and returned other medical cards dated for a final injection tomorrow.

Everything moved *fast*. Keeping the count was quite exhausting work. At 9.30 a.m. Ina Buckley brought me a mug of coffee and two sandwiches. As I took a bite, a passing child grabbed the sandwich from my hand and absolutely shovelled it into his own mouth, and then looked at me pleadingly for the other. I have never seen such desperate hunger — I could do nothing but hand the child the second, and watch it disappear in a few wild, famished gulps. Oh, if only folk could see the pathetic need!

We were finished by 11.00 a.m. — every flake of oats had gone: every drop of milk was finished. 4,885 people had passed through and each received some help at least. Tidying up, sorting out, writing reports — and an early lunch.

The continual noise and crowds, pathos and needs, have been very wearying and we are all feeling that a week is all we can manage at a stretch.

Saturday 23 July. Our time at Wamba has ended.

In some ways, a success story: over ten thousand refugees helped with food and clothing and medical care. Yet this was one small group, perhaps one per cent of all that needed doing. Already the Government was talking of plans to repeat this week in some fifty other needy areas, but they have not the personnel or the supplies to implement their plans. And we realized that we had hardly scratched the surface of the tremendous and appalling needs.

4
How Could I Be So Foolhardy?

In the welter of need, each of the returned missionaries and of the church elders sought to find his own priorities. It wasn't easy, in the middle of everything, to see the wood for the trees. Why were we in Zaire? And what were we meant to be doing, individually and as a group?

After three weeks at Nebobongo and in the area, soaking in the needs of schoolchildren, patients and refugees, I went back to Nyankunde to discuss and pray with Dr Becker, as to what we should tackle first.

Dr Becker had already made his own decision: that all interested missionary societies and church congregations should create a new medical team, and that together we should build one good, central hospital for the vast region, where Africans could be cared for in body, soul and spirit, to the highest possible standards.

Would I join him?

For a week Dr Becker had to be away from Nyankunde, working at the mountain hospital of Rethy. So I went with him and we worked together, doing ward-rounds, general surgery, outpatient clinics and special eye clinics day after day. All the time we discussed the various possibilities of this tentative plan. At one moment it seemed possible that we might approach the Government and offer to take over one of their hospitals, as at Bunia, and run it for them. But as we discussed it, all the impracticalities became so abundantly clear that we dismissed the idea. We became more and more certain that what was needed was a Christian centre, where Christlike behaviour as well as teaching formed the essential basis of all the activities. We needed the right to appoint, discipline and dismiss staff, in order to maintain spiritual and medical standards. We needed the right to select students for our training college from our respective church secondary schools.

As we discussed and worked together, a definite over-all plan began to form itself in our hearts and minds. Our vast region was some 500 miles square, a great basin of tropical rain forest, bordered to the

195

east by the mountain range on the foothills of which Nyankunde was situated. If we could develop a 250-bed hospital at the Centre with facilities for 1,000 outpatients daily, and first-class medical and surgical, obstetric and pediatric care, all this could support a training school for twenty-four students annually in a three-year course. Young men would be trained as medical auxiliaries to run rural hospitals and dispensaries, and young women as auxiliary midwives to run the accompanying maternity units. We envisaged a network of a possible dozen regional hospitals, in the care of European nurses at first, helped by Nyankunde school graduates, until these could be upgraded and able to take over the leadership: and each of these regional hospitals to be surrounded by some ten or a dozen rural dispensaries.

Our imagination ran on, and saw every one of these medical health centres served by radio-contact to the Centre at Nyankunde, so that any nurse or auxiliary, national or foreigner, could discuss difficult cases directly with a doctor and receive all possible aid from the Centre. Then we realized the essential need of a small plane and pilot, to link up every outpost with the Centre, with half-mile long airstrips to be cut out of the forest at each dispensary and hospital.

Quickly our minds moved on to the problem of medicines and equipment. We would need a central pharmacy at Nyankunde to undertake all the problems of import licences, customs duties, transport, reception, checking, stocking, sorting. From here each outlying hospital and dispensary could order its monthly needs.

The next step in our thinking was easy: one doctor from the Centre should be freed from other responsibilities each week to fly to one of the regional hospitals to do a week of medical oversight and surgical care, to help the nurse in charge with administrative problems, and to distribute the needed drugs and equipment. Thus the benefit of our work at the Medical Centre at Nyankunde would be spread over the largest possible area, and give the maximum help to as many as possible of the five million inhabitants.

Throughout our discussions, my mind kept flicking back to the need of a training school, to train Africans to the highest possible standards of nursing and medical care for their patients, as well as in diagnostic principles and practice; to train them for the job that most needed doing, in all the outlying regional hospitals and dispensaries. Already I was mentally listing the subjects to be taught, how many hours of each to each class, methods for combining practical with theoretical training, report sheets to record the progress of each student. I was picturing class-rooms and laboratory, nursing arts' demonstration room and assembly-hall, offices and record filing. I could visualize dining-hall and dormitories, uniforms and entrance exams. Each evening after prayers, as I went to bed, I scribbled all my thoughts down, covering reams of paper. I drew up lists of suggestions, lists of possible students, lists of proposed courses practical and theoretical.

My heart and mind were caught! Already I was visualizing the future years, seeing graduates from our training centre serving all over the region, not merely as skilled medical workers, but above all as medical evangelists. With my whole being I believed in the rightness and necessity of teaching and training others to do my job. To me, this was virtually an obligation laid upon me, in exchange for permission to live in Africa. My principal desire was to train medical auxiliaries whose prime objective was to show Christ to their patients, not only in preaching, but through the standard of their medical practice and the loving care given to each individual.

Back at Nyankunde the following week, we paced over the 40 acres (20 hectares) of land that we were being offered for the Medical Centre. Dr Becker had already commenced building, and had already in his heart and mind a vision of the whole. We were situated in the bowl of two hills. Around the hills, as we looked up the valley, were to be the homes of the medical staff. The school and playing-field, dormitories and dining-hall, would be in the centre. Then spreading out down the slope below, away to the north, the hospital, with laboratory and pharmacy, X-ray and maternity, operating theatre and intensive care unit. Twin wards were to be built on either side of a central corridor: and finally the administrative block and offices, outpatient hall, clinics and chapel.

There was room already assigned for a 'self-help' village, for distant patients who did not require hospitalization: also for a small tuberculosis village, leprosy-care centre, and psychiatric wards: for laundry, garages and workshops.

So I returned to Nebobongo again, churning over all the exciting new possibilities, and wondering how I could 'sell' my vision to the Ibambi church elders. I needed the local church to be with me in this project, or I felt sure it would fail. I wanted them to release me from my immediate task at Nebobongo, of helping children, patients and refugees in our own church area, to go far away — 350 miles of rough roads, two days' driving to start a school. It all sounded a little lame, put like that. Would it sound like running away from overwhelming, obvious, pressing need, to hide myself in a small, comfortable spot doing a small, enjoyable job? How could I convince them that ultimately it was for their own good? If I can train some of their sons and daughters, I told myself, to obtain the new Government medical auxiliary diploma, they would then have workers for several hospitals and dispensaries, instead of just me alone at Nebobongo.

I knew this was true, but I also knew it didn't sound convincing. A bird in the hand is worth two in the bush. A doctor now seeing to their multitudinous needs at Nebo seemed much more worth while than the vague possibility that in a few years' time they might have some half-qualified help. 'They are never going to be doctors, are they?' I could hear them asking.

Throughout the long, tiring fight against mud and ruts, during nineteen hours of journeying, including being pushed and tugged out of two giant-sized mud-holes, my mind ploughed on at the problem. Was it right? Could it work? Would the others agree? Could I 'sell' it to my WEC colleagues, nationals and missionaries, by promising to visit them twice a year, to supervise our medical services? The awfulness of those 350 miles appalled me, and then I would have to add a possible further 1,000 miles' circuit to visit our three northern, central and southern hospitals and their many dependent dispensaries. The road surfaces were all deteriorating rapidly; some bridges were dangerously near to collapse; many of the hills were practically impassable after rain. My heart failed at the prospect of regular trips.

Back at Nebobongo, I met the church elders and nurses to tell them of all our deliberations at Nyankunde, and the proposals for the new school. They were stunned. I had only just got back to them; they had no other doctor; how could I ask them to agree? Even the suggested twice-yearly visits raised little enthusiasm. The prospect of a monthly visit by a doctor/ surgeon by plane certainly fired them to set to and cut an airstrip out of the surrounding forest, in order to make this dream a reality. The fantastically high fees proposed for students at Nyankunde Nurses' School were terribly discouraging to them in their abject poverty, and I vowed in my heart to procure scholarships from somewhere.

For two days I prayed over this with them, and we sought God's mind. Then together we went to Ibambi to meet the church council, and again I rehearsed carefully all our proposals. Their discouragement was hard to accept. They just couldn't bear to think of my going away again, and no-one to replace me. I dared not even encourage them over much by promising visits from the 'Flying Doctor Service'. Our small hospital at Nebobongo suddenly seemed so utterly primitive, after I had visited various medical centres of the other Missions, with their electricity generators, running water, permanent buildings and huge crowds of outpatients. I had become ashamed of our little medical centre. Had I been so immersed in my own inadequacy that I had fatalistically accepted poverty and inadequate buildings and supplies? I seemed to have done so little for them — and yet I reminded myself that many hundreds had been healed in body and spirit through the work at Nebobongo during the previous twelve years.

Another two days of prayer, and we discussed the problem from all aspects. On the second day, they received a letter from a missionary who had been the director of our secondary school. We all knew that, during the year of the Rebellion, he had gone to work for another church area. Now they were anxiously awaiting his return to re-open the school. He was their one hope for the thousands of children needing secondary education, and also for the training of national teachers for the hundreds of primary schools. But his letter came to tell of the overwhelming needs down south, with over 1,000 boys finishing sixth-form primary school that summer, and only one teacher available to accept them into secondary school. Therefore he was asking the church to allow him to stay down in the south for a further two-year period. Our church council was stunned. Their own over-whelming need was so appallingly apparent that they simply couldn't believe that their one secondary-school director was not returning. They felt deserted.

And there was I, doing virtually the same thing. How desperately we needed reinforcements in the way of school teachers, doctors, nurses and secretaries, as well as mechanics, builders, electricians, radio technicians, air pilots and general administrators. Where were the workers to fill all the gaps?

Eventually, by the end of the week, albeit grudgingly, the council agreed to wish me God-speed, and allowed me to go ahead with the new vision that had started to burn in my bones. I left immediately on the long journey to Kinshasa, the capital of Zaire, to lay the plans before the central Government and to secure their rubber-stamp on our blueprints.

The country was, of course, still emerging from the torture of the two years of internal strife and bloodshed, so ordinary methods of communications and transport were almost nonexistent. I hitch-hiked the 1,500 miles in an army transport plane, noisy, cold, uncomfortable, but free! Then started three weeks of foot-slogging and dogged perseverance, to seek the right people for our cause, and to persuade them to be sufficiently interested for a sufficiently long time to grant us some sort of pledge of their co-operation and assistance.

At the same time as I was presenting our plans for developing a Medical Service centered at Nyankunde, I was also endeavouring to procure residence visas in the passports of the five WEC missionaries. What a thankless task! We had applied for these over seven months previously, and had not heard a word since then. The Christian travel agency which handled these affairs for us was non-committal and discouraging. I was not the only one seeking a visa, it appeared! And no-one really knew how to tackle the task, or hurry officialdom.

A taxi-ride two miles up the main boulevard; a vast flight of steps, a wide corridor with many doors; folks hurrying here and there, doing nothing apparently but carrying huge portmanteaux; others holding up the walls as they discussed at length, in high-sounding French, why they should not do what their superior had ordered, and why he had no right to order them to do it anyway. Down a narrow flight of stone steps, to Chancery. It was truly Dickensian, even in the elaborate, outdated vocabulary. A large, elderly African came forward and I explained my need.

I was nervous and anxious not to offend or to appear in any way critical of their right to make me wait seven months. Yet I was eager to state the case clearly, even if apologetically, trusting they would then serve me. He retired to his desk and began searching in the only file in it, among some twelve sets of application papers and photographs. Eventually he sorted out our five and came back with them. Again I went through all our reasons for applying for permanent visas. At last he motioned me to leave that room, pass through a door in the corridor, and re-enter the same room by the next door, to the same counter but farther along.

Here I explained to the same man all that I had already told him twice. After a short delay he led me into another, larger room, almost empty except for four large desks around the edge and Congolese officials perched on high stools behind them, through an opening to the second half of this hall, with a further four desks, only here the officials sat on chairs!

I was led to one senior official and introduced to him. I repeated my story, clutching the five sets of application papers with their photos. He took our passports and examined our expired visitor-permits. As he had not fully understood me, I repeated again the circumstances of our arrival in Zaire during January and March. He went and discussed the matter at length with another official. They returned together, and I recited again the tale of my distress! Conferring together, they decided to send me to 'Immigration' — 'just over there, by the momument'. He gave me a note of introduction to 'Immigration', asking that I be treated with courtesy and alacrity as I had already waited seven months.

I set off to walk 'just over there, by the monument' and took a quarter of an hour to reach the monument, and a further five minutes to discover the office. I waited in a queue, and showed my letter of introduction. I moved to another queue at a window and repeated the performance. From there I moved up two rooms and joined another queue. They passed me on to an office at the 'back', but the official there was obviously not pleased to be found, just twenty minutes before closing-time. The argument grew fairly heated, but all he assured me was that I was 'unofficial' and must become 'official'.

A Belgian technical adviser offered to drive me back to the Ministry of Foreign Affairs, guided me back to Chancery, introduced me to the same large African to whom I had already told my story three times, who escorted me back to the high official who had sent me 'unofficially' to Immigration. He accepted all my precious sets of applications and photos, promised to 'process' them the same afternoon, and told me to go to Immigration the next morning, by which time I would find that I was truly 'official' — but by then I had no letter of introduction! I felt I had moved a distinct step forward, but subsequent conversation with others who had shuttled for months between Chancery and Immigration brought me a large measure of doubt as to whether I would

201

ever see our forms again, officially or unofficially.

So, next day, to Immigration — no news, but forcefully told not to go again! Back to Chancery, where I drew a blank: just 'Come again at 2.00 p.m.'.

Back again that afternoon, and that time I actually saw our five names on a list that had been sent to Immigration for indexing. When (and if!) that list returned, I could collect our visas. Chancery said hopefully that they might be ready in three days: everyone else prophesied they might be ready next year!

Three days later, in the torturing heat, I presented myself once again at the Ministry for Foreign Affairs, looking for our visas. From there I was once more directed the mile to the Immigration Office. But no luck! The applications had passed through the first office, to another — but who would stir them out of there, no-one seemed to know!

A week later the search was still on, but by then I had got an able assistant, Jessi Nkoma, a very accomplished, educated African. Under his pressures the application papers were eventually found and transferred to the right office, and the man in charge promised them for the next day.

So Jessi went back for me the next morning, but was told to return in the afternoon!

That evening, he burst into the home where I was staying, waving my passport triumphantly in the air, duly stamped with the required resident visa! But . . . not the other four! 'Tomorrow....'

Meanwhile our main business was to gain recognition for the Nyankunde project for a medical centre and training school. During my first week in the great city I had made my way to the Ministry of Public Health to see the Secretary General, Mr Nandu. While I was waiting for him in the ante-room, Dr Trieste, the inspector of all medical and paramedical education in Congo/Zaire, came in. Recognizing me from that traumatic inspection at Nebobongo three years previously, he was gracious and even courteous, and arranged to see me in his office at the end of the following week, when I could present him with our proposed school programme.

Mr Nandu arrived and received me in audience most enthusiastically. He listened patiently and keenly to all my explanations and to our three main requests, namely:

a. recognition for the new school, immediately;

b. a five-year period for the war-stricken north-eastern region, during which candidates might be accepted for paramedical education with less general secondary education than demanded elsewhere;

c. upgrading and recognition for our older para-medical assistant nurses, trained between 1950 and 1964.

It seemed obvious that I was not the first doctor to approach him about these burning questions. He felt that if I presented all this to Dr Trieste immediately, before the meeting of ministers the coming week, there was a very good chance of the first two points being granted at once. This would then allow us to bring in the older assistant nurses, who showed capabilities of being upgraded, during the five-year extension programme.

I was really amazed at how quickly he had assimilated all that I had presented, especially as I myself was becoming increasingly tired, with the strain of talking and thinking in and listening to French all day, and keeping exactly to the appropriate points with each different official to whom I was presented.

When I eventually reached Dr Trieste's office I was even more tired, from ten days' foot-slogging to get the necessary documents signed for presentation to the Ministry, and not a little discouraged by it all. Dr Trieste walked in ten minutes late for our appointment, nailed me with two sharp, piercing eyes, and demanded brusquely: 'What do you want?' There were no preliminaries, no introductions, none of the courtesy of our earlier encounter, and a hint of: 'I've no time for you — two minutes at the most. I'm a busy man. . . .'

'All I want is . . .' — a moment's hesitation — 'sympathy' I added quickly, remembering that inspection at Nebobongo three years ago, when he had declared our training school unsuited for Government recognition, despite our ten years of sweated labour.

I think he was taken aback momentarily by my reply. There was a pause; then he actually smiled!

I leapt in and outlined hurriedly the whole desperate situation in the war-torn north-east; and, refusing to be daunted by my obvious inability to get the subjunctive tense or right concords into my utterly ungrammatical French, I rushed on into the plan forming in our minds to meet those needs.

He listened, at first idly, doodling on his blotting-paper; then more intently, eventually becoming caught up by my enthusiasm into jotting down notes. Then things started happening.

'O.K. How concrete are your plans? Have you a time-table for how you can achieve all this? Building plans? Curricula?'

I gulped — gazed — and pledged anything he wanted!

'Give me the use of a typewriter, paper, carbons and a pen, and I'll produce all you want.'

'Go ahead then — use my desk. I've a meeting with the Minister in ten minutes. I'll tell him that I want to see him again tomorrow with your proposals.'

He left, and I started to work, from 10.00 a.m. through to almost midnight. I drew plans and drawings of proposed buildings; I worked out time-tables for a four-year course both for students and for staff; I made out a decidedly optimistic budget with no suggestion of where the funds would come from. Then I worked on proposed record cards and diplomas, methods of organization and suggestions how to bend the present law to allow for the recovery of the north-eastern region over a five year period. It all seemed a wild gamble of imagination! I nearly got cold feet as I realized I had no authority from our team at Nyankunde to commit them so completely.

At midday I managed to contact Dr Becker through the Missionary Aviation Fellowship radio network, and got his permission to go ahead. I'd no idea how much he then understood of what I was promising to do in his name! But he was wholly in the project and prepared to back me all the way.

By midnight I had left the completed file on Dr Trieste's desk, drawn up as an eight-year project to establish the training school, with buildings up to the required Government standards, curricula following the suggested Government scheme, and all the staff necessary to implement it. And I fell into bed in a daze of doubt. How could I be so foolhardy as to think I could ever achieve it? But God . . .!

For two weeks I had to wait for a word from Dr Trieste, but at last the word came. He then took me on a wild tour of various departments, from one end of the city to the other, seeing secretaries, functionaries, administrators, and eventually the Under Secretary to the Minister. As we went we gathered up papers, documents, forms; course material, models, books for our non-existent library (though most of this material was for a course either junior or senior to our proposed one: there just wasn't any available material for what we wished to teach); and an

204

enormous quantity of enthusiasm, goodwill and encouragement.

'Go ahead with your plan. We'll send inspectors up as soon as we can;' and with this I had to be content. No written word, no signature, not even a firm promise, but I inferred that recognition would follow inspection if we could complete our side of the bargain in the stipulated time.

And so back to Bunia to give a full report to all the team at Nyankunde; to start work on preparing entrance examinations, and building plans for the first phase of the new training college.

A week later I set out for Nebobongo, despite many transport problems. I managed to hitchhike a lift on a cargo flight to Kisangani with two and a half tons of pork! I had been waiting two days at Bunia for a regular flight that never came, when I saw a DC3 come in and begin unloading cargo. I went quickly through the waiting-hall and out on to the tarmac, to see if I could possibly get a ride. A Greek was loading pig carcases. A Belgian gentleman also wanted a place. Two passengers would be allowed by the pilot if two carcases were unloaded. Much heat ensued, and argument in many languages. 'Impossible', the Greek roared, working out his financial loss through such an arrangement.

I just stood quietly by, with my suitcase, in the shadow of the wing of the plane, and waited.

Fiercer arguments — greater heat — still he shouted: 'Impossible!'

They all went off to the office and I heard the altercation continuing. Someone came out to the plane; two carcases were taken off, carried back to the hall and weighed, and my heart rose.

More shouting, gesticulating, fury; the Greek returned, and the two carcases were thrown back on. Still I waited.

Then it all occurred again. . . and the pilot and co-pilot arrived, obviously furious. 'Get in quickly: go up to the cockpit and sit in the co-pilot's seat — make yourself conspicuous!' Totally baffled by the last part, I did as I was told. The pilot revved the engines up, we taxied out, and climbed up into the air — when I was told to make my way back to a seat amongst the pigs! I gathered the pilot was mad with the trader for thinking a miserable pig's carcase more important than a lady doctor! He then made it clear that he took me in his seat at his expense, and the old trader could care for his own conscience!

Our students who had been in training before the rebellion sat their entrance exams for Nyankunde. Papers came in from eleven other centres and schools, and I spent a day marking and sorting, finally selecting four classes of twelve students each for the first year at Nyankunde.

The fantastic activities of the week among the refugees at Wamba came as a surprising interlude in all our other activities, including steady preparation to leave Nebobongo to start a new life at Nyankunde. As the date to move grew nearer, all sorts of alarming rumours also grew. Kinshasa radio reported violent uprisings between Katangese troops with mercenaries and the National Army, involving the death of Colonel Chache. Colonel Yossa went from Isiro to Kisangani to verify reports, and found himself landed in prison. General Mulamba was expected in Kisangani from Kinshasa, and the air was full of speculations.

I met with the Greek traders in Isiro and discussed how all this might involve us. It seemed probable that there had been a planned 'coup', as the Katangese troops had all left our region some weeks before and there seemed no obvious reason for their return. Some were frankly optimistic, other hopelessly pessimistic. When the evening news stated that the 500 whites in Kisangani were 'safe', it sent a shudder through me, to hear again the sort of language we had heard all through the Rebellion. In Isiro, there were two or three days when officers were having difficulty in maintaining calm and order among the excitable troops. The major had even wanted to blow up the bridges on the Kisangani road and cut down trees as roadblocks. As excitement and rumour mounted, all the soldiers were made to lay down their arms. We missionaries were requested to stay at Ibambi, despite the rising tensions, as the sub-lieutenant said that our presence would give assurance and exert calm in the explosive atmosphere: he promised to send an armed escort should we need to be evacuated in a hurry.

But when 26 July, the day for leaving, dawned, we all felt that it was right for me to go ahead with our programme and to start the journey to Nyankunde. Our Land Rover and trailer were loaded to capacity. Pastor Danga of Wamba and my friend, Jacqueline van Bever, were in the cab with me, and behind, like sardines, were John Mangadima, his elder brother Naundimi, Benjamin, my house lad, and Cornelius Balani, a senior nurse from Poko with his wife and two little boys. Over half a ton of goods were packed in tight around them!

We spent a night at Isiro, and set off at six o'clock on the Wednesday morning, 27 July. Within fifty miles our troubles began. There followed 150 miles of the worst roads I had ever travelled. We struggled through deep ruts, thick mud, and potholes into which the whole front of the van would sink. Water channels careered crazily down every hill, cutting the road into uneven halves. We travelled, one wheel each side, weaving to and fro with the crevasses, and holding on for dear life to avoid slipping and slithering into them. The road was an endless switchback, and every hill a nightmare, every valley worse.

We travelled mainly in low gear, often in four-wheel drive, several times in low-ratio gears. We stuck twice, at a crazy 60° angle. We pushed and prayed, and ploughed through. My hands were nearly blistered, my shoulders ached. Time and again I waded through in wellington boots to measure the depth of a hole, or test the firmness of a narrow ridge.

We arrived at another Mission village, Lolwa, at 9.30 p.m., utterly exhausted, having been the first truck to make it after a terrible storm the previous night. We were held up at barriers and chatted our way through, with smiles and sweet meats, till the soldiers laughingly waved us on.

The next morning, Thursday, on the last 50-mile lap of the long journey, we burst a tyre on the trailer! Not carrying a spare, we had to set to and repair it somehow, despite a four inch slit right through the outer cover! We crept the last ten miles at five miles an hour, until we arrived at the large cement signpost by the roadside, Nyankunde Mission and Hope Hospital. The words suddenly spurred us on with renewed courage. We swept up the side road for three miles' climb towards our future home, the engine roaring out our conviction of hope for the new adventure starting on the morrow.

5
You Build, I Teach!

Two days later I stood on the terrace outside the home where I was staying on the mountainside, and gazed out, as dawn slowly broke across the valley. The opposite hills were wrapped in low-lying mists and just the peaks reflected the pink glory of the new day. Bird-song chorused on all sides. I watched as the distant hills drew nearer, their contours rising from the dissipating mist, through the foothills to the rounded summits. The air was tangible with the fragrance of the frangipani and the stillness following heavy rain. Here and there I could see clumps of gum trees and golden acacias. Suddenly there was a vivid flash of startling blue as a weaver bird swooped by, drawing my eyes nearer across the valley. Fields of pasture land, scattered farmsteads, rounded hummock hills, the lush green following the winding riverbed, and so my eyes came to the hospital buildings below me, part hidden by bright yellow acacias and rose-pink flowering shrubs. Four wards, theatre and pharmacy to my left, laboratory, X-ray and maternity to the right: beyond were the foundations of administrative and outpatient departments. Nearer, there were the pupil midwives' temporary quarters: and then just below me, and stretching up the mountainside, a wilderness of long grass and brambles, a field of some 4 to 5 acres — this was our school!

For a week I looked, and planned, and measured, and thought, and tried to envisage, in the place of wild elephant grass and rough brambles, a training school for national medical auxiliaries to serve the church of the northeastern region of Zaire. I dreamt of dispensaries opening up all over the quarter million square miles, staffed by Zairian graduates of this school — able, responsible, spiritual; and I saw the streams of refugees, of hungry, naked and sick, adequately cared for by well-trained, conscientious health officers, nurses and midwives, trained at the Medical Centre.

I walked and stumbled in this field, measuring its slope and realizing the difficulty of levelling and building: slithering in its mud — thick, black, heavy alluvial soil, washed down from the mountains,

208

covering an impervious red-clay subsoil holding the water, damp and unsatisfactory for drainage or hygiene. I carried the mud back home, up the hill, in inch-thick clods on my sandals. As I gazed across the valley, imagining the immediate needs of temporary homes and class-rooms, and the future replacements of dormitories and dining-hall, laboratories and library, trying to see into the future, I could see only *mud*! Acres of mud, and difficulties, and frustrations.

I had come to Nyankunde full of faith and vision and enthusiasm...and now, was a little bit of mud going to discourage me? No! I was sure that God had said: 'Go forward' and so 'go forward' we would. During the coming week I expected students to arrive. Just how they would come was hard to say, but we had sent out messages by modern radio and ancient bush telegraph to invite any young men or women, with a minimum of one year's secondary education and a desire to serve as medical auxiliaries, to come during the first week in August. Some who had done entrance exams probably wouldn't turn up; others who hadn't done the exams might well turn up. So I waited expectantly.

Meanwhile the news grew steadily more unsettled. Fighting had broken out only 50 miles from us, between two frontier tribes, and several were injured. One hundred miles south, a 'gang' of about one hundred armed rebels (Simbas) came down from the mountains and attacked the population. The local National Army lieutenant rose to the occasion and practically wiped them out with machine-gun fire and mortars: but there was an uneasy tension around as a result. Two wounded National soldiers were flown to Nyankunde for surgery.

Then we heard that, to the north, another missionary and his wife had had their new 6-ton diesel lorry commandeered. Katangese and mercenary troops appeared to be pouring into Kisangani from all sides, and whites were said to have been evacuated. Some even added that all 'Simbas' in prison had been liberated and given arms. Greeks added to the gloom by telling us that Isiro had been stripped bare and all vehicles commandeered by the mercenaries. They said that all whites had fled the area, several over the border into the Central African Republic.

Added to this sort of news, we had our own 'extras' in the way of fairly violent earth-tremors, almost daily. Nyankunde had been considerably shaken in March 1966 by the earthquake that hit the Ruwenzori mountain range, and these rumblings now shook our hills fairly constantly.

Despite the happenings around us, the medical team went ahead and held their first official meeting of the 'Board of Directors'. It lasted from 11.00 a.m. to 9.00 p.m.! We drew up statutes for the new intermission medical project, got everything decently translated into correct French and typed up in five copies. Now we really felt officially 'launched'!

I filled in time while awaiting the arrival of students by visiting the local chieftain to pay my respects, and to ask permission to cut poles in his afforestation area, at 3p for a 10 foot pole. We needed some 1,500 such poles for the plan I had made out for our initial building programme. I also managed a trip to our local township of Bunia, some 30 miles to the north-east, to lay in stores for the school kitchen. It was quite exciting thinking and ordering in large quantities, such as half a ton of rice, ten sacks of flour and ten of sugar, ten cartons of soap at a hundred pieces each, forty-gallon drums of petrol, paraffin and palm oil: besides looking at bales of cloth and blankets, dozens of buckets, bowls, lanterns, mugs and plates, huge cartons of matches — there seemed no end to the list.

And then *they* came! There were twenty-two students in the first batch. I can still picture them as they arrived. Manasse, tall, debonair, light-skinned, wearing sun-glasses and looking down from some lofty height of self-importance — he managed to make me feel very small! Jack, short and thick-set, very dark-skinned, not bright judging by his entrance paper, but with an air of knowing all the answers which I found a little intimidating — accompanied by a quiet, inoffensive little wife and four rowdy children. Peter — oh, dear me! — from the first, Peter and I clashed. I remember one day in class: two of us staff were struggling to keep three classes going, and we were teaching in shifts, from 6.30 a.m. till 8.30 p.m. every day. It was necessary to make some slight adjustment in their time tables to allow Miss Fuchsloch to fit in the necessary hours of practical supervision in the wards. The change was written up on the blackboard, and Peter stood and drawled, in his near perfect French, with a superb disdain for the usual student/staff relationship: 'Has the Government approved this change?' The class held their breath, never quite sure whose side to take. I held my breath and counted ten — and then quietly replied that the Government had *suggested* the change. A gasp— and then the class clapped, and the bubble was pricked for that round — but there were many such rounds in the ensuing two years.

I remember most clearly those who gave most challenge, but there were others: quiet, gracious Joel, who had been with me at Nebobongo before the Rebellion and stood by me fearlessly when I was nearly killed — back now to finish his courses, with his unobtrusive young wife; Joseph and Ganisius, Ruandese refugees, taller than the Zairians, a little aloof perhaps, or else only shy and reserved, good-looking young men, hard workers, always courteous and helpful; Job, dull and heavy — he had not passed the entrance exam and we never quite knew how he got in, except that he came with the crowd from the south with a 'good story' — but he never quite rang true to me; Seth, small and wiry, like a house sparrow, bright as a button in appearance and speech, but completely the reverse where academic achievement was concerned! How he ever passed the entrance exam remains a mystery, unless he had been helped by Jack. He became known to everyone by his invariable response to each and every request throughout his three years with us: 'No problem, no problem' — and then, equally invariably, a howler would follow.

They had arrived in groups of four and five, each group from different directions. Some were chatting nonchalantly, self-possessed: they felt they knew the ropes and were just coming to continue their ordinary way of life, but in our setup: they knew the medical director, Dr Becker, and were prepared to show other newcomers what to do. Others were shy, withdrawn into themselves, very fearful of this new start in their lives. Yet others, like Peter, were proud and rather disdainful — they had already completed three years of secondary school and considered themselves a cut above the rest, a little unsure whether we were worthy of the honour of their presence.

Nevertheless all were tired, dirty and hungry. The fortunate few had been brought the hundred miles down the escarpment by car, Manasse among them: the less fortunate had spent five days hitch-hiking in transport lorries over 300 miles of wild jungle country, often helping to push the heavily-laden vehicles through seas of mud, or even to unload and later re-load their transport truck in deluging rain, for a spring to be repaired. A few local students, such as Joel, had cycled or walked across the valley, carrying their precious bundles of all they possessed tied up in bright-coloured cloths, or packed in rough soap boxes. All were expectant, wondering, and a little dazed after two years of suffering to be given this chance to continue their schooling.

Two years ago, some of these were in our Nebobongo nursing aids' school; others were in different primary and secondary schools throughout the region; ordinary, teenage students, happy, free . . . they didn't have much in the way of clothes, or housing, or personal possessions, but that didn't count much. They studied when they felt like it, and played when they didn't! Football was more important than textbooks: yet at the end of each year, like students all the world over, they suddenly became stuck to their books, the football field deserted: and then, all smiling, they passed their final exams with flying colours and looking as though they thought they deserved it!

And then the holocaust of the civil war, the Simba Rebellion, had swept across their horizon, absorbing everything before it. They were the lucky ones, still alive — many, many of their classmates were gone, killed, murdered, liquidated. They had seen whole class-rooms of fourteen-year-olds rounded up, herded into waiting lorries, driven off to the 'front' — singing, shouting slogans, their morale boosted by liquor and drugs, and the pledge of the power of witchcraft to bring them back victorious. Hardly any had returned. And these others, after two years of hide-and-seek in the dense forest, avoiding involvement in the tragedy of war, had survived and were seeking to pick up the threads again.

Slowly they gathered in the driveway behind Dr Becker's house. I took their names and welcomed them, sitting at a camp table on a wooden chair in the open yard. In front of us was our field, 5 acres of steeply-sloping land in the bowl of the hills, shoulder-high with rough grass and thorn bush, and huge clumps of elephant-grass towering above. Their eyes strayed across the valley, wondering where the school was, where the dormitories, as I and John Mangadima, once again my assistant director, gave out blankets, plates, mugs and spoons, lamps and bowls, matches and soap.

Manasse strolled forward from the group. 'Where is the school, Doctor?'

With as cool a wave of the arm as I could manage, indicating the field and rising mountain-slopes, 'Over there,' I replied.

Their eyes slowly turned and followed my pointing hand.

'And the dormitories?' Manasse continued, refusing to show any

212

reaction.

'Also there,' I replied, my eyes now challenging his for further comments. It began to sink in — there was no school, no dormitories. Yet . . . hadn't I invited them to come? For the moment I left the subject, and turned to the immediate needs of sleeping accommodation for that first night.

The local headmaster was lending us two primary-school class-rooms during the summer holidays; several church elders had offered to house one or two students; some of the missionaries managed to squeeze in one or two in their already overflowing homes. As we called each name and assigned them to a home or room or dormitory, we were conscious of mutterings and murmurings, and I seriously wondered if we were going to be able to win them round. These young men, mostly seventeen to twenty years old, all secondary-schoolboys, representing nine different tribes, from six different church areas and backgrounds, presented us with a tremendous challenge. Could we win their confidence? And would they trust us to direct them during the coming crucial years? Not only were they young men at the cross-roads of their individual lives, but they were young citizens at the cross-roads of emerging African nationalism. The problems seemed to loom higher than the elephant grass. These proud young men, full of their own importance at having secondary-school education, with all the determination to assert their independence, would they agree to weed, and clear, and cut, and build?

Later that afternoon they drifted back, and we surveyed the valley together. We pushed our way through the tangled undergrowth, measuring out ten-yard plots. Then we scrambled up another steep rise through a forest of elephant-grass and came out on a small level platform, and, laughing and breathless, looked back down the valley. 'That is our school,' I said, with a sweep of the hand across the waving green maze. Students eyed me quizzically, some almost hostilely. Could I be serious? Again they looked at the waste below us, and ourselves heavy with thick black mud, and our clothes full of thorns and burrs. And I appealed to them openly.

'You build, I teach.'

Are you willing to get your shirts off, take up the tools, and turn that valley into a school village by sheer, dogged, hard labour? Will you clear and dig and weed the ground? Will you go out into the afforesta-

213

tion areas, 6 to 10 miles away, and fell trees, hauling them back on your bare shoulders? Will you build and roof and thatch? Will you stick at it till we have a school village to house us all and all the families of our married students? *Then* I will teach you — my word, I may not know much French, I may know even less about politics and economics, but I can teach, and those of you who want to learn to be dressers, orderlies, nurses, health officers, medical auxiliaries, I'll teach you all I've got!

A stunned silence met me, as the reality of the proposition sank into their minds. So I really was serious. This was no joke, no white man's sense of humour. I actually meant it: 'You build, I teach.' It was fantastic. It just couldn't be real. Some closed their eyes and shook their heads, as though to shake off an unpleasant nightmare.

'We'll meet tomorrow at 6.30 a.m. in the courtyard for your decision,' I said jovially, inwardly quaking with doubts lest they would not respond. So we made our several ways down the hillside to our homes in search of an evening meal.

There was a special welcome service arranged in the church that evening, led by church elders and medical staff, Zairians and foreigners. The students all came, possibly as they had nowhere else to go. The theme was 'workers together with God'. Slowly, as different ones spoke and through the singing of the hymns, I felt some of the students begin to thaw towards us, accepting the challenge. Others, however, remained withdrawn, their eyes wary and suspicious, if not actually hostile.

Next morning dawned misty with drizzling rain. I went out to the courtyard and rigged up a couple of planks on some broken cement-blocks that I rolled into position. I put out my chair and camp table, and sat down to wait for the students. I began reading my Bible, a short morning portion. They did not come, and my reading continued to the end of the chapter. Still they didn't come, and I continued to the end of the book. I was wet and chilled, and very nearly discouraged. So much lay in the balance.

During the previous week many of the legal representatives and senior men, African and European, of the six participating mission/churches had met to form an administrative council. During the meetings I had proposed that the students themselves should build their own temporary homes in the school village. If we started at once, building through August and September, I reckoned we could start classes in October 1966.

My proposal had met with incredulity and open laughter!

All the available finance at the Centre was already allocated for wards, outpatient departments, homes for the missionary staff, drug supplies, medical and surgical equipment. The school would have ended the list. We should have to wait till the fall of 1967 to get started. But I was impatient. My own particular 'bee in the bonnet' had always been that 'no white man is justified in working in Black Africa unless he/she is teaching'. I could see no ultimate justification for the Medical Centre, except for the college. There had to be a Centre as the college could not function without the hospital and all its ancillary departments; but equally, there must be the college to give the Centre credence.

But could I really build the school with nothing? The other council members were justifiably sceptical. It must have sounded a wild-cat scheme. Strangely enough, no-one actually asked me how much money I had available or how I would feed the students during the three months of building or how I would procure the necessary supplies for the first term. No, the one burning question had been: 'Do you honestly believe that you, a foreigner, and a woman into the bargain, can persuade secondary-schoolboys, nineteen/twenty-year-old youths, with a consciousness of their own dignity as the "white collar" workers of the future, to build?' No-one asked me what I knew of building myself, nor who would measure out the land, plan the over-all development, collect the materials, construct the homes. No, they had just asked: 'Can you make *students* do it, willingly?'

And I had staked my reputation on it.

At 8.45 a.m. that first morning they arrived, and I had won!

I tried to pretend that I hadn't noticed they were over two hours late. I tried to ignore the fact that I was wet through with waiting in the drizzle. I tried to appear as though there was no question hanging in the air. We sang a hymn; I gave my prepared Bible study; then I started assigning work. The students let out their breath. I don't know where they had met, who was their leader, what led them in the end to agree with my proposal; but it was obvious that they had agreed, even though they said nothing.

In a businesslike way we divided ourselves into three groups. Each group had a set of tools and appointed a group leader. One group of nine had axes to go to the nearest afforestation area and fell trees; the next had hoes to clear a dormitory site. The third had knife-like scythes to mow down the jungle of tall grass to the south of the dormitories, where we would start a football field and, beyond, food-gardens. Granted there was not much enthusiasm, and it was soon apparent that some had never handled an axe before. They certainly were an ignorant bunch where building was concerned. But suddenly someone said: 'O.K. You win — we build and you teach!' and everyone started laughing at the sheer impossibility of the suggestion.

The ice was thawed, the tension gone, and I began teaching in earnest how to handle tools. We drew up the plans together, we paced out the land together, we marked off the plots, and I offered a bonus prize to the first group to complete their assignment. Two groups of nine youths each, to the two dormitories, each with a 6-yard deep toilet-pit: and ultimately five groups of three married men each, to do three small homes, each with cookhouse and toilet. They even managed to become excited. But in no time their unaccustomed hands were raw and sore, and it wasn't always easy to keep them at it from 6.30 a.m. through to 5.30 p.m. each day.

I went out with the first crew of tree-fellers, walking the three miles across the rough hillside to the nearest afforestation area. We worked all day in twos, an axe between each pair, felling blue gums (eucalyptus) anything from 6 to 18 inches in diameter, and some 25 feet high. As they fell crashing to the ground, the second of each pair lopped off all side branches, clearing these of leaves and smaller branches, and stacking them for roofing framework. The first day, in our enthusiasm and ignorance, we overdid it, and as dusk quickly fell we were suddenly all of us just too dog-tired to make the journey home. We lay out there on the mountainside between the poles we had cut, and slept soundly. By next morning I was so stiff and sore that it was hard to believe we would ever achieve our target. We struggled home in the early morning dawn for breakfast — and were inwardly furious to find that no-one had missed us, let alone considered sending out a search party for us!

We made the most of every encouragement: the first poles erected called for 20 gallons of sweetened tea! The first roof on (it was Jack's house — they feted him, but there was a gnawing corner of suspicion in my heart that he hadn't really acted honourably. The other homes in his group were far behind, and he was obviously working as a lone wolf and not as a member of a team, often a danger sign) demanded an after-noon off for a football match!

We pulled together, and slowly the students began to realize that we *could* do it. Neat rows of houses began to appear; each day toilet-pits went down a few more hard-earned inches, and we felt ourselves approaching our target-date for completion. It was the driest wet-season on record, or we could never have got that far. Others willingly helped us, hauling in lumber at all hours, or preparing meals for us. This involved more problems, as students from the north had never eaten the local manioc porridge and southerners could not stomach the palm oil; several said they could not digest corn flour, or beans, or other items of staple diet. But again, we learnt together.

The political news those days — or rather, the lack of news was disturbing and distressing. The mercenary and Katangese units in the National Army were in mutinous revolt against Colonel Mobutu, the Head of State. Kisangani was cut off from us, and four prospective students from that area still had not arrived. Isiro was likewise cut off, and the eleven prospective students from the old Nebobongo school, coming directly into their third year of studies, still had not come. Mail arrived only intermittently, and told us of the evacuation of missionaries and Europeans from both these towns. A general sense of tension underlay everything, and one felt that at any moment a spark could ignite a new conflagration.

Then sickness attacked us, to add to our difficulties. Several students went down with severe bouts of malaria; then bacillary dysentery put nine boys on their beds for several days; then two developed typhoid fever. We were well into September, and really only half-way through our project. I wanted to provide decent eating and sleeping accommodation before starting classes. But it was clear to me that we would need three months to create a habitable village, especially as work now slowed down considerably for ten days. Small problems began to loom large. Grumbling started over the food rations, the housing conditions, the long hours I drove the students to keep them at the building. We had to evacuate the primary school buildings at the start of their new term, before our own first dormitory was ready. Tribal differences reared their head and became focused in the missing group from Nebobongo. The former students were all WaBudus by tribe, as was John Mangadima, my assistant director.

When it was obvious that classes would not start on 1 October and I proposed to postpone the official school opening till 31 October, feeling was running dangerously high. Someone muttered: 'She's holding out for her WaBudu students to arrive.'

So I temporized: 'O.K., let's aim at 15 October — see if we can finish in ten weeks from starting.'

Then we had a fortnight of torrential rains. Our fields became a quagmire. Roads were impassable for hauling poles. Grass, urgently needed for thatching, was beaten down and damaged. Morning after morning we woke to drenching mists shrouding the hills and soaking the valley, only to be displaced by heavy banks of dark, scudding clouds with more rain and yet more rain. It needed so much courage to believe we would ever finish!

Meanwhile, in between measuring and checking, weighing and building, and a multitude of other jobs to help the project forward, there was also a mountain of office-work to be done. Each student needed a personal file prepared, with past and present details of educational attainments, plus family history, medical records, and a word on his spiritual state. Accounts had to be kept, for all the building material, transport costs, kitchen utensils, food, soap, paraffin and firewood, and all the essential equipment for starting a new secondary school. Lectures had to be prepared, time-tables arranged, and a hundred and one other responsibilities seen to, often between eight and eleven o'clock at night.

As the work neared the end, the problems seemed to intensify and multiply. Manasse walked off one day, over his strong-willed refusal to eat beans. The group of students working on the southern dormitory became sullen, as their building had to be taken down and re-done due to carelessness. Their determination to finish first had allowed slackness in accuracy, and poles were not properly measured, so that the roof supporting poles were not absolutely horizontal. Had we allowed this building to continue, the roof-thatching would not have stood up to the heavy tropical storms for the length of time we planned, so those responsible were told to pull it down, and they didn't like it. Within a few days the Mission's 5-ton lorry and the Medical Centre's tractor, both heavily laden with roof-truss poles, twine and grass, were bogged down four miles away in thick mud.

By the end of that week, however, Manasse returned — with a letter from an elderly lady missionary who had brought him up in a church orphanage, to say that he honestly could not eat beans, and we agreed to supplement his diet with animal protein. The southern dormitory group rallied and made a tremendous effort, working late into the evenings, to catch up with their northerly neighbours — and we helped them all Saturday afternoon (while the others played football) to fasten the roof-timbers in place. Our Land Rover went out and succeeded in towing the tractor up the hill, and eventually helped to deliver all the lumber we needed to complete the frameworks to our village buildings.

At the same time as all this, other activities were pushing forward. We cleared paths up the mountainside and staked out twenty-eight plots for food-gardens. We completed clearing a full-sized football field and attempted to level it a bit. We employed a local village tailor to get going on making shirts and shorts and aprons for the nursing students. Considerable time was spent three times a week at local markets bargaining for our food needs. With no difficulty at all I found sixteen hours a day full of activity and sufficiently hard work to ensure eight hours' solid sleep by night — and no time left for preparing lectures.

After almost continuous rain for seventeen days the sun returned, and work went forward again at a pace. The students were finding it easier now to do ten hours' hard work, without blisters or grumbles. But the opening date had been put back once more to 30 October and I could sense annoyance and frustration in many of them. So I wasn't altogether taken by surprise at their next move, even if hurt by their lack of trust and seeming unreasonableness.

A representation of each of the three proposed classes for the coming year, with John Mangadima as spokesman, went to see Dr Becker, the medical director of the Centre, with four main questions, which he sought to answer both fairly and clearly.

'Who is finally in charge of the school?' And one sensed the underlying question: 'Can Dr Roseveare expel a student, or have we a higher court of appeal?'

Dr Becker replied: 'Dr Roseveare has been appointed school director by the unanimous vote of the Administrative Council, African and foreign leaders of the participating churches and missions,' and we stored away the knowledge that a disciplinary committee would have to be created as a satisfactory court of appeal.

'Why has the date of commencement of lectures been several times put off?' If the first question had raised an optimistic hope of intelligence, the second reversed this, as the answer seemed so obvious: 'The change of the date of commencement is due to the unsettled condition of your own country and through no fault of the missionary,' not even mentioning that we had been quite unprepared earlier, with no homes, no books, no lectures.

'Why can we not start school till the northern students arrive?' They were speaking of those from the Nebobongo area, delayed by the mutiny in the army causing transport chaos in their area. These students were mainly for second- and third-year classes, having begun their studies before the Rebellion. All were from the Nebobongo church area and mostly of the WaBudu tribe; and the question really meant, 'Is favouritism going to be shown to the WaBudu students, at the expense of the others?'

Amongst those expected from Nebobongo was the church elder appointed to be bursar/chaplain to our new school, Basuana, who had been with me during the previous twelve years. Dr Becker replied calmly: 'Obviously Dr Roseveare needs the school administrator to relieve her of many of her multitudinous duties if she is to be free to teach you in the class-room.'

Finally, 'Who has arranged the programme?' they asked, almost belligerently. In other words, was the whole plan merely a whim of mine, a fantasy, a hair-brained scheme, or could they be assured of receiving Government recognition at the end?

Now I myself longed for real satisfaction on this point! But the Government, who had given many verbal promises, had sent no letter, no statement, no signature. They just were not prepared to commit themselves. It was all a gigantic gamble yet I felt a spiritual assurance that God was saying 'Go ahead'. But could one build a school on that? Could one ask intelligent youths to risk their future on that? To put in four years of studies, paying school fees, for a mythical diploma and therefore a precarious salary at the end?

'Dr Roseveare spent three weeks, at her own expense, on your behalf in Kinshasa searching out and obtaining the official Government programme, and pledges of full recognition.'

They were partly satisfied, though still suspicious. One could not blame their suspicions. I sensed the struggle of the newly independent against the feared 'neo-colonialist', and yet their hunger for the education I could give them. It wasn't going to be easy for them or for me.

At last, however, the initial building programme was practically completed. Water-piping brought fresh drinking-water to the village from the mountains. A 48-foot flagpole was cut, cleaned and erected in the centre of the compound. Rubbish was cleared away; final touches put to finished buildings 'hair-cuts', as we called it, given to the thatches; shirts and shorts were issued to the thirty-two male students, and blue-and-white striped dresses to the three girls; household equipment was provided for each of the eighteen married students. Some of their wives and children began to arrive.

Yet there was still no sign of the northern students, or of Basuana who would carry all the administrative load of the village, and so release me for the duties of the class-room. Could I go forward without him? Yet rising tensions among a few of the strong-minded students made us feel it was imperative to get going on 'Phase two'.

6
So We Were Launched

On Saturday 29 October, three months after we had started building the school village, we dedicated the college with a moving flag-raising ceremony, and launched out into the job of teaching.

Thirty-six students had arrived by then, and some two-thirds of the initial temporary-building programme had been completed. During the last week of October there was a sudden rush of final tidying — weeding, digging, sweeping, planting bright red canna lilies — to have the central courtyard cleared and each house standing in its own neat area. Fifteen missionaries and many Zairian colleagues had gathered on the newly cut road to the north of the village for the simple ceremony. The thirty-six young men in smart air force-blue shirts with school pocket-badges, and olive-green shorts, and our first three girl students in blue-and-white pin-striped dresses, marched into the compound forming a large semicircle around the flagpole.

We sang; Dr Becker and others prayed; John Mangadima unfurled our new flag; Jack Sibaminya blew heartily on an ancient trumpet. All came smartly to attention for the National Anthem as the flag rose slowly to the top of the mast, uncurled and waved out bravely against a clear blue sky.

Suddenly the moment passed, solemnity disappeared, and dignified students turned into ardent footballers. Blue shirts and hymnbooks were speedily exchanged for white T-shirts and a ball, and 'marrieds' played 'singles'.

'Well, how do you feel now?' one senior missionary jocularly quizzed me over a cup of tea. 'Not bad, eh? You made it, despite all we prophesied!'

I hesitated, and sensed a sudden wave of fear: I was scared. There had been difficult, even tense, moments during the past three months — as one might expect amongst any group of thirty-six senior teenagers. Yet I felt suddenly sick with apprehension. Could we carry out what we had set our hands to? The whole scheme seemed so futile, really, looked at worldly-wise. Here was I, intensely proud of my developing new village, but in the cool light of reason I knew that it resembled a corner of the slums, over-crowded, extremely poor, muddy, and inevitably underfed. Why had I done it? My whole being had always longed to give the Africans as good as the Europeans had. We called our Village 'temporary', but it had cost a cool £1,000 already, and finance was running out.

Could I really run the school and the administration? What if Basuana did not come? Was my own knowledge any longer up to today's required standard of teaching? The difference between American and British medical methods appeared to be considerable. Was I sufficiently adaptable to be willing to teach in theory as the Americans would be doing in practice? I suddenly felt very small and very weary. Was I young enough to carry the load any longer, and the long strenuous hours which would undoubtedly be involved?

'Helen,' chided a colleague, 'a penny for your thoughts!'

'Not worth it!' I exclaimed with a grin, and came back to earth and the job of pouring out cups of tea.

So we were launched.

I remember that first Sunday, marching three abreast the half mile from school to church, all dressed alike with maroon trousers or skirts and white shirts — startling, to put it mildly! Certainly eye-catching, and I dared not turn my head to catch the varying expressions as we passed an admiring crowd. Some were curious, some sceptical, some amused no doubt: and yet probably all were hopeful that this hailed a new start. Dr Becker preached that morning, and John Mangadima gave a short word of personal testimony. It was a good service, and the student body seemed attentive and interested.

Liliane Fuchsloch had arrived back from furlough in Switzerland, in time for the opening ceremony. She was to become deeply involved in the teaching programme of the college, practical and theoretical. We had walked all over the new school compound, discussing all the plans and proposals. We had visited the new hospital and dispensary sites, and the old dispensary buildings. These, we felt, could be converted without too much difficulty into class-rooms, to serve until our own new buildings were ready. We spent hours discussing courses and time-tables.

Liliane had already completed two terms of service at Nyankunde and in the immediate vicinity. She had served the local community as nurse and midwife, and had helped on the staff of the nursing aids' school which had previously been at Nyankunde, from 1955 to 1960. She knew something of the pressures of time-tables involving theory and practical classes, lectures and supervision, with insufficient staff. She was French-speaking by birth, and knew something of the pain of listening to British and Americans hashing up her language in the wards. Could she stand it also in the class-rooms? The radical changes that I and others were so glibly suggesting were to a work dear to her heart, that she had helped to build up and establish. How would she take it all?

'I think it is magnificent!' she exclaimed enthusiastically, as we finally got back to my room and a cup of coffee. From then on we worked closely together, and found we were on each other's wavelength!

We prayed over each decision and sought God's mind together on each problem facing us. We were both conscious that the coming year might prove decisive in the history of Zaire. No-one knew how long we had in which to offer any help in re-establishing educational and medical services. Would the whole economic structure crumble? Would the malcontents start a counter-revolution? Would the ultra-nationalists insist on the withdrawal of all foreigners before we could hand over properly?

It was no good theorizing. I could be neither philosophical nor political. There was a job to be done and we set about doing it After that first Sunday of dedication, we had two days for final preparations before classes were to start on the Wednesday. We cleared an old store-room that the church was lending us as a class-room. We arranged shelves, desks and forms, made by a local carpenter. We found two tables and chairs. We 'blacked' some boards, sorted exercise and text-books, pencils and blackboard chalk, all brought out from England nine months before. The carpenter mended two broken window frames and made fixtures for our charts and models. Two missionaries installed electricity for us, with a line from the generator which served the local printing press. Liliane and I completed what preparation we could give to the time-tables, drew up a simple set of rules for the school, created a committee from local national church members and medical staff, and planned staff meetings for routine school direction.

So the stage was set and our training college launched. On the

Wednesday at 6.30 a.m. the students assembled, all in their new nurses' uniforms, all expectant and curious, some probably a little fearful. After an opening hymn of praise I spoke briefly on our college motto: 'Unto Him, without limits' taken from the Campaigner youth movement, of which most of our senior students were keen members. We tried to set out clearly and deliberately (albeit in hesitant French) the aims and ideals of the college. It was being formed as part of the local church to train them, not only as medical auxiliaries, but also as Christian evangelists. Our standards and rules were unashamedly based on the Bible. In our opinion, as staff, whole-hearted commitment by each individual to the keeping of God's first and great commandment: 'The Lord our God, the Lord is one; and you shall love the Lord your God with all your heart, and with all your soul, and with all your mind, and with all your strength,' would knit us together as a family, and create from the outset the right sort of atmosphere that the college hoped for.

As I was writing my diary at the end of that first week, jotting down a few of the manifold happenings and listing the jobs that must have priority in the coming week, there was a great longing in my heart for the arrival of our eleven students from the north with Basuana Bernard, our college bursar. These senior students needed to get into classes at once with no further loss of time if they were to complete their courses in the year. Basuana was urgently needed to take over the oversight of the kitchens, the tailors, the new building programme and a hundred and one other jobs that I was still having to do between and after classes.

Suddenly my thoughts and day-dreaming were shattered.

'They've come!'

The courtyard was full of crazy noise — laughing, singing and crying. We helped them down from the lorry, thick with mud, weary from sixty hours on the road, many painfully thin from two years of under-nourishment, several sick and feverish. Many of the younger children were fretful, sore from the bruising treatment of the truck over the atrocious roads, through days of deluging rain. Basuana, eleven students, plus the six wives, twelve children and all their goods were eventually disgorged into the drive, to a tumultuous welcome.

There was Basuana, solid and tough at forty, utterly reliable and loyal, my right-hand man through our ten years together at Nebobongo, up to and during the Rebellion. He had been school chaplain and administrator as well as maintenance man and my own close friend. His wife Andugui and five of their nine children were with him. He just stepped straight into my shoes, and carried all the burdens of building, feeding and direction with a quiet, unruffled efficiency.

On the second morning after their arrival, at breakfast-time, he came to me with a list in his hand.

'Doctor, I've just checked the tool-shed. Three axes, five hoes and two machetes are missing. May I have permission to put a padlock on the door and keep an inventory?'

I swallowed my desire to apologize for my inefficiency and told him to go ahead, fine by me!

At the end of that week he came again with another list.

'Doctor, we really need to employ a second cook for the school kitchens, and a couple of gardeners for the school food gardens. I've interviewed several people, and suggest we take on the following for a month's trial.'

Again I gulped and grinned. It was good to have him back, and this sounded like old times!

'Go ahead, boss. Fine by me.'

All I was asked to do was to sign their contract in their workbooks and to pay them at the end of the month!

On the following Thursday three students arrived from the 'big city', as we called Kisangani, the capital of our northeastern region. They came into class at 8:15 p.m., just as we were to start evening prayers. They were given a tremendous welcome by everyone, escorted back to the village where they were taken to the dormitories, given a bed each with mattress and blankets, and then served a hot meal. How different from our arrival three months earlier, when not a single building was yet erected, and no hot meal available!

But the next morning two of the three were waiting for me when I returned from school at eleven o'clock. They were full of complaints.

'Don't you realize that we have already done two years' secondary school? Why should we start again in first-year studies?' grumbled the lads, revealing their ignorance by their inability to comprehend that any new course of studies must start at its own first year.

'Don't you understand that we are *secondary* school boys, and therefore should not be asked to *build*? And any way, if we should build, you would certainly be obliged to pay us full wages.'

I was just weighing up how to tackle their attitude when they continued belligerently: 'and the food! We have been accustomed to...', but I found that I had switched off, so to speak. This was what we had been given to expect from any coming from the 'big city', in sharp contrast to the gratitude of the forest-born students.

I allowed them to continue in their own strain, asking a question here and there, or expressing a doubt in the midst of their reasoning, for about an hour, and then felt I had had enough.

'Are you, or are you not, called by God to be medical auxiliaries? We are at present the only college in this vast region accepting students for any of the three possible option courses. If you are called to this service, you'd be well to accept what we offer and settle down. If not, it is well that you leave before I enter your names on the register.'

I suggested that they should leave me then, and come back at 2.30 p.m. when my assistant director would be with me. John and I sent for them at three o'clock only to learn that they had already left.

On Sunday 6 November I went the 30 miles to our nearest town of Bunia, after morning service, to meet the midday plane. We were eagerly expecting Jill Thompstone, an English nurse/midwife with teaching qualifications, who was coming to work at the Medical Centre on the college staff. However, there was no-one on the plane that I knew, not an uncommon experience where plane services were concerned!

Most days my waking hours, from 5.00 a.m. with coffee till nearly midnight, were packed tight with activity. School hours were from 6.30 a.m. morning prayers to nine o'clock evening prayers just before the generators were turned off for the night. We managed twelve lecture-periods between the three different classes, with meal breaks and school staff meetings sandwiched in between. Then home to light pressure-lanterns, and to start marking books and preparing tomorrow's lectures. Through the first four years this daily preparation continued, always for tomorrow's lectures. We never seemed to be able to get ahead of ourselves. The subjects had to be decided on, read up, thought over, simplified, written out, translated into French, typed on stencils and run through the duplicator, the latter process sometimes being at about one o'clock in the morning.

At first the French was a tremendous strain for me. Until the Rebellion I had used French only sparingly, talking mainly in Swahili, the trade language. Now French was obligatory for all secondary school and higher education. I was never quite sure how much of what I said the students followed, nor how extensive was their limited vocabulary. Each Saturday we gave simple test papers, often on the multiple-choice question system, in each subject, on the one week's work, just to encourage them to study regularly throughout the year. These began to reveal how much (or how little) they understood. One of the best howlers during the first month was an answer to a geography question in the general knowledge paper, 'Describe the structure of the earth.' One student wrote: 'A nucleus of molten metals, surrounded by a sort of cement-paste to hold people on, so they won't fall off.' An attempt, perhaps, to explain magnetic force?

At last, on Saturday 19 November, Jill Thompstone arrived! We were thrilled to welcome her. Once the students heard her near-perfect French, they gave her an even warmer welcome than the staff had done! When Liliane and I prepared the year's time-tables, we had prepared one for Jill along with ours. Jill had been preparing for her life's work as a sister-tutor in Zaire for a considerable time, as she had been delayed two years by the events of the Rebellion. Now that she had arrived, she was as excited as we were to get launched.

Then, ten days after her arrival, one Monday morning, Dr Becker sent for us. He reminded us of the urgent, almost desperate need of the hospital for trained nursing help. In other words: 'Couldn't you and Liliane carry the teaching programme for this first term, or even the whole first year, without Jill's help, Helen?'

Dr Becker's eyes seemed to bore into me, and yet held an urgent sense of appeal. Just for a brief moment I reeled as under a physical blow. We had so counted on Jill's aid to cut the heavy hours of teaching and preparation: but I could see clearly the force of all the arguments he began to assemble. Without an efficiently-run hospital, our students could not receive the necessary training. Jill herself would obviously benefit by working, for a time at least, in the hospital under our local tropical conditions, before trying to teach the students techniques suitable for African nursing practice.

I glanced quickly at Jill, and sensed the fight in her heart. She was longing to get into the teaching for which she was specially trained, and to which she had been looking forward for so long. Yet she was willing to fit in where she was most needed. I caught her eye, and we smiled as we understood so exactly what was going through each other's mind. Together we agreed to Dr Becker's proposal. That very afternoon Jill went to take over responsibility as theatre sister, continuing to give her mornings to language study and evenings to helping prepare lectures.

Another job Jill offered to take on immediately was to sort out the college accounts! I had tried almost in vain to balance these, between all the other activities. I never had been much good at this, back in my Nebobongo days, and obviously I had not improved at the exercise over the years. The vastness of the figures now involved, compared to those old days, staggered me. In the first four months we had gone through over £1,000 in freewill offerings and personal gifts from friends at home.

'Phew! If it has taken that much just to launch us, whatever is it going to take to keep us afloat?'

Somewhat daunted, I had fought on at the books, to get them ready to hand over to Jill in the New Year. Looking back and reviewing the achievement of those first four months, I was not only thinking of the £1,000 finance, but also of all the nervous effort, as well as physical, that had gone into each aspect of the initial building programme and launching. Could we really achieve what we were aiming at, in the eight years that I had specified at Kinshasa in May? The mountain of difficulties seemed almost insurmountable — physical, material, financial, medical and spiritual.

The next day a letter came out of the blue, to encourage us. It was from the American consul in Kinshasa, proposing to give the college some financial help from their American A.I.D. (self-help) programme, on certain conditions. We, the college authorities, must guarantee the balance of the finance needed to complete the building programme; it must be completed in 'reasonable time'; and we must employ local voluntary labour, including the students. It was an encouragement, certainly, but also a challenge. Could we accept the conditions?

In Friday school, during the daily hour given to general science and applied mathematics, I took the students into our confidence and explained what might be involved by the proposed conditions. Together we drew up scale-plans of the proposed new college complex, classrooms, offices and laboratory block, dining-hall, kitchen and stores block, dormitories and living quarters, and finally sports facilities and grounds. We prepared a budget, including the hiring of a contractor, ordering materials, paying workmen and transport. I explained the need to submit progress reports to all those financing the project. The students easily became more excited than I was, as they conveniently could not see all the thousands of snags and difficulties that might crop up.

As they worked on their plans, I was busily calculating how many tons of cement we would need, how many thousands of bricks, sheets of asbestos roofing, cubic metres of timber, panes of glass. I was reckoning out the cost of masons and assistants at the present scale of salaries, how many weeks of labour would be involved, and how many miles of transport. Multiplying, adding, subtracting. I decided not to contract out to anyone but to 'do-it-yourself'. Eventually I came up with a tentative figure of costs per square metre of surface area. Then reckoning on inevitable rises in costs of materials and wages, the figure began to look astronomical, in the realm of £25,000 for the total project. Over a five-year period, that would be £5,000 annually, and this to be divided between the five main mission/churches participating in the Centre. I began to get excited too, as I realized that it *could* be done.

I tried to explain to the students that the 20,000 hours of free labour that they had already contributed while building the temporary village could be counted in balance to this new permanent project, even though this would have to be done by skilled paid labour. That they found harder to understand, but decided to take my word for it, when they discovered that this meant they were not being asked to contribute more hours of labour!

Had I known then that costs of material would quadruple and salaries treble before the project was through; that months would pass with no cement or other vital commodity available; weeks possibly with no-one available for a particular job needing specialist skills; that Zaire currency, and later both the dollar and sterling, would lose their value— I might not have been quite so sanguine in signing my name to the American A.I.D. proposal. Perhaps it is just as well in this life that we do not know too much about tomorrow while we still have today with us. Suffice it to say that, six years after signing that contract and accepting an initial gift of £2,000, the programme was almost completed in every detail. But we faced formidable and unforeseen problems along the way.

7
Extra-Curricular Activities

Sundays began to take on a particular pattern. The students had been going out preaching each week with a local church elder in another missionary's vehicle. One Sunday I was woken at 6.20 a.m. to be told that the chauffeur who drove the students to the surrounding villages was ill: could I please drive them? Momentarily displeased at being woken so early on a Sunday, after working till after midnight every day the previous week, I checked a hasty comment and got dressed. After a quick cup of coffee I drove down the hill in the Land Rover to collect some eight or ten students, and then thought of Jill. I ran across to her room and tapped on the window.

'Jill, we're going out preaching in the villages up the Irumu road. Would you like to come with us?' — and in five minutes she was there!

It was a perfectly lovely day, clear, with a low heat-haze over the hills and a cloudless pale blue sky. Jill and I chatted in English as we went, mainly of the students and their problems. One particularly was worrying us. He was a third-year student from the Oicha pre-rebellion school, clever and capable. He worked hard and was obviously determined to do well. There were periodic 'troubles' in school, as there will be in any large group of senior teenagers — student pranks that go too far; minor disobediences that nearly end in disaster; strikes over the time-tables, or the food, or some such current problem — but Hezekiah kept apart from each episode, determined not to be involved in any insurrection. We were conscious, however, that he was not really pulling with us. I almost felt he despised me, for working with the students on the buildings, for talking colloquial Swahili more fluently than the official French, and for being a foreigner and a woman at that!

About eight miles out from Nyankunde we drew to a stop at the roadside, under a large mango tree. Two students scrambled down, clutching Bibles and hymnbooks, and a pile of tracts and Gospels. The rest of us moved on towards Irumu, as the two pushed their way up the narrow track leading through the waving maize to a hidden group of round huts, to gather children and adults together for a service. Just before Irumu two more students got off, at a long lane of thatched houses winding down into the valley, full of laughing children, goats and chickens, and various wary adult spectators. On again to the Irumu prison, with its twenty or thirty inmates. They were mostly ex-Simbas, largely in their late teens or early twenties, all bored and disillusioned, and glad of the interruption to prison routine, even at the price of singing a few hymns.

Two more students stopped at the hospital: two at the further outskirts of Irumu, near the army camp. We continued into the country, over the river, up a steep, winding hill, to a group of houses in a wide plateau of maize fields. Here we called a halt at what we came to know as 'our village'.

Honking the horn as we approached, we watched the children come running from all sides. A youth started to beat an old iron wheel-hub suspended from the beams of the palaver hut. The village elder came smilingly across from his home carrying two dilapidated chairs (the very best he had) for his 'honoured guests'. Handshakes and greetings all round, chatter and laughter, as slowly some sixty, or even eighty, folk gathered, it would seem miraculously, from nowhere. All were largely naked or clothed in torn tatters: they sat on branches or on the dusty ground: and they listened intently.

Hezekiah led the worship and he was excellent. He seemed to enter right into the lives and thoughts of the people, and talked as one of them. Jill gave her testimony that first week, in Swahili, and I remember how thrilled we were that we had gone. We went regularly after that first Sunday, and began to get to know the villagers.

Twin boys came regularly, sometimes in shining white T-shirts and little red pants, sometimes just tied around with a scruffy piece of cloth. An intelligent little eight-year-old girl always sat on the front row, with her small sister, and drank in all that went on — the hymns, the reading, the message and prayer. In two weeks she was singing the hymns by heart, her whole face lit up by an inner happiness.

One week, as the assistant student was preaching, her little sister, uncomfortable on her bit of the tree trunk, punched the little girl next to her, pushed her off and took her place. The second little mite, dirty as they come, with a filthy cloth round her, lifted up her head and howled dismally. Hezekiah quietly slipped across, picked her up in his arms, slipped back to his seat and sat and soothed her. She sat through the rest of the service in his arms, her head nestling against his chest trustfully and silently. That little act of loving sympathy, where another would have slapped the child, or told her firmly to be quiet or to get out, spoke more to the congregation of the reality of the gospel of love that we preached, than even the words we used. We thanked Hezekiah on the way home, and found that we *were* pulling together, after all!

Then there was our first Christmas. We had only two months to prepare an 'item' for college participation in the festival services. By then we had fifty young men but only three girls in the student body. What could we sing, and whom could we inveigle into helping us as sopranos? We wanted something definite, to mark the first Christmas of our Training College, to involve us all and to glorify God. It should be sufficiently difficult to demand hard work and some sacrifice regarding time, if it was to be of any value as part of the curriculum, yet simple enough to be well executed, if it was to be truly part of the worship of the congregation. We chose the Hallelujah Chorus of Handel's *Messiah.*

We had sung this before, at Nebobongo, at Christmas in 1961, and I still had our tonic solfa rendering and Swahili version. Practices began in November. Qualified and pupil midwives agreed to join us, as did also three of the European nurses. A time had to be chosen to suit both groups from the college and from the maternity unit, and these had to be during daylight hours, as the church lighting system had not been restored since the Rebellion. So we fixed rehearsals each Wednesday afternoon at 1.30 p.m. The first week I turned up, armed with tuning-fork and blackboard already covered with solfahieroglyphics for the first page. I waited. By 1.45 p.m. a few had wandered in. By two o'clock there were about fifteen, and my patience was wearing thin. At last we started, and did fairly well for an introduction.

Next week, despite all our urging, the start was equally delayed. They appeared to remember very little of what we had previously studied, until I realized that they had all swapped places, basses deciding to sing alto, and tenors preferring bass. We started all over again, dividing them into four voices and taking their names to prevent too much changing in future. While I was teaching a section to the sopranos, the altos and tenors started chattering. Silencing them, we started again, and then several late-comers arrived and had to be sorted out into their places. I asked the altos to sing their part alone and a somewhat unmusical 'cat's chorus' resulted: the sopranos all roared with laughter. The male students were deeply offended and almost refused to try again. The basses, bored by the proceedings, were doing homework, and failed to respond at all when their turn came.

The practice finished in grim silence, and I left in glum frustration. During the following week I painstakingly typed out stencils and duplicated one hundred copies of the Chorus with the tonic solfa. Next week, most arrived on time, waited in uneasy silence, sang as demanded— and it needed half an hour to win their co-operation again and persuade them to *enjoy* the exercise instead of only suffering the agony. Slowly it took shape. I pressed for more practices — after evening studies; after lunch; each voice separately; in various groups. Time was running out. We were far from perfect. Could we really do it? Was it just a publicity stunt on my part?

Christmas Day dawned bright and clear. The students marched across to the church in their well-pressed Sunday uniforms, singing hymns, to the accompaniment of trumpets and drums. Slowly the church filled with a capacity crowd of 1,500, and many more outside the doors and windows. There was community carol singing, special items from different groups of primary school children, two good messages on the wonder of the coming of the Christ to redeem us from our sins, and then, as a glorious finale, the college was invited to sing the Chorus. It was beautiful and very moving, especially knowing all that had gone before in the preparation. A great hush of wonder settled over the whole congregation, who had never heard such music before, and one sensed that all hearts were lifted and filled with praise to God. As they finished, there was a long, silent pause that eased into a shuddering sigh of satisfaction. For us, it had made our Christmas complete and memorable.

At the end of that first term, in mid-January 1967, Jill and I filled the ten-day school holiday with a rapid and exciting trip back to my old hospital at Nebobongo. The seventeen hours' driving to cover the 350 miles, mostly in sunshine, were accomplished with practically no difficulty. At one road-barrier, where a soldier was checking my driving licence and stamping all our road-passes, a discontented chicken started loudly protesting. The soldier then demanded road-passes for all our livestock. We just managed to suppress our laughter, and assured him that we had only one chicken which was to be tomorrow's dinner. Eventually we persuaded him to accept our plausible explanation.

Florence Stebbing, my colleague through the eleven years' work at Nebobongo, had arrived back that same week, on her return after the Rebellion, and she had hardly had time to settle in before we turned up. Daisy Kingdon, one of our veteran missionaries, was staying with Florence, as it was considered unwise for any foreigner, especially a woman, to be on her own at that time. Colin and Ina Buckley, missionaries from Isiro, were also there, with two tons of supplies to help the hundreds of destitute refugees still pouring out of hiding in the forest to the south.

When Jill and I drove in, unexpected despite letters and telegrams (which eventually arrived after our departure), at 9.30 p.m. in the dark, the house which had previously been my home for many years seemed almost uncomfortably full. Camp-beds were everywhere, and bales of blankets, cartons of drugs and sacks of foodstuffs were stacked along all the walls. If our quarters were cramped, however, our welcome certainly was not! The unbounded joy of our Nebobongo team that I was back among them, even if only for a week, was very moving.

The week sped by. A visit to Ibambi to deliver stores that we had brought from Bunia turned into a busman's holiday, with a crowd of a hundred really ill patients to be seen. Then we went to see their new maternity-unit. Senior midwife Martha Anakesi had been responsible for its construction by the husbands and friends of her clientele. It was spotless in its fresh whitewash, and filled to capacity with contented mothers and babies. This visit was one of the highlights of our week. It was a great encouragement to me to see something of what the African staff could achieve on their own, and to know that we had had the privilege of some little part in their training.

Two days were given up to journeys to Isiro, the local township 40 miles north, to do essential shopping for food and stores; and to Egbita, another church centre some 40 miles north-east, to do a clinic for the sick and to examine eyes for reading glasses.

Our two Sundays were filled with 'missionary activity', preaching to a packed church, Bible study with the nurses, fellowship meetings with the church elders. As always, the abandoned happiness of the singing of the Christian family caught at my heart, and I realized afresh how much I was part of them.

Then five packed days of doctoring. Everything had to be included. One day included four hours in the leprosy-care centre examining fifty-two new patients and checking over one hundred others, writing up their report cards, checking on drugs and dosage schedules, and generally encouraging them. Another day we arranged a clinic for the eighty primary schoolchildren, checking teeth, eyes, skin, blood and stools, looking for anaemias, due to intestinal worms or chronic malaria, leprosy or tuberculosis. Yet another day we spent many hours in the pharmacy, cleaning, re-arranging, listing, making up quantities of stock drug mixtures and injection solutions, and a list of urgently required replacements.

When we had arrived, everywhere had seemed a little dilapidated and rather dirty. Thieves had broken in the previous week and taken all the operating-room linen, quantities of penicillin and vitally needed drugs, syringes and instruments, and the African staff were somewhat discouraged and depressed. The stores and enthusiasm that we brought with us did much to restore courage and replenish shelves. Everyone set to, with scrubbing-brushes and disinfectant, sewing machine and rolls of cloth, firewood and sterilizers, and the operating-theatre was soon transformed into its usual dignity. Seven drums were packed with new cloths, gowns and gloves; three small autoclaves were all hard at work; floor, tables and trolleys were spotless; rows of instruments, trays and catgut had all been sorted into four general sets; and we were ready to start!

We managed five major surgical cases each morning, mostly hernias and fibromes, with a couple of emergency Caesarian sections. Afternoons were given to clinics — tuberculosis cases, leprosy patients, schoolchildren, eye diseases and those needing glasses, as well as regular outpatients' clinics with chronic malaria, undernourishment, intestinal worms, all complicated with severe anaemia. Each evening, a ward-round to see some fifty very sick patients. Only the most seriously ill came to hospital, as their abject poverty made even our heavily-subsidized fees seem exorbitant. How we longed to do more for them, but how? and with what?

An incident occurred during our visit to Isiro, which somehow illustrates the problems of black/white relationships of that period. I had ordered a 40-gallon drum of petrol, and entered the shop to pay for it. While I was there Jill hurried in to tell me that the drum had fallen on to the toe of one of the helpers and that 'the toe is half severed off!'

I'm afraid Jill was surprised that I did not go at once to see the

236

man, but instincts, developed during eleven years in Congo, restrained me. I turned to the shopkeeper and reported the matter to him in Swahili. He at once went to see, and I delayed a little longer in the shop. Then we went out and saw the shop keeper standing on the kerb, arms crossed behind his back, four assistants working hard in sweating silence to load the drum on the trailer, and then to fill the four jerry cans and tank. Glancing round I saw the 'bystander' two or three yards away, squatting, holding on to his bleeding toe, and scowling at the shopkeeper. Jill urged me (fortunately in English) to go and see him. I gently pushed her away towards the van. Gathering our shopping-lists and handbags, and locking the van doors, I guided her away from the scene to do our other errands.

'Why?' she asked. 'Aren't you a doctor? How could you possibly leave him? And he was actually *helping* you when it happened!'

I tried to explain what might occur if we became involved, thus revealing that we felt responsible, which would be interpreted as guilty — a court case, two or three days' delay, insurance claims, lots of unpleasantness. I assured her that I was willing to give the man all he needed to be taken to the local hospital, but that I was not responsible: and that in 'these days' it would be very unwise for a white person to be involved in an accident in which an African was injured. Jill remained sceptical and was not too pleased with me, and I wasn't too sure in my own heart just how plausible it all sounded.

Ten minutes later I went back to the van with a load of groceries, to be met by two policemen with open notebooks, and we were quickly surrounded by an interested crowd. Fortunately I remained outwardly calm, though the fear, born in the Rebellion, was nearly stifling me. Asked for an explanation of the 'broken toe case', I said the least possible, stressing the financial element in the knowledge that in African law this would absolve me from direct responsibility.

'I had *bought* this drum of petrol, which was being loaded on to my van by the shopkeeper's workmen, when this bystander apparently came too near and was hurt. Actually, I wasn't present at the moment of the accident as I was in the shop *paying* for the petrol and labour.'

Fortunately the police (and crowd!) were satisfied, and turned to the shopkeeper.

'I'll willingly examine the man's toe, if you wish it,' I offered to the policemen, 'and drive him to the hospital should this be necessary.'

They assured me that this was not necessary; that they would see to it directly themselves — and they thanked me for my 'generous offer and obvious concern'. We left, and I couldn't blame Jill for the look of scorn that I had so easily accepted such undeserved praise; yet we were deeply relieved that what might have led to considerable unpleasantness had ended so peacefully.

Jill and I wanted our home at Nyankunde to be African in style, a home where Africans could always feel at home. We wanted it to be like our school buildings, so that there would be as little difference as possible between us. We wanted it to be made almost entirely of local material, by village workmen, so that Africans might be encouraged to build equally good homes in their own villages. It had to be within our income, and yet pass the fairly strict standards set by our local building committee.

The European family had asked Jill and me to consider building a duplex (two-in-one semi-detached bungalow), and by January 1967 the housing situation was sufficiently urgent to ensure that when we presented our plans to the building committee, they were passed with very little opposition. We were delighted!

We tramped over the hills to the south of the hospital and college, to choose our site. Higher up the views were glorious, but the land very exposed to the strong easterly gales: lower down, it would be much easier to reach the site with building materials, much closer to the college for supervision, but we would sacrifice some of the views. We timed ourselves clambering up and down from college to various sites: we cleared small patches, spent an afternoon at each, studying and reading, and eventually we picked a site to the west of the main valley, 'half-way up', really 'neither up nor down'!

Once again, in mid-January, when we presented our plans in greater detail, including the site and direction and drainage, we were thrilled that they were passed at once. On Monday 6 February four workmen started clearing the site; eight went to local afforestation areas to cut poles; others went farther afield for grass for thatching before the annual burning of the fields in early March. Yet another group went daily to dig out sand and gravel from various pits in the vicinity; and we began to watch the materials arriving.

Every day we would go up to the site to see how things were progressing, but it seemed such slow work. The ground was rock hard, and digging out a site from the mountainside really demanded great effort, especially with our very primitive tools.

At last the site was levelled to take our 40-ft by 26-ft bungalow. Then to drive 2-ft-deep holes in the rock surface to take the poles, four main supports of 1-ft diameter, sixteen other supports of 10-in. diameter, and then almost 300 for all the framework poles of 8 in. diameter,— what a task! Hands were blistered, one crowbar was broken, several pickaxes made useless before the job was completed.

Meanwhile others had cut poles to the right length, prepared the top end in a forked notch to carry the ridge-poles, cleaned and prepared ridge-poles for the five main support-lines.

The first week in April was a school holiday for Easter, and so, early on Tuesday morning at 6.30 a.m., Jill and I joined the work force and watched as the wall-frames suddenly went up. Then the sixteen subsidiary supports; then the four main central supports — eucalyptus trees, straight and strong, almost 24 ft high — hoisting them slowly upwards, slipping their bases into the prepared pits, fixing them upright with forest-twine pulleys on all four sides. Quickly the workmen roped scaffolding branches 2 yds high to hold the whole framework in position: standing on these, another circle of scaffolding 3 1/2 yds high completed the preparation.

On Wednesday we hoisted the ridge-poles. The outside wall ridges first; then scaffolding across the house at ceiling level; then the formation of a 'human scaffold', five workmen to each side of each of the four main support-poles, each standing on another's shoulders. It was an amazing and somewhat frightening sight to watch as we hoisted the main central ridge, a 40-ft long eucalyptus trunk, up the human chain of scaffolding, from ground to outstretched hand, up to shoulder level, up again with outstretched arm to the down-reaching hand of the man above. Students stood around and a great silence fell as the huge pole slowly rose, and rose, and rose into the blue sky. All necks stretched back, eyes glued to the pole. The slightest slip by any man would have been disastrous. The final pushing upwards by the fifth team of eight men; the straining of every muscle . . . .

'It's up!' - a cheer went up, as bated breath was released.

The roofing timbers went up quickly in the following week. Then the whole roof was closely covered with line upon line of strong stalks of elephant-grass, bound on with forest vines.

Others were preparing grass. Twenty-four tons had been carried in. It all had to be cleaned from bracker and foliage: gathered in lengths, tied in 2-yd-long bundles 6 ins. thick, and then cut in half. Bundles were neatly stacked all round the house. Coiled lengths of split vines were soaking in waterbutts.

Amazingly, the dry season held. Rains were two weeks overdue. Each morning the sky was filled with dark, lowering clouds, but they blew away by midday and the building progressed.

The slope of the roof, at almost 45°, scared the local workmen. Basuana, from the northern forest region, was accustomed to it, but they were unwilling to believe him that it was really safe. So I took a day off school, and scrambled up and sat astride the top ridge to encourage them when they started the thatching! This seemed to go very slowly: methodically setting the first line along the lowest edge with the cut end towards the ground and the long, loose leaves up to heaven, and binding each bundle to the framework; then line after line, binding on to alternate rows of elephant-stalks, patiently, accurately, knotting the soaking vine; twisting and knotting, twisting and knotting, slowly moving around the house, line upon line. At last it was complete, except for the final ridge.

Then bundles of longer, uncut grass were thrown like javelins from ground to ridge, and bound on strongly astride the ridge. The next night it poured with rain for five long hours!

This firmly beat the thatch into place. After three such storms another row of grass bundles was attached astride the ridge. After yet further storms a final third row was fixed into position and the roof was secure. Probably 18 tons of grass were up there, held by a few forest trees, tied down with thin twists of split vines. It seemed incredible that this could hold up against the fantastic tropical storms, gale-force winds and thundering rains. The thatch was 15 ins. thick when completed, and planned to last a probable ten to twelve years, before needing replacement.

Sheltered from the rains now, as the seasons changed, and working under the roof, a framework of thin branches or bamboo stems was attached horizontally outside and inside the pole structure, to all the outside and inside walls. We were into May when 'mudding' started and the wall-framework was stuffed with mud, smeared with mud, plastered with mud. Then it was left for two weeks to dry out before a final plastering inside and out with mud mixed with cow-dung, which set hard like cement.

Window-frames and door-frames, prepared by a local carpenter, were set in. Water was brought to the home by pipes from the hospital water-supply system, and Richard Dix, a missionary construction engineer in charge of the over-all building programme at Nyankunde, gave us bathroom and kitchen taps and toilet. Cement floors were laid, doors were hung, walls were whitewashed, windows were put in. The outside was swept and cleared, and flowers planted — and by 30 June, Independence Day 1967, we moved in!

It really was exciting to be in our own little home. A local carpenter had made us some lovely bedroom, dining-room and office furniture, all in grained red-wood. Curtains had been measured, cushions prepared, rush mats for the sitting-room acquired — and we were in, five months from starting to clear the ground. True, another month was needed to complete the small garage and cookhouse behind the bungalow, levelling the drive, clearing up the garden, but the job was completed in and around all the regular duties of lecturing and administration and hospital practice.

As our first school year drew to a close and Jill and I had a moment to assess the situation, various pointers prompted us to make a trip to East Africa. First, we urgently needed equipment for the new College laboratory, both for the first-year orientation classes in elementary physics and chemistry, and also for the third- and fourth-year students in medical procedures, requiring microscopes and chemicals. Secondly, my father was planning to visit us for a week and hoped we could meet him in Kampala and drive him back to Nyankunde. Thirdly, there was growing unrest amongst the troops in the National Army, with disturbing rumours of the possibility of an attempted coup to restore Moise Tshombe to power.

We packed up a minimum of supplies for the journey and set off early one morning, at the start of the long summer holidays. We travelled in the Land Rover with trailer, and took with us two Africans who had not previously travelled outside their own province, Basuana Bernard and Gandisi Benjamin. As we crossed over the great central mountain range at 8,000 ft, from Zaire to Uganda, and dropped down the escarpment to the east to the source of the Nile, our two African colleagues were tremendously thrilled. The motor-driven ferry across

241

the Nile; the hundreds of enormous elephants calmly munching at the water's edge, eyeing us disinterestedly like ruminating cows at home; the thundering water at the Karima bridge near the Murchison Falls, with spray thrown up to form a fantastic rainbow arched across the valley; these impressive sights drew exclamations of wonder.

Walking up the streets of Kampala, a pleasant tropical town to us Europeans but an overwhelming city to our African colleagues, completed their amazement. The shops, the traffic, houses of several storeys, Indian temples, the lights at night, the airport and the arrival and departure of great planes with over a hundred passengers each . . . the days were not long enough to satiate their curiosity.

We acquired the laboratory and other school and household equipment we had come for, and packed the van and trailer to capacity. We met my father and started the long journey back to Nyankunde, going through the National Park to see the Murchison Falls in all their glory.

Then followed a lovely week, in our new home which had been finished only two weeks before, but all the time we were nervously listening to radio broadcasts indicating the worsening situation and danger in our area. I must confess that I was glad when the week was up, and we set off for the border again before trouble broke. Once out of the country, into East Africa, I could relax and enjoy the long trip to Nairobi from where my father flew on to Malawi.

Jill and I spent a week camping near Nairobi before going to the Kenya Keswick Convention, where I had been invited to speak about our experiences in the Simba uprising.

Then the long trek back to Kampala, as the first lap of the journey back to Zaire, only to be checked by a request to visit the British High Commissioner. He asked us not to proceed to Zaire at that time, as the situation was so uncertain and they feared a fresh outbreak of hostilities.

Frankly, I was pleased to be stopped by Authority. I feared to go back in. I had had enough in 1964, but I didn't want the responsibility of making the decision. Jill was champing at the bit to get back to the job at Nyankunde, and must have found my easy acquiescence most irritating, especially as I was the driver and she was entirely dependent on me for transport.

We were not the only ones 'shut out' at that time, and we soon met other missionaries. Some had just got out with great difficulty from farther south, due to the mutiny of the mercenary troops serving under

General Mobutu. Others were on their way to Zaire for the first time and were understandably hesitant. We all waited for a green light from the British High Commissioner.

Meanwhile, to fill in time profitably and to try to prepare for the new school year ahead of us, we visited the University library for several days. We then travelled to the eastern border of Uganda to Mbali to visit the medical auxiliary training school there, to study their programme and course material. After a week there as welcome guests with the headmistress of the local girls' school, we journeyed back to Kenya and spent a wonderful month on a farm of friends of my father, whom we had visited a few weeks earlier. The holiday was a real refreshment, with plenty of time for reading, writing and preparation for the new school year.

At last, impatient of receiving no news, no letters, no word from the Embassy, we set out on the journey home and made an uneventful entry! There were no difficulties at the border, no customs duties to pay on our few purchases, no accident to the van, in fact nothing worthy of report at all. We drove into Nyankunde late on Saturday evening, hoping to start school on the Monday, and what a welcome awaited us! One would have thought we had been gone a year, instead of a month or so. Apparently that Sunday had been pin-pointed as D-day. If we were not back, all senior students were to be sent home, as the remaining staff felt they simply could not cope with all three classes, as well as all their own hospital and dispensary responsibilities.

Students poured out of the village and we were mobbed. Laughter and singing, crying and clapping. Missionaries seemed to arrive from every direction, and our hands felt limp from shaking, before we eventually reached home and settled back into routine for a new school year.

8
Seeking Recognition

After my visit to Kinshasa in May 1966, it was obvious that one of the very basic requirements, if we were to gain Government recognition for our college, was that we should have permanent buildings to 'specified standards'. It was almost impossible to discover what these standards were: some said one thing, some another. I gathered that a certain cubic metrage of air per student per class-room was demanded, which was an interesting requirement in the wide-open spaces of our mountain site! Internal flush-toilets had to be included, even though the students would have to be trained in their use, never having met such things in their village life. Obviously the building would have to be constructed in permanent materials, and this posed plenty of problems, compared to the simplicity of putting up our own small home.

We decided to tackle first a class-room block with auditorium, laboratory, library and administrative offices; and later, to construct a separate dining-hall with kitchens and foodstores. Many and varied plans were prepared and studied and turned down for one reason or another. Eventually a very simple plan of a130-ft-long building, 40 ft wide, with a long central corridor and rooms along both sides, was found to be the most economical as well as the most useful plan. The completed building would be four times as large as our home and would probably cost eight times as much. Richard Dix, the builder attached to the hospital, was basically in charge, but he had an enormous building programme in hand for the hospital and staff homes. So he agreed to allow Basuana and myself to tackle the job of school construction under his supervision. Eventually the necessary permission was granted by the local building committee and we started to prepare the site in June 1968.

Fifty thousand bricks were available, from a newly-built kiln that Richard had completed. Six tons of cement and 500 sheets of corrugated asbestos roofing were purchased. Louvre window-frames and glass were ordered.

Twenty-four workmen were employed in four groups of six, each group with a semi-qualified mason in charge, assisted by a villager who showed enough intelligence and initiative to be trained as a mason, and four locals for digging trenches, carrying bricks, making mud, and generally helping to complete each team. Basuana had the immediate oversight and direction.

The land was cleared and levelled; then Richard came, complete with instruments, to lay out the foundations. Basuana was fascinated! He and I had always squared our corners with the old three-four-five measurements and pegs, checking with equal diagonals, and making sure that all was level with a spirit level laid on our strings. *This* was quite different, efficient and accurate, and Basuana drank in every detail.

Then the digging of trenches, while others quarried huge stones from the mountainside near the local river. The trenches were filled with stones, carefully laid and levelled in concrete. Then the four groups separated to the four corners, and the walls started to creep up. Between classes I used to rush over the half mile from our temporary school quarters to the new building, to check on corners and levels, bonding and mudding. Students used to rush over in break, and stand around in the dinner-hour, to watch. Everyone became excited as the gaps for windows began to appear. Then window-frames and door frames were bolted in. Then reinforcing irons and concrete slabs were laid all round the structure, and a further five lines of bricks brought the huge building to ceiling height.

Students would wander round inside in the evenings, trying to decide which room would be what, and getting a real thrill as they were allowed to help on Saturdays to speed the work along.

The dry season came and we were ready to put the roof on. But here we paused. Basuana and I had never tackled so large a building before, and we felt that we just could not manage a roof of such dimensions. Richard's workmen, under his supervision, had prepared the triangle trusses for us, and all was ready; but Richard had several other urgent tasks on hand and simply could not spare the time to put the roof on yet. So we started praying that the Lord would send us a 'roofer'.

Meanwhile we did every conceivable other job that we could find. Richard sent a plumber over to help us prepare for putting in the water-system. The masons got ahead with pointing the whole building. The carpenter hung doors and fixed window-frames. The workmen carried gravel for preparing the floors for cement. Still no 'roofer'.

We squared the corners of the roofing; we stacked the triangle trusses in place around the building; we carried sand for plastering the inside walls; we prepared timbers for surrounds under the eaves. We even cleared away all debris, smoothed the paths, planted grass and flowers, and cut a giant eucalyptus for flag pole. Still no 'roofer'.

One Thursday evening in January 1969 Basuana came to me.

'Shall I dismiss the workmen and tell them not to come tomorrow? There just isn't another job to be done, and there's no point paying them for doing nothing.'

We eyed each other. We had worked together for fifteen years and just about knew the thoughts going through each other's mind.

'No,' I said, grinning suddenly. 'No. Let's trust for the roof tomorrow.'

'O.K. by me,' and we let the matter rest.

That night I was woken by a car coming up the hill, and peeped through the curtains to see if I was needed. No; the car drew up next door, at Dr Ruth Dix's house. Lights went on and I could hear voices. Shortly I saw Ruth leave and drive down the hill to the hospital. I prayed for her that all would be well, rolled over and went back to sleep.

Next morning, going down the hill at 6.20 a.m. to prayers with our workmen, before starting school, I passed a young American going up the hill. I greeted him and he nodded, but looked too weary to bother to speak. Suddenly Basuana came running up towards me.

'Do you know who that is, that you passed on the hill?' he panted excitedly. I didn't.

'He's a roofer!' — and as I realized the import of these words, the two of us turned and hurried back up the hill.

'Sir,' I called out breathlessly.

He turned politely, if with a puzzled look.

'Please do excuse me, I don't even know your name, but is it true that you're a roofer?'

'I beg your pardon?' he said in a confused way. 'I'm Ruscoe Lee, but I don't quite understand what you asked me.'

Hardly surprising! We explained our situation, and he explained his. He had driven in during the night to be with his wife Rachel, who had been flown to Nyankunde the previous day for urgent hospital care under Dr Ruth Dix's supervision. And he was a roofer! During Rachel's two weeks of care and convalescence, Ruscoe worked hard with the African team and achieved our goal — the roof on!

There still seemed so much to do, though. Ceilings, electrical wiring, plumbing, flooring, plastering, painting — the jobs seemed endless. Then furniture began to arrive: forty desks and forms, fifteen tables, 180 chairs, cupboards and shelves. All had to be sandpapered and varnished. Blackboards had to be plugged to the walls. Laboratory equipment, pharmaceutical scales and drugs, nursing arts' teaching models, charts and library books: all had to be listed and put in place.

Then in May 1969, at the annual meeting of the Board of Directors, we had the college officially opened, singing the National Anthem, raising the flag, cutting the red tape, and we were truly launched. The service, the speeches, the choir, the thanksgiving feast all soon became items of college history, but the sheer joy of teaching in good and adequate premises is a permanent present-tense reality.

Before the college building was finished, the Inspectors had arrived! Since classes had started in 1966 we had kept Kinshasa in touch with us. We regularly sent them progress reports of every part of the Nyankunde programme. We continually put together what we considered necessary for a 'dossier', despite great ignorance as to what was really needed. Local educational authorities were loath to help us, as we were under the direction of the Ministry of Health rather than of Education. Now and again I'd catch a hint of a better way of presenting our material and at once we would re-compile the whole dossier, typing out several copies and sending them off to all the authorities which we felt might be even remotely interested in us.

For over a year we heard nothing from Kinshasa. Then someone passed us a verbal message that applications for recognition must go first through regional channels, then provincial, before approaching central. With unflagging willingness we started all over again, and actually achieved regional 'consent', for what it was worth. I rushed off to Kisangani, the provincial centre, clutching the regional letter of recommendation and all the carefully-prepared copies of our dossier.

A week of dogged perseverance followed. I went back to the same office twice a day, till eventually the provincial medical director was persuaded to give me an audience. Most graciously he added his signature to that of the regional authorities, and suggested that I go next to the Governor of the Province (as he was then styled).

Another week of equally dogged perseverance, only at the last to be told that I had broken etiquette by going to the medical director before the Governor.

'The Governor will not look at a document already signed by a subordinate. His signature authorizes medical and educational authorities to continue with their investigations into the suitability of the application.'

Back to square one. Another set of documents was rapidly prepared and taken to the Governor, who graciously signed them. Back to the medical director, only to find that he had just left on a six-weeks' tour of the interior. Over to the director of education, and roughly the same procedure through another week till I found him in, and willing to listen; but it took several more visits to persuade him to take action. Even then, he would not sign our documents till he had had time to send an inspector up to see our standards.

I flew back east to Nyankunde and got back into school routine, teaching some twenty-four periods a week with all the preparations involved, as well as office administrative procedures. Everything was made ready for the promised inspector; no-one came.

At the start of a new school year, in September 1967, we actually received a specimen document from Kinshasa as to how to apply for recognition. We speedily re-prepared our ever-fattening dossier according to this newest formula, and sent off three copies to the address specified.

We waited in vain for an acknowledgment from Kinshasa.

We waited in vain for an inspector from Kisangani.

We sent letters of request to both. Eventually Kinshasa replied that they had never received our dossier. We did it again and sent it off by registered mail. Two months later, it was returned to us with a cryptic message that we deciphered to mean that we must submit our papers through the right channel.

What was the right channel? We sent to the local regional authority, to be told that their jurisdiction did not extend to para-medical schools. We went to provincial authority, to be told that they could do nothing till our previous papers of application were duly completed and signed. We reminded them that we were waiting for an inspector, only to be sharply told that this was now quite unnecessary. I promptly produced my earlier forms, carrying the Governor's signature, photostat copies of the medical director's signature, and the space waiting for the educational authority's signature.

He actually signed — and I sent them all off the same day by registered mail to Kinshasa, accompanied by our precious dossier.

Three months passed by.

In May 1968 the papers all came back, without the dossier, saying these forms were now obsolete, and would I please procure and fill in the new forms for requesting school recognition?

Where did one procure such forms?

Teaching and preparation continued.

In September, we received a new application form. Somewhat automatically we filled it all in, re-did the dossier, affixed all the end-of-the-last-year reports, and all the beginning-of-the-new-year reports, and sent everything off.

Teaching and preparation continued, in our cramped temporary buildings, while every effort was being made to speed the construction of the new permanent building.

Rumour reached us that inspectors were on their way. We tried to school ourselves to ignore such rumours: they only built up to frustration and disappointment. Yet one day they would prove true, so we did all we could to prepare. All student dossiers were checked and brought up-to-date. All didactic material was listed and catalogued. Our Swiss staff put in overtime to check and correct the French of our course material.

The inspectors arrived! In November 1968, one Tuesday afternoon, the Government doctor from our neighbouring town of Bunia drove out to us, with two European ladies (a Yugoslav and a Britisher) accompanying a Zairian from the Ministry of Health at Kisangani. This was it!

That first afternoon, in a continual drizzle, pushing our way through mud and rubble, we set off to inspect the new school building, then up to ceiling height (and awaiting its roof!). It was the biggest building I had ever been involved in and I sometimes felt guilty at its size, in those days of economic uncertainty. Would we be able to complete it, and would we really have enough students to fill it?

The national inspector asked endless questions about the size of each room, the lighting, ventilation, electricity and water supplies and sanitation arrangements.

'My one criticism is that it is all too small. The minimum size of a class-room of a secondary school has been set up by my Government as 48 square yards, or at least 5 cubic yards per student.'

I did some rapid calculations, quickly making a mental note of each room and its proposed usage. I then led him down the central corridor to the first- and second-year class-rooms, where only the foundation was in for the dividing-wall.

'Will not this satisfy the requirements?' I queried, motioning to the one large, undivided room, 11 yards long by 5 yards wide. He paced it out, and no more was said. We never built the dividing-wall. Honour was satisfied on both sides, with no loss of face.

Up to our temporary mud-and-thatch village, through the two dormitories, the dining-room and cookhouse, the home of a married student with his cookhouse and toilet facilities. The students hadn't been warned: would they rise to the occasion? And anyway, could anyone really think our village satisfactory? Even in my own heart, proud though I was of the students for having achieved this village and being willing to wait for better accommodation, I knew that this was little better than the proverbial 'shanty town'.

'I think this is wonderful,' one inspector commented. 'All local materials to meet local needs, within the local economy. Very commendable!'

Was I really hearing aright?

'And the rooms are so clean and tidy: a real credit to the college.'

Boys, thank you!

We moved away, through the hospital compound towards our temporary school buildings. By now darkness had descended, and the students were in the class-rooms studying. We went first to our tiny office, where I tried to interest the inspectors in the filing system and the students' private dossiers, but they were obviously tired and not interested.

Next door, the five senior students were studying. All of these had been in our Nebobongo school before the Rebellion. They were older men, most of them married, and some with very rudimentary French. Before the Rebellion much of their teaching had been in Swahili, and I had not worried over much about this aspect when they came to complete their schooling at Nyankunde. The two ladies were watching them and making towards them. I tried to edge them away and into the large first-year class-room, where we had a crowd of keen teenagers with good French and an ability to express themselves. Unsuccessfully!

Moving into the fourth-year class-room, the inspectors started to ask the students questions about public health, the care of the tuberculosis patient according to the latest proposals of the World Health Organization, and I licked my lips in apprehension. Joel looked across at me, in hopeless bewilderment; Lawi was turning the pages of a book, at least knowing where to find the answers; when suddenly Gaston saved the situation, sailing into an excellent extempore dissertation on the care of the tuberculosis patient. There may have been some wild guesses; there was certainly some very original thinking; grammatical howlers filled every phrase; but sheer enthusiasm for the subject of preventive medicine could not have been more abundantly portrayed if they had been schooled to it.

We did eventually enter the first-year class-room, where students were painstakingly copying down a very elaborate diagram of the interaction of hormones in the control of the health of the body. Their notebooks were beautiful. The blackboard diagram was the pride of my heart.

'This is absurd — quite outside the scope of the curriculum and of no possible real value to the work they are going to do.'

I felt like a deflated balloon. The national inspector had to leave us to return to Kisangani, and I was left to the mercy of those two highly-qualified, high-powered, W.H.O. lady inspectors.

The next two days were agony. They grilled me. Nothing seemed to please them. Mostly we sat in our sitting-room going through course materials and programmes, while other staff kept the school time-table going as best they could. The subjects that the inspectors were keen on were those that I knew practically nothing about, such as the growing importance attached to the teaching of preventive medicine and public health. The subjects I knew best, and loved teaching, and had spent patient years developing, were to them of minimal importance, such as basic anatomy and physiology, the science of diagnostic medicine, the principles behind the surgical procedures we employed. We just didn't seem to have any common ground. The more they talked and reasoned and explained and instructed, the more I felt that I was on a different wave length, and had been altogether wrong in my whole approach to the establishment of the college and its standards.

Was the whole college, as I had envisaged it, only an outworking of my vision and individuality? Had I really felt I knew just how it should be done and, if they would let me, I'd prove to the Government that I was right, until they would actually turn and thank me, even would eventually adopt my plan and method? Had I allowed some basic in-born feeling of white superiority to drive me along, irrespective of what the local Government was demanding? Was I really training a new generation to be discontented and maladjusted, because their courses would not fit them to take their place in their developing country? Would they really feel underpaid according to Government salary structure, because I had taught them too much for a junior diploma?

Could I really be all that these inspectors implied?

It certainly was a terrible blow to my pride. I simply couldn't face the enormity of the consequence of these allegations: all I could do was to pack and go home. What a fool I'd been, what a proud, stubborn fool — and I really had dreamt I'd be thanked for all my effort or, at least, I'd be satisfied by the worthwhileness of all that was to have been achieved.

By Friday midday I could take no more. I broke down and cried, and asked them please to stop. 'Better you talk to the other staff. They'll be more able to adapt. I've just made a mess, a proud stupid mess. I'll leave. The others will know how to benefit from all you're saying.'

My house-help, Benjamin, unable to understand as we talked English, and hardly better able to understand when we used French, could easily understand atmosphere and now tears. He was furious that these two strangers had so upset 'his' doctor, and tore off down the hill to the school to collect Jill and Liliane.

Meanwhile the two inspectors were equally horrified. Whatever had they said to upset me? 'But of course, the college is wonderful. It is one of the very best that we have seen in the country so far.'

But why on earth hadn't they said so before?

'But our job is to show you the one or two areas where it could be improved.' Liliane and Jill arrived at this point, followed by an almost savage-looking Benjamin, who was quickly dispatched to prepare coffee and biscuits all round. And we started again.

By that evening, the two inspectors had had a meeting with the students to encourage them, and to promise them that everything possible was being done to acquire the coveted recognition, and that, meanwhile, they had a college to be proud of. They had also a meeting with all the staff together, to present their final findings and to promise us that they would recommend us for immediate recognition and, following that, for upgrading to the status of a senior technical college. Furthermore they had a meeting with all the missionary personnel of the Medical Centre, and explained again the great importance of close cooperation between hospital and college, the need to increase our bed capacity to 250 as soon as possible, and our qualified nursing personnel to a minimum of one to every fourteen beds, more than double what we had at that time.

On Saturday, Jill and I went out with the two ladies for a picnic, to the escarpment overlooking Lake Albert. It was a lovely, still, hazy day, and we enjoyed chatting about one thing and another, nothing to do with the college, until it was time to take them to catch their plane back to Kinshasa.

Arrived back at the college, we were immediately surrounded by students.

'Did it succeed?'

Did what succeed? We looked puzzled. Everyone talked at once. At last we made out that the student body presumed our 'outing' for the day was in order to bribe the ladies to give us what we so dearly longed for. We were tempted to roar with laughter — the whole concept was so completely foreign to our very English way of doing things — till we realized how utterly serious they were. This is what we should have done, as our students saw it; and if we failed to become recognized now, it was indeed our own direct wilful fault.

And it was to be two and half years before we heard any more. That 'fault' was going to cost us dearly.

The first real indication of growing irritation among the students came during the final week of the 1969-70 school year, eighteen months after that inspection. Nothing had apparently come of it, and so, in frustration, the students staged a revolt against the staff: minor, perhaps, but no less traumatic.

They were impatient with their Government for not providing legal diplomas. These had been virtually promised for June 1970 or so I had said. They hadn't materialized. Had their Government failed them, or was it possible that I, school director but foreigner, had lied? Had there perhaps never been an agreement, and was it all my bluff, to — to what? To satisfy my 'neo-colonialist' instincts to make them do what I wanted? Or to satisfy my 'imperialist west' plan to achieve cheap labour for the hospital that we foreigners were running? Such were the thoughts fed to the students daily over eastern radio broadcasts. Perhaps they were true after all?

Anyway, it was easier to strike out against local known leadership than the far-distant unknown Government, so we had to take the brunt of their frustrated dissatisfaction.

We were within a week of the final oral examinations. Petty irritations began to occur in all classes. Students came in late with no apology; others deliberately sat when answering questions, where the custom was to stand. Some refused to make any attempt to take part in discussion groups; all of them seemed suspicious and sullen. We had a meeting in the assembly-hall to try to heal the breach before the fuse blew, but we got no co-operation. Eventually one asked to see the diplomas that they were going to receive at the end of term, and with an almost audible sigh of relief we felt that we had discovered the root of the trouble.

Knowing that they would be disappointed that the official documents still had not come (weren't we all?), we had had new diplomas printed locally. They were as near to the coveted Government ones as we dared to approach, using the same format, but keeping our college name and crest in evidence, and our motto clearly printed at the base: 'The Son of man came not to be served but to serve, and to give his life a ransom for many.'

I went along to the office and collected one of each of our college documents — diploma, certificate, report card, annual bulletin, as well as road-passes and student passes for reduced rates on public transport. Back in the hall, staff and students awaited my return in strained silence. I showed each document in turn, beginning from the last, and briefly explained both its value and also its format. When I held up the diploma I was booed. Everyone started talking at once, and in the general hubbub I caught phrases:

'Why on earth is there a Scripture verse on a diploma?'

'What value has that piece of paper, with no Government signature?'

'Who's going to sign it, anyway?'

'How dare you imitate a Government document?'

'Who do you think you are, anyway?'

At last the noise exhausted itself, and I briefly answered some of the criticisms I had managed to distinguish from the torrent of angry comment.

'We have written permission from the Government to produce our own diplomas again this year . . .' angry booing interrupting me as I spoke; '. . . so long as we show clearly that it is not in fact legal,' and the angry shouts drowned anything else I could say.

'Listen, fellows, give it a chance. The exams are on Tuesday. If the examiner comes as promised, if the exams are fair and you pass, if he stamps these diplomas with a Government recognized seal and duly signs them as the Government appointed official, won't that content you?'

Obviously not, as the torrent of noise increased again and ugly looks were being exchanged.

'I promise you that I have done all that I can to get the official documents here, and I won't cease to go on badgering the Government till they come' — but my words were silenced in mocking jeers of 'wretched impostor', 'imperialist white', and 'it's all been a hoax'.

On Saturday morning I received an anonymous, badly written, poorly-worded, scruffy letter on a sheet torn from an exercise book. We called their bluff and sent it back for signature. Triumphantly they returned it with all but four of the senior students' signatures.

On Sunday I carefully answered the letter, point by point, in polite, accurate French on college notepaper, explaining again all they already knew.

On Monday both sides watched each other warily, and no one moved.

Tuesday was our big day. Staff had worked hard all Monday to prepare the library for the visiting examiner, to prepare the questions for the oral examinations, to prepare diplomas and certificates to be duly filled in as each student completed his quarter-of-an-hour oral, so that all would be ready for signature and stamping at the end of the four-hour session. On Tuesday morning fresh flowers were placed on the table, trays for mid-morning coffee prepared, students alerted as to their order and practical details for the smooth running of the day: and we waited.

Promptly at 8.00 a.m. the Belgian doctor from Bunia drove in, alone. We had expected a Zairian doctor too, but we accepted the change philosophically. He worked hard and efficiently. The exams were quick and fair. Every student of second- and third-year classes successfully passed the required 60% mark. Diplomas and certificates were filled in, checked, signed and stamped according to recognized international custom. And the doctor left us shortly after midday.

Normally all the students would have been in the assembly hall to greet the examining doctor and hear the results. Then speeches would be made by both sides, and considerable freedom of expression allowed to let off steam. That day the hall was empty, no-one came to hear the results, no-one thanked anyone. With some embarrassment the staff saw Dr Marchland off and sincerely thanked him for his services and time.

Turning back into the school, we sensed the gathering storm but met no-one. We cleared up and went home for lunch.

Then they came, a fairly small group at first, climbing the hill in silence. A last, fleeting hope that they might be coming to thank us for their schooling was quickly squashed as they lined up outside our small verandah and angrily shouted abuse at me. Two held batons menacingly. All looked hard and disagreeable. It was inconceivable that these were our own students, our friends, for whom we had cared, whom we had clothed and taught for the past four years. Their threats were sinister, using gestures and vocabulary learnt from the Simba rebels, and therefore even more frightening to my ears.

Through various stages, up and down the hill, they besieged our little home for the next twelve hours, and we were, quite honestly, scared. They sang lewd songs, they threatened us and shouted abuse at us, they threw stones at the doors and windows . . . but that was all.

Next morning, no students reported to the hospital for work. There should have been twenty-six of them, in the six wards, outpatients' department, laboratory and operating theatre. There were none. Graduate staff, foreign and national, worked round the clock and saw that the patients did not suffer. Letters went to and fro; conciliatory offers were made; veiled threats were returned. Eventually at 4.00 p.m. they agreed to meet with Dr Becker as arbitrator, on condition that he went alone. Normally one would never question 'going alone', but even the tone of voice in which they demanded this was calculated to strike fear in my heart.

Then it all fizzled out. By the end of the week all the ringleaders of each class had left for summer vacations. Those who were prepared to sign a statement of compromise stayed on to work in the hospital. Diploma day and festivities were all cancelled, but not before the staff and the four senior students who had refused to sign the original protest had all had their fill of insults and threats. The students suffered worst: their property was seized and fouled, buckets of water poured over their beds, everything they owned rendered useless.

It was perhaps only a petty show of frustration, as some tried to persuade me, but it left a dark stain in my heart. When I drove the first group to Bunia to put them on public transport for their various destinations, all at our expense, they had spat at me — and that burnt deep. Oh, granted that they were only students, and did not really represent the general feelings of the population; nevertheless they were our students and it mattered to me tremendously what our relationship was going to be in the future.

The very next week, at the end of the first half of our projected eight-year programme, I left for England for a quick three-month holiday. I needed a breathing-space to look at things from a distance so as to assess the real situation. Also I wanted a short time with my mother, who had been ill during the previous two years. She had spent many months in hospital, having operations on both her knees, and was then limited to two crutches and a wheelchair. While on holiday with her in Cornwall I weighed up carefully whether I honestly wanted to face the students again.

What was being achieved? Were our results worth the price that was being paid? As I looked back over the twelve years of my medical career at Nebobongo, where I had been a fulltime doctor — surgeon, physician, obstetrician and pediatrician all rolled into one — I asked myself again: 'Is it worth giving up all *that* for *this?*' That is: giving up being in charge of a medical service for the problems of running a training college to staff such a service.

Many of my close friends were quite sure it was not worth such a price. Yet I remembered times at Nebobongo, too, when I had seriously questioned if being in charge of a medical service was worth while. At first, when I found myself so involved in building, and buying food stores in the market, and caring for orphan children, and developing the student nurses' school, that there was no time for being a doctor, I had grumbled.

Eventually I had been persuaded to see that all these activities had brought me nearer the people. When my hands were raw with throwing newly-burnt bricks down from a kiln, the workmen understood and accepted me as one of themselves; whereas when I was drawing on sterile surgical gloves to operate on a seriously ill child, I was a thousand miles away from them, on a pedestal of respect and awe. When I fumbled around in the Kibudu language down at the markets, the village-folk roared with laughter and loved me; whereas when I was teaching in school in French, even the students held me apart as an object of discipline.

Later on, when I found myself so overwhelmed with medical responsibilities, endless surgical emergencies day and night, hours needed in the pharmacy for making up accurate solutions of drugs, time spent in the laboratory coping with tests and analyses beyond the ability of our students, so that there was no time for being a missionary, I had grumbled. Eventually our evangelist Agoya had persuaded me to look at things differently.

'Listen, there are 300 people coming to our hospital daily. Why are they there?'

I wasn't going to be drawn.

'Because you are here! If you, the doctor, weren't here, they wouldn't come. And what do you think *we* are doing?' Agoya and his wife Taadi were both Bible School trained evangelists, and Basuana and his wife Andugui were catechists, appointed by the church to full-time ministry in the hospital.

'All day and every day the four of us are fully occupied talking to patients in the clinics, the wards, the health centres. Do you realize that five, ten, sometimes twenty people are finding Christ as their Saviour every week through this ministry?' He paused, and then added quietly: 'You know, Doctor, we can't all be the last link in the chain!'

My thoughts moved on to the recent four years at Nyankunde. I never did surgery now; I hardly ever entered the wards and only rarely helped in outpatients. The students did not respect me as a doctor, but merely tolerated me as a teacher. Even my teaching ability was now in question and was to become more and more so in the three years ahead. I was becoming an office-boy rather than a teacher, let alone a doctor. Was this reasonable or worth while? Did this really make sense under the title of a 'medical missionary'?

Someone else was to take over first-year teaching, including anatomy and physiology; another the youth club and sports activities; another had been nominated to represent the school on the executive medical committee of the Centre which handled school disciplinary problems. More and more, I was to sit and type out seemingly hundreds of Government forms, adding up seemingly endless columns of figures and statistics, filling in seemingly useless reports and documents.

Why? Was something really wrong? Had I made a mistake, and somewhere got out of the line of the Lord's will? Basuana, on our school committee, had tried to talk sense back into me during the previous year.

'Listen, Doctor; think for a moment of Cornelius, and Isaac, and Bernard, and Mordecai; cast your mind to Poko, Aba, Nala, Oicha, . . .' and he named a whole list of college graduates, and the places where they were then working.

'How many graduates from our college are now in full-time church employment, do you think? And how many patients are they reaching daily, not only with medicines but also with the gospel?'

I knew what he was heading towards without doing the calculation; however, he wanted an answer.

'Well, I suppose some forty graduates so far, and they're working in twenty-two of our hospitals and dispensaries, and so I suppose they are seeing at least 3,000 patients daily, and might be even more — and that is not counting the thousand patients daily here at Nyankunde.'

'O.K., and how do we come to have these graduates?'

I thought back quickly over all the trials and tribulations of those first four years at Nyankunde, all the staff and workers involved, all the preparations, teaching, demonstrations, as well as office work that had achieved even our present position.

'You know, Doctor, the Government demands a doctor's signature on all the forms and letters to authorize the very existence of this college. And really . . .' and he used the same Swahili idiom as I had heard years before at Nebobongo from Agoya: 'we can't all be the last link in the chain.'

As I remembered all this and reviewed things from the perspective of the cliffs of Cornwall, in the quiet peace of a summer day, I let the impatience in my heart simmer down, and I made arrangements to go back to Zaire at the end of the month and to carry on.

9
Recognition At Last!

Without doubt, the Government was grateful for all the funds chan-
nelled into its medical services from overseas by private agencies,
including the enormous contribution made by the missionary societies,
but they could hardly be expected to take this into account when planning a new national health service. We also had to realize that a country's self-respect cannot accept endless voluntary contributions, especially if these are in danger of dictating policy by their very largeness in
comparison to the national effort.

So we were not altogether surprised when a move was made to
change the pattern. Almost out of the blue we heard that our application
for Government recognition of our college had apparently been (or was
about to be) granted, and so the country's treasury had been authorized
to pay a subsidy towards the salaries of the four registered, qualified
teaching staff. With this short notification came four pay-sheets, and the
assurance that the money mentioned could be withdrawn immediately
from the local bank.

Rather exciting, even if the cheques were small compared to home-
land equivalents: about £60 a month for our nurses, £80 for the sister-
tutor, and just over £100 for myself as medical director. I wrote at once
to all those who by their sacrificial giving had kept our college going
during the five years since the Rebellion, to let them know that the
Government intended to carry one-third of the responsibility in future.
This would be increased by increments until they could economically
afford to accept the whole budget on the national grid.

Accordingly a certain degree of overseas support ceased. Simulta-
neously the Government-promised aid failed to materialize. Hadn't God
known the latter when He agreed to the former? There were a few
'light' months with hardly enough to pay the workmen. Then came the
long summer vacation, when college feeding-bills and running costs
reached their annual minimum and we maintained par. However, these
same months usually included stocking for the coming school year.

Tons of rice, beans, groundnuts, dried fish, flour, sugar and palm oil: thirty local-made beds with mattress covers and blankets for the new first-year students: uniforms, stationery and class-room supplies all needed replenishing.

I had been ill in February of that year with a mild attack of tick-borne typhus fever, and the rather severe depression that followed this made it advisable that I should go home to England for two months to regain strength. At home, on holiday, I made out lists of all our college needs; I prepared lectures and time-tables; and I tried to rest and relax, rather than chewing my nails over the enormous, unresolved problem of turning my paperwork into practical realities.

I arrived back at Nyankunde on the first day of September with four days before the college was due to re-open. On my desk, amid a mountain of mail, was a statement from our regional educational authorities of a gift of almost £1,500!— unsolicited, entirely unexpected, and probably unprecedented. Doubtless God had already arranged this provision when He allowed other sources to dry up temporarily. Even after twenty years of experiencing His unfailing faithfulness in such matters, and His amazing accuracy in timing, I still had not managed to accept the period of uncertainty with equanimity.

Now, with this generous gift in hand, we went the next day to Bunia and turned all the prepared lists into acquired realities, and then found we still had sufficient funds in hand for the first quarter of the new year.

Despite repeated efforts to correct our Government paysheets, my own remained obstinately at just over £20 a month for several months, and then stopped altogether. The following April I, along with others, attended a teach-in at the regional educational offices in Kisangani, some 400 miles to the west. It proved to be an excellent and valuable, if intensive, three days, dealing mainly with various financial aspects of our service. This included how to fill in forms to apply for subsidies for salaries, equipment and didactic material, and then how to fill in more forms when the response to the first set was not satisfactory.

During one session, the national lecturer told us of the dubious excitement being enjoyed at that moment due to the installation of a vast new computer to handle all national grid salaries for the armed forces and police, the tele-communication service personnel, educational, medical and general transport personnel. He explained a little of the vast programming involved for each service, to include basics, educational bonuses, family allowances, transport and lodging expenses, all deductions for pensions, national tax, health services and others. He explained how the punch cards were prepared from statistics provided, and the checking system employed before the final feed-in ticker-tape was actually ready. With all this, he indicated some of the thousands of possible hold-ups or pitfalls. Finally, various listings would reach regional, and then sectional, sorting offices, post offices and banks, for distributing to groups of services, through to area representatives, and so ultimately to the individual.

Pinpointing some of the hazards of the system, and how easily mistakes could get in but how hardly they could then be got out, he told us a story.

'We have a medical doctor as a director of one of our secondary school extension programmes, training medical auxiliaries. The punch-card code is DD, but when the computer met this for the first time, it queried it as a mistake, and so substituted D6. When this came through, the computer realized the error, as D6 would mean a secondary school director with only six years of secondary school education, an impossibility in our revised educational system. So the code was duly changed to d6, temporary director with six years of post-primary education: and the salary came through at about £20 a month. After a few months the computer caught up with its error, that a qualified medical doctor was earning only £20 a month, so it cancelled the pay-sheet and fed it back into the machine for correction, including back-pay. By now this totalled over £600. The computer had been taught that any monthly pay sheet over £500 must be an error, so again the result was cancelled and fed back in.'

Amid growing amusement as the story unfolded, the lecturer further explained that this school director had thus received nothing at all for several months. He looked across at me then and grinned, concluding: 'I confess I'm glad she's white, or she would doubtless have been on strike these months, living on my office doorstep, till we could sort out the computer!'

The school year 1971-72 went remarkably smoothly until the last month. As usual, an application had been made to the central Government in February for a Jury to be formed in June for our finalist students. Hearing nothing, we wrote again in April. As there was still no acknowledgment or response, we telegraphed Kinshasa in May. In the first week of June we received a telegram asking if we wanted a Jury that year or no, and if so, when. Frantically we sent an answering telegram, and also an unofficial verbal message by radio. The examinations were due Tuesday, 12 June. We had one week left for arrangements.

We had a radio message on Thursday, 7 June that the central Government had authorized the regional authorities to make all necessary arrangements, and they were glad to delegate their authority to sectional level. Would I therefore contact Dr Biki, the national Government doctor at our local hospital in Bunia, and also the inspector of secondary schools at the local offices of the Ministry of Education, to arrange details?

We set off, on what proved to be a long trail. Dr Biki was not in. The Educational Office said that it would agree to whatever Dr Biki suggested for Tuesday the 12th. Dr Biki was not found in at all on Thursday the 7th nor on Friday the 8th. On Saturday, I managed to waylay him as he left his home in the early morning.

'No,' he said emphatically. 'I certainly cannot accept delegated authority by word of mouth. There must be written confirmation.'

Back to the post office to send a telegram to Kisangani, and to sit there four hours waiting for a reply. They were about to close at midday and I was growing frantic. Eventually our local post office relented and allowed me to use their radio telegram line myself, and I contacted the head postmaster at Kisangani. Understanding the urgency of the situation, he agreed to send a runner round to the Ministry of Education and to radio me back in half an hour.

I sat on by myself in a now-closed post office, not even sure if I knew how to let myself out, let alone how to handle the radio, telegram and telex machinery.

Two hours ticked relentlessly by, and I felt it was a wasted job. I might as well give in, and return on Monday morning. I put my things together, turned off the machines, went to turn off the lights — when a sudden hunch made me try once again. Switching on the machine, I called in Kisangani post office, and they replied!

'We're doing all we can for you. A telex has been sent to Kinshasa, as the Provincial Medical Director who nominated Dr Biki as his delegate is away, giving examinations at Isiro, and we cannot contact him. We may hear by 5.00 p.m. and we'll radio you.'

I had to be content. I went back to tell Dr Biki this news, and he nonchalantly started talking about the examinations. Had we set the questions yet? Yes? Good, he'd like to see a set. Oh, you've got them with you? Excellent. Thank you very much.

He started flicking through the patiently prepared lists of thirty questions in each of twelve subjects.

'Have the students seen these?'

'Of course not,' I exclaimed.

'Why not? You must show them to the students at once. That is only fair.' You couldn't win with this man.

I went back to the post office and waited till six o'clock and tried unsuccessfully to call Kisangani several times. At last I gave up and went home. Monday found me back at the post office as soon as it opened. There was no telex, nor telegram, nor letter. Nothing. Eventually we established radio contact with Kisangani.

We're doing all we can. We have no contact today with Kinshasa. We have sent copies of all telex of the weekend down on this morning's plane. We'll radio you as soon as we hear anything.'

Time was running out. The date set for the examinations was tomorrow. I managed to contact the missionaries in Kisangani by radio and asked them to get anyone possible from either the Ministry of Education or the Ministry of Health to their radio by 11.30 am. to rendezvous Dr Biki, and so give him the needed authority to act. I rushed off to persuade Dr Biki to come to the radio; but he refused. Back by myself, I spoke with the Kisangani authority and explained my difficulty to them.

'But we have sent Dr Biki a telegram nominating him for tomorrow's Jury.'

'Please, can you send another, now, and I'll stand by for its delivery and take it out to him.'

'Certainly.'

I stood by till the office closed at 4.30 p.m. No telegram. What could I do next? I went back to the Ministry of Education. The inspector was ready for the following morning and obviously irritated by the unnecessary fuss. I retired. Eventually I decided to spend the night in Bunia. Early Tuesday morning, I contacted Dr Biki at his home.

No, he had heard nothing.

No, he was not willing to act without proper authority.

I went back to the Ministry of Education, where the inspector shrugged his shoulders.

All day, I hovered from one to the other. Eventually at 4.30 p m. there was a telegram for Dr Biki. No, the post office would not give it to me to deliver. No, they had no runner available to take it: it must wait till tomorrow. No, it would be no use my going for Dr Biki, as they were closing.

I felt frantic, when suddenly Dr Biki himself appeared! He took the telegram, read it, and brusquely said: 'All right, we'll have the examinations on Thursday, 8.00 a.m. Be ready! 'and swinging round, he left. I rushed off to the Ministry of Education, but everywhere was closed: all the personnel had left for home. I'd no idea where they lived.

Once more I drove home and told everyone the news. On Wednesday I drove again to Bunia to be sure the Inspector of Education would be available for 8.00 a.m. Thursday, and to arrange for his transport.

'I'm sorry, Miss. The inspector leaves today on the plane. He has other examinations booked elsewhere tomorrow. No, he hasn't left any instructions. No, nor has he left his rubber stamp.'

How could this happen? I stopped short as I realized that I was running round in ever-narrowing circles. I took a grip on myself and had a short time of quiet prayer.

Then I set out again. By lunch-time I had persuaded the Ministry of Education to send a primary school inspector to us. They had discovered the needed rubber stamp, and contacted their senior authority for permission to use it. I had the address of the junior inspector and knew where to find his home.

After lunch I went back to Dr Biki to ask if his chauffeur could go to pick up the inspector at 7.00 a.m. and bring them both to Nyankunde by 8.00 a.m. for the Jury. I gave the address, and started on the explanation as to how to find the place.

'Over in the suburbs? Good gracious, no! My chauffeur is not going over there. Why hasn't he got a car of his own? If he must come with me, he can walk into the city.'

I was furious. The sheer snobbery, that 'we of the city' were a superior class to 'them of the suburbs', left me dazed. I knew this sort of thing back home among Europeans but I'd never met it among Africans.

'Please don't worry. I'll come in for him myself tomorrow morning.'

I turned to leave, when Dr Biki called me back. Picking up the copies of the examination questions lying beside him, he leisurely tore them across and delicately dropped them into his waste-paper-basket.

'Those are useless. No good at all. We need clear, simple questions on each subject, such as...' and for ten minutes he rattled off suggestions. I grabbed a pencil, dipped into the waste-paper-basket for a torn remnant, and scribbled as fast as I could.

'Oh, and my chauffeur will collect your inspector tomorrow,' he threw at me as he finished.

I left him, seething inwardly at my own impotence. I was sure this had just been an idle show of power to put me in my place, but it all seemed so unjust, so unnecessary. I raced the thirty miles home, tore round to collect all the staff up to my home and explained the situation to them. Then we all worked half the night preparing new questions, typing sheets and rearranging things to fit in with the last-minute suggestions that Dr Biki had given.

At 8.30 a.m. they arrived and a grim day started. Nothing pleased him, nothing was right. Why ever didn't I know how to organize things better? At Kimpese they had done it this way — or that way — but never my way! Contrary to custom, he asked questions in the main, instead of the staff, and many students could not even follow his rapid French. They were all so nervous. Many questions were far too hard and simply not geared to our syllabus. He argued with the staff over almost every answer even. We felt the day would never end; yet as each student stumbled out of the room in a daze, Dr Biki wrote down a mark on his report card, invariably higher than any member of staff would have given. No student failed.

At last it was over. All certificates and diplomas were filled in. Augusta Johannessen, an elderly Norwegian lady who had been living with me all the year and tirelessly serving the school as our secretary, had everything ready for Dr Biki to sign within a few minutes of the last student leaving the library. Then the next row started.

He certainly wasn't going to sign anything. He had only been asked to witness the examinations. If Education wanted to sign, that was fine by him. No, he was adamant: he would make his report to his superiors, as to just how unsuitable the examinations had been, how poorly organized, how 'altogether wrong'. He then strode into the hall to face the rows of dazed students, waiting in bewildered silence, to hear the end of

the strange day. He faced them all belligerently, and swung round to me.
'Where's the list?'

All was ready, Sir. Here at once, Sir.

And he read out, to the dumb-founded college, the amazing list of 100% unqualified success. After an unbelieving pause, the whole student body burst into cheers. The senior student made a good quick speech of thanks, to which Dr Biki replied with extraordinary graciousness.

The following school year, 1972-73, started off quite normally. The previous year had been a good one. Mordecai Kasereka had been an excellent head student and diploma day had been a happy occasion for us all.

There was a large new first-year intake, including six girls. We were under pressure on all sides to take girls, to give them two years' general nursing training, and then a third year concentrating on midwifery. The whole north-eastern region, with a population of some five million, was urgently needing qualified midwives, women who could not only undertake responsibility in rural maternities for the care of normal deliveries, but also the care of complicated cases. Since the Rebellion it had been hard to recruit girls: there were not many in our secondary schools, and all who reached a sufficient level in general education seemed to want to go on to university, to prove their equality with the boys.

For the first time we had four girls who had finished the two years' general nursing training and were admitted to the third year to train as midwives. The staff spent considerable time and care planning their course and time-table, to make it not only efficient and practical, but also attractive. There were not really enough of us on the teaching staff to carry a four-year programme, and so considerable doubling of classes had to be manoeuvred. Third-year women midwives and third-year male medical assistants could follow almost half their programmes together with very little difficulty, and each would benefit from the extra material given to the other.

We had four weeks' training school with the new first-year students, while second- and third-year students had their annual vacation, and during this period the main preparation was done for the school year for all four classes.

In October we started full classes, with all third-year students, men and women, in class, and second-year students working on the wards. We were excited and expected a good year, with enthusiasm for the new courses. Application had been duly made to the Government to recognize our midwifery section, as our nursing and medical auxiliary sections were already accredited.

From the start we found it heavy going, to say the least of it. By the end of four weeks, all the staff were tired of encouraging, persuading, cajoling the third year to work and study and co-operate. They simply wouldn't. A sort of don't-care attitude pervaded their class-room. Slowly it became clear that the girls were the ringleaders. We invited them home to coffee and cakes, to share with them more informally our hopes for the success of the year's programme, and their prospects as the first qualified midwives under the new Government plans. But no response. No enthasiasm.

Another staff member invited them out. Every effort was made to 'get through' to them, and eventually someone tipped me the clue we needed. I sent for them again.

'Someone tells me that there is an absurd rumour going round that you will not get diplomas of equivalent value to the men's.'

Silence.

'You know of course that this is rubbish. They are identical in value.'

Silence.

'Are you worried about the salary-scale at the end of your training?'

No answer.

I produced copies of both finalist diplomas for third-year studies. I produced the Government wage-scale for para-medical workers, male and female. I produced the law-book, controlling para-medical training colleges, course materials and programmes.

No response.

I nearly lost patience, and told them to stop wasting their time and mine, to start working and putting their backs into their studies, to pull with the rest of the class, and to help us all to make it a good year.

They left, unimpressed — and school continued under strain.

Another hint reached us, so we tried again. All the staff got together and invited Dr Ruth Dix, the obstetrician in charge of the maternity unit, to join us. We discussed together, prayed together, and then invited the four girls to join us for coffee and cakes, in a relaxed atmosphere.

'Have you any questions you'd like to ask me, about the syllabus this year, or the opportunities for service next year?' Ruth asked them.

Vague indifference; monosyllabic answers.

'You know how much we are looking forward to having qualified help in our maternity units. I'm prepared to do all I can to help you to get all the skill and knowledge possible, to rise to the top of your profession.'

Polite agreement; nothing more.

Studies dragged on interminably, with none of the usual joy and fun. Quite honestly, we all became a bit bored with the effort of winning their confidence or trying to help them. Petty disobediences, frequent late arrivals, unwillingness to do any public service such as cleaning the school and grounds on Saturday mornings, refusal to attend church or weekly fellowship meetings, uncooperativeness at choir practice: all this harassed and aggravated us.

Then, during the ten-day Christmas vacation, the storm began to burst. A letter was written to Dr Becker demanding student representation at executive level. A meeting was called, and the students produced a list of some twenty demands, mostly involving pay for practical service in hospital during their training, redistribution of hours of service giving more to theory and less to practical, the right to know what staff did with their Government salaries and a continuing angry demand to know why we were not yet a legally-recognized college with Government diplomas.

Each demand was answered as reasonably as possible. All the staff managed to remain calm and polite, even in the face of outrageous demands touching their own salaries. Students were allowed to examine the books, to see the Government pay-roll and the Government schedule of distribution of hours for theoretical and practical teaching — all of which they had seen before; but every effort was made to satisfy them.

They tried to threaten that they would not work in hospital unless they were paid. The whole executive committee balked at this. Every student was being heavily subsidized already for schooling, housing and clothing. Their practical work was part of their training. We all gave our hours voluntarily to teach and train them. Anyway, there simply was no money available to pay them.

'O.K. then, we won't work,' was the student ultimatum.

'O.K. then, we don't teach,' was the staff rejoinder.

Stalemate. I left the room. Why continue? We, the staff, did not need them, the students. We owed them nothing, but were willing to give them everything, as I saw it. Until qualified, they did need us, however unpalatable the truth might be. I was almost tired of serving them as a slave, with just no response at all on their side.

The students went back to work.

The staff returned to teach.

But the tensions in the class-room increased rather than eased.

Classes were to divide after Christmas, girls having their own programme, practical and theoretical, until Easter, and the men theirs. That was when we finally found the underlying cause of friction. No girls turned up to their practicals; they all came to the boys' instead, and they came in a militantly aggressive way as Mrs Pankhurst of the English suffragettes might have done!

'We will not be treated as inferior to the fellows. We are equal. Give us our rights. We intend taking the same courses, the same exams, the same diplomas. We are equal.'

To suggest that to attend their own courses showed their superiority, as the men were not invited to be midwives, was to court disaster. The four militant female students were in no mood for reasoning. They had made up their minds — or rather, their minds had been subtly made up for them — that the only way to show their equality with the male students was to force this particular issue. We soon discovered that they had been systematically brainwashed during the first three months of the school year, over the radio. Broadcasts in French from Kinshasa, broadcasts in Swahili from farther east, had been repeating day after day that the women of Zaire must insist on their rights, demand absolute equality, refuse to be made out less than their male counterparts.

At Christmas, the final thrust had been made over the Voice of Zaire radio network.

'Girls in Medical Auxiliary Training Schools! Don't let your staff tell you that you can only be midwives! Don't listen to their specious reasoning why it is better for you to be a midwife than a health officer! Demand your rights! Fight for equality!'

And our four were going to fight!

We didn't give in easily. As we assured them, it was for their own

270

good that we did all we could to persuade them to do midwifery. They were needed as midwives by the population.

'Isn't the first object of our political leaders that we should serve the people?'

As midwives, they would have jobs assured, but no-one would employ them as health officers, as we couldn't send a woman to a rural village on her own.

'Are you threatening us? We'll report you to the Party!'

And they meant it. And we didn't like it — and they knew it!

So they joined the men's classes. We closed the midwives' class for the year. We sent a report to the local Government doctor and the educational authorities. The year crept on much as it had started, with a veiled campaign of passive resistance, no co-operation and less-veiled glances of contemptuous superiority.

However, the truth remained that we urgently needed qualified midwives, and that African culture made it strongly preferable for our girl students to train as midwives rather than as health officers. Ultimately we, the staff, felt sure that these same girls would regret the action they had taken. So we made plans to ensure that this would not occur again. At the end of term, when reports were to be given out, each second-year student was asked to sign a request form to be admitted to third-year studies subject to their exam results; and the men's form, all made out in the masculine, requested entrance to 'the health officers' course of studies, while the girls' form, written with feminine concords, requested entrance to 'the midwives' course of studies.

We sent for the six second-year girl students, explained the whole situation to them again, and gave them their request forms to sign. Forms were in duplicate, so that they could send a copy to their parents or to their local Party member, should they so wish. No pressure was put on them. They could sign and do midwifery, or not sign and go home. As simple as that. There was no option open to the girls to sign for the health officers' course. We merely stated that the latter course was already full with sixteen male students.

We waited. One girl went home without signing, to 'discuss it with my father'. Three girls came up to see us to 'talk it over more fully'. Staff were nervous: students were edgy. The local Government doctor, who had initially backed us and given us his authority to take this course of action, withdrew his support, and warned us that we might be heading for trouble with the Party.

At four o'clock one Tuesday afternoon there was a knock at my front door.

'Good afternoon, Doctor. This is my father and brother,' spoke a second-year girl student, indicating the two visitors she had brought up the hill.

'Good afternoon,' I responded, and we all shook hands.

I suggested to the girl student that she go back to the girls' quarters, while I talked to her parent. I turned to go in and make them tea.

'No,' the father snapped. 'She stays.'

I paused, took a deep breath and turned to face them. The very air felt menacing. Then a mud-slinging contest started, voices were raised, tempers became heated and I knew fear. I had no witness, no-one to quote me accurately, no-one to defend me against the outlandish accusations that this man was making against me. I knew fear of direct physical violence, that he would strike me, and I knew I dared not defend myself. I knew fear for the college, that, after all we had done to establish it, one foul slander from this man could lose us our Government recognition. It was all so weird, so unreasonable. It was useless to reason with him: he had already decided on his course of action before ever he approached me. He was almost demented, beside himself with rage.

At last, others came and took him away, talked with him and appeared to reach a conclusion. They went, and I breathed a little more easily.

Two days later a letter came, a copy of a letter of bitter accusation that this man had sent to the judiciary powers in Bunia, to the special powers that controlled the movements of foreigners and held our dossiers, to the Party and to the National Army. He claimed that, as a foreigner, I was acting for a foreign power, against the best interests of Zaire, that I had ridiculed the Party and the Flag, and that I had stood in the way of his daughter receiving the best possible education provided by the Government, showing sex discrimination and anti-Party colonialism.

The case dragged on for nearly three months. Several times I had to appear in court in Bunia, costing not only £5 each trip, but also several hours of precious time. Reports were written and submitted, explanations were prepared and given, advice and consultation on all levels was sought and received. Lumbabo Eugene of our educational office was a tower of strength. He knew the right people to give us the legal help we needed, particularly with regard to court-room custom and language. He gave me his friendship and time without measure. He represented me several times, when he felt that an African could cope better than a foreigner. His report to the court officer on my reputation and relationship with local Africans was generous to an extreme.

Eventually the affair 'blew over', or was allowed to settle. I was acquitted, I presume, although no-one quite said so. Someone would have lost face had that been done. Those three months of court appearances and uncertainties were almost like the proverbial straw that breaks the camel's back. Not one word of appreciation from this parent for all we had taught his daughter; not one word of apology for his cruel lies and absurd accusations; not one word about reimbursement for all that the court case had cost me. No, but next term he was to come to Dr Becker and ask the medical staff of the Centre to employ his daughter in the hospital, as though nothing had ever occurred!

Despite Government salaries for the staff and a Government doctor for our final examinations, we still had no paper to say we were truly recognized and accredited as a Government college. We needed a legal identity number to put on all our Government communications. We needed a formal statement with a clear signature to say that the Government had agreed to our request for recognition. We still had not received any Government diplomas for our graduating students with which they could obtain official posts with recognized salaries in the Government health service. All we had was the salary for four foreign teachers. In the eyes of the Government this was our personal money and we were not expected to account for its use, only to sign for its reception. If in fact we each ploughed it all back into the running expenses of the college, this was our own private affair and of no account to the Government, however grateful they might be for what, to them, must be obvious generosity.

The students heard that we had received Government subsidies, and so they concluded that the college was recognized. This should have meant that the college was also receiving direct subsidy money for the use of the students, but this was not yet so. The facts were explained to the students, but they chose not to believe us. The only alternative was therefore to believe that we were lying, hiding from them the truth, presumably (in the thinking of the students) because we were stealing the college subsidy for our own private use. They were shown the books and the Government-salary pay-sheets. Members of the district educational office explained the situation to them patiently and in considerable detail. Still they could not, or would not, believe what we said: and a growing spirit of criticism and suspicion crept in between staff and students.

We applied repeatedly to the Government to have some Africans on our pay-roll. True, we had no national with full teaching qualification available for our school staff, but we had some fine young men, graduates of our college, who stayed on at the Centre to help train first-year students. Their main responsibilities were in the realm of the art of nursing (bed care and ward routine) and to control discipline in class-rooms and dormitories. We felt that, if even one of them were on the payroll, students would be more likely to believe them than at present they were to believe us, when only foreigners were paid.

In October 1972, to our delight, three Africans were added to the pay-roll. All seven of us, black and white, went each month to the local educational offices to receive our 'salaries' and sign for them. Everything was open; each one could see what the other received; and we hopefully expected the underground mutterings and discontent and suspicion to subside.

What a vain hope! By Christmas, while women students fought for their rights, men students clamoured for cash. Their conviction appeared to be that the Government money we were accepting as our salaries was meant to be their pocket-money! At their request (as I have mentioned) I showed them my monthly pay-slip, totalling about 32 Zaires (£30), on official computer form. They were dumb founded, and yet still not convinced. True, they did not know that my salary-subsidy was so low due to a mistake in the computerization, but even they must have sensed something a little bizarre, when a qualified doctor with over twenty years' experience, director of a training college, was receiving the same as one of the college graduates with only two years' experience.

For six months the undercurrent of grumbles and suspicions rumbled on, periodically flashing into the open. I was ill for five weeks during February and March, and to make up to the students for all the lectures they had missed in that period, we offered to rearrange their time-tables. It would mean very heavy hours for the staff, perhaps especially for myself, but very little ultimate change for the students. However, the third year representative student came to see me to refuse categorically all the changes we had suggested, unless we paid them 'for the inconvenience'.

It was almost incomprehensible to us as a staff. Our African colleagues tried in vain to reason with the students, to show them that only they would be the losers: the staff were not sitting their final exams! To the students, apparently, it was equally incomprehensible that we were willing to put ourselves out for them with no ulterior motive. They refused to believe it possible, convinced that we were putting something over on them. They sent us their suggestions for the final three months of the school year, with an apparent ultimatum stating what they were willing to do if we did not pay them for their services.

We accepted their suggestions, just as they stood. It meant far fewer teaching hours for us. We determined among ourselves to carry the extra hours of practical service in the hospital, rather than make any further appeal to the students.

Then suddenly we heard that the scholarship grants were on their way!

We heard a vague, unofficial report that these grants were to be paid to individual students, and not to the college as previously indicated. Then we heard from a school in Kinshasa similar to our own, that they had received their grants. The next week we heard that violent trouble had broken out in that school due to a misunderstanding of the use intended by the Government of this scholarship money. A visit to us in the Easter vacation by a staff member of another similar school helped us to understand a little better the problems involved, but gave us little guidance as to how to avoid the same violence in our own college.

Letters were sent to Government officials at our local township and regional capital. Visits were made to two senior educational establishments in the area where scholarships had already been received. Gleaning all the information we could ahead of time, we prepared a document as to how we felt we should disburse the money when it came. Copies of this document were sent to the central Government in Kinshasa and also to church leaders, regional educational directors and local directors of other subsidized schools, to elicit their comments, corrections or criticisms. We received no response. No-one was willing to commit himself.

A Government conference in Kisangani on medical education enabled two of our staff to ask again for clear direction as to what we were expected to do when the cash arrived. Once again, there was no answer. Basically they would only say, rather cryptically: 'Wait until you have the cash: it may never come!'

Two members of this regional conference then flew up to inspect our College at Nyankunde. I shall tell more of this inspection in a moment, but during it they had an unpremeditated meeting with the student body, when they were faced with the same question direct from the students. On being asked what I proposed to do, I produced the document that we had prepared, not without considerable trepidation, as it was not a Government document and we never quite knew how far we could go on our own initiative.

The inspectors read out the document, line by line, painstakingly explaining each phrase, as to how the monthly 10 Zaires (£8) for each second- and third-year student would be allocated, to housing, schooling, clothing, feeding, and finally 20% as pocket-money. After checking various figures against our annual accounts, the inspectors eventually said that they considered it an extremely good document, the allocation fair and reasonable: if they had any criticism, it was only that 20% was too high for pocket-money. The Government reckoned that this was the money needed for existence, and pocket-money should be provided by the students' families.

I let out my breath with relief: the students almost hissed.

The atmosphere was electric, and I felt embarrassed before our distingushed visitors. Later on, over coffee, I asked if we had permission to allocate the 20% as pocket-money, and they assured me that, as director, it was entirely left to my discretion what I did, particularly as it meant that I was still subsidizing their fees to that amount out of my personal money.

We went ahead on this authority, albeit verbal only, and prepared documents in detail for every month of the current year, for each student, in duplicate, ready for the day the cash arrived. We trusted that, when it actually arrived, the students would be so thrilled to get their 20% that they would drop their mutterings, particularly now that they had heard their own authorities say that we were being more generous than others!

At the beginning of May 1973 a radio call informed us of an important conference in Kisangani for all those involved in para-medical teaching, particularly arranged for national and foreign nurses. I had been ill earlier in the year and missed many lectures. It was therefore felt wisest that I should not go. I was also leaving the country soon, and it was obviously more sense for those who would be carrying on to hear all the advice given. So Vera Thiessen, an American sister tutor in charge of the class-room teaching of nursing arts, and Camille Djailo, the national supervisor of students on ward practice, were nominated to represent our college at the conference. We prepared our 'file' of school dossier, information, statistics and questions, briefed the two of them on all we wanted to know, and sent them off.

Then an urgent radio message three days later from Vera.

'They want to meet you, and are coming to Bunia tomorrow.'

'Who? Can you repeat that message, Vera?'

Nothing but crackles and static interference answered us: we could make out no more, but were left to guess at the inference. In fact, we were prepared. We had lived six years in a state of preparedness for this moment. All our files were up to date, our teaching material in order, our time-tables carefully balanced. School accounts and statistics were all ready for instant inspection. Nevertheless, there was a wild rush of activity, to polish and tidy and lay out everything available; to prepare beds and meals; to clean dormitories and iron uniforms. A sense of expectant excitement filled the air.

The next day I went to Bunia with one of our African staff members and met the inspectors, a lady sister tutor from Kinshasa and a man from the Ministry of Education in Kisangani. We chatted happily and freely on the journey back to Nyankunde, where we arrived in time for the midday meal, generously provided and graciously prepared by Dr Ruth Dix. Then the afternoon was given up to the inspection. We did not spend long on the buildings: they were obviously pleased and satisfied. We spent longer in the class-rooms and offices, in the laboratory and nursing arts' demonstration room. They asked many searching questions and listened carefully to our replies and explanations.

The blackboard layout of all time-table programming for each staff member and each student for the whole year, in a fairly complex double-entry eight-colour system that we had devised, drew the longest discussion, and they were obviously impressed. Accounts and book-keeping, lists and statistics honestly did not interest them, and only with difficulty did I persuade them to sign these for me as being satisfactory. We discussed in detail the balance of practical experience with class-room theory; different pedagogic methods and approaches; student-staff relationships; the place of Party political involvement, especially where the Saturday active participation in manual labour was concerned, for medical workers. In everything they were clearly satisfied.

The next morning they met informally with the students for an hour and invited us, the foreign staff, to be present as well. There was an obvious element of suspicion. The students felt that the inspectors had probably sold them to the white staff and that we, the white staff, had talked the inspectors into accepting our point of view, as though we had something ulterior to gain through this inspection. Both inspectors did all they could to dispel this attitude. They openly praised the school, staff and students, for the obvious achievements: buildings, curriculum, uniforms, esprit-de-corps, examination results. All spoke of success, which in turn revealed hard united effort.

'Are there any questions you would like to ask us?'

I drew in my breath and waited.

'Is it essential that we girls should be midwives?'

A moment's stunned silence. I had not prepared the lady inspector for this particular problem of women's lib. in our midst.

'Essential?' she parried. 'But no. If you wish to remain with your second-year training diploma in general nursing, and work in the hospi-tal, of course you may. We offer you the privilege of continuing a third year in midwifery.'

'Why can't we study with the boys, as health officers?'

This went on relentlessly for twenty minutes, just as the staff had had it all year. The lady inspector refused to lose patience, nor did she use sarcasm, but she clearly stated exactly what we had so often repeated. It was a privilege for a girl to train as a midwife, but a girl health officer was not wanted by the population, and service to our people must be our guide.

Eventually the Educational Inspector swung the question, and so a male student brought up next the vexed question of money.

'We hear there are to be scholarships, back-dated to January. How is the money to be handled, and by whom?'

Again the inspector replied with care and courtesy, examined in detail our prepared document, and agreed that what we had planned was exactly in line with Government policy except that we were being too generous to offer them 20% as pocket-money! The students were furious, certain that I had previously primed the inspectors, or bribed them into saying what I wanted said.

Despite the hour of rather unpleasant questioning, as it seemed to me, both inspectors were very impressed by everything, including our student/staff relationship! They were quite amazed that we were able to encourage some 60% of our graduates to go back to the rural areas when they finished their studies at the Centre, as most other schools found that only 10% were willing to leave the city life.

I remember, as I gave them mid-morning coffee before driving them back to Bunia for the midday plane, asking them hesitantly if we could know the final 'mark' that would be attached to our inspection report. We needed seven out of the available ten to become officially recognized. It was so important to us, I hardly dared to breathe as I awaited some response.

The man shrugged and spread his hands. 'What can we say, really?'

This left me still quite uncertain and on tenterhooks of anxiety. Had he any idea of the importance of that moment to me as the climax of twenty years' hard work?

'Listen,' said the sister tutor. 'You are the last of the forty-three schools in our vast country of this standard of paramedical education that we have inspected. We have already given two schools nine, so what can we give you except ten? There is just no comparison.'

I nearly fainted.

'Thank you,' I whispered. 'Thank you.' I was addressing them both, yet I was also addressing in my mind and heart all the staff and all the students, all the helpers and workers, all who had been involved. 'Thank You, God.'

10
Apparent Rejection

It seemed that our immediate goal, Government recognition for the college, resulting in legal diplomas for the graduates, was almost achieved. I confess I was thrilled. For seven years I had been working for this. In fact, quite honestly, for twenty years we had been working towards recognition, even if not always at Nyankunde. We had asked the Government in 1966 to give us eight years to achieve the standards required in permanent buildings, course material and qualified personnel. Now, in only seven years, one year ahead of our proposed schedule, we were in sight of completion.

When Government-subsidized salaries arrived for the teaching staff in 1971, we really knew that our request for recognition would be granted, as it was inconceivable that they would pay us unless they were content with our methods.

When Government doctors were sent for the final oral examinations and were authorized to use the legal rubber stamp on our diplomas, we were even more certain of our ultimate acceptance.

When the inspectors had arrived and spoken so favourably, and shown us the copy of their report recommending 'immediate recognition, and speedy upgrading', it was obvious that it was only a matter of time before the coveted official document would arrive, recognizing us as a Government school for training national para-medical workers. Add to this the fact that the inspectors had brought with them the blank legal diplomas for us to fill in for each finalist student of that year, and our joy was full.

Monday, 26 June, only four weeks since the inspection and eleven days after the final oral examinations, dawned like any other day of our tropical year, at 5.30 a.m., bright and clear, with a mild haze over the distant hills. I went down the hill early to college as we had a lot of work to get through. The other staff soon joined me in the library, where we prepared for the day's activities.

Each student had a six-week summer holiday to visit his own people and to collect his fees for the coming school year. Half of each class would go on holiday from 27 June till 11 August, while the other half worked in the wards and outpatients' clinics of the hospital. A week of overlap from 11 to 18 August made allowance for transport difficulties, and also enabled us to arrange our 'Big Day' with the whole college together.

We were inviting the 1968 graduating class to come for an 'old-boys' reunion on 14 August. The 15th would be a welcome meeting for two new doctors, Philip and Nancy Wood, who were expected to arrive early in August to take over the direction of the college. In the afternoon there would be the presentation of the diplomas to the new graduating class. The 16th was to be a farewell meeting and evening party for me, as I felt that the time had come to leave Nyankunde and to hand over to younger workers.

Arrangements were well in hand. Transport had been arranged for all those hoping to come. Local Government officials had been invited to be with us and to share in the programme. The choir had been practising for five months. I hoped to have cassette recorders running throughout the three days and had acquired films for my camera, in order to have a permanent record of the final achievement of my twenty years' work in Africa. After the three days of festivities, at the end of the week, the second half of the student body, including all those finally leaving us at the end of their three years of study, would go for their holidays till the end of September. Those back from their homes would take over the hospital duties.

Before leaving for holiday, each student of the first group needed to receive his annual report card and class bulletin, a certificate in lieu of diploma, a road-pass and student identity card for claiming reduction of fares on public transport, and various other items, differing for each area and student. Usually we gave them their tickets if we had managed to secure these ahead of time, and some pocket-money to enable them to reach their homes without hardship. Added to this, each student needed to check the wording and spelling on his diploma which had to be sent to the Government for ratification and signature.

Besides all this, this year each senior student was to receive a bonus gift, as we thought of it, from the newly-arrived Government scholarship money. We had worked hard to decide how to allocate this money justly. The Government had sent almost £10 for each second- and third-year student for each month from January to July. When we completed the annual school accounts for 1 July 1972 to 30 June 1973, it was obvious that this £10 a month per student would barely cover the cost of feeding, clothing and schooling the students, let alone housing and administration. However, we felt we wanted them to have at least some of the money, as pocket-money, while we accepted the responsibility to continue a certain amount of subsidy.

Eventually we decided to give them 20% of the money for the six months January to June, and all the July allocation if they were on vacation. The 80% that we retained (for 35 students this came to about £1,500 at that moment) would enable us to prepare adequately for the coming school year, as the regional educational authority's gift had done the previous year. In future, the regular monthly income would help the college to run smoothly without being so dependent on foreign subsidies; doubtless this was the object of the Government's scholarship scheme. We had already prepared carefully-worded explanatory forms for each senior student for each of the seven months involved. Each student would be asked to sign in duplicate for each month's allocation.

At 7.00 a.m. the first three students came in together, all third-year students who were being invited to return after their vacation to join the staff for a year as hospital supervisors. They would be largely responsible for the training of first-year students in the art of nursing. Albert Amuli was one of these, and he showed every promise of being an excellent and capable leader in the future.

Basuana, Vera Thiessen and I had sorted out all the 'piles' of certificates, road-passes and money for each student. We explained things again carefully to these first three, getting them to check each document for signature, the correct date, the spelling of names: to check the road-passes and tickets for the correct destination. They knew the routine well from previous years. We then gave them a certain allocation of gift money, approximately the price of their journey home plus 50p for every night spent on the journey. Amuli lived six days' journey away to the south-west, almost 1,000 miles by road, and he received approximately £12 for this.

Then we explained again all that had been discussed four weeks previously when the inspectors had been with us, concerning the scholarship money. We showed them the duplicated receipt-forms and how the money was being used. We then offered them £22 each as pocket-money to take home, and asked them to sign for it.

Probably my own subconscious fear didn't help the situation. I knew it might not be smooth sailing, though I tried to carry it off with an easy optimism. I knew that there had been mutterings among the students ever since they had heard that scholarship money was coming. And even before that they had believed that, since the staff received Government salaries, there must have been money sent for them which I was not handing over. They simply couldn't believe that their Government would pay us, foreign staff, a salary without sending anything for them, the students. It mattered so much to me that all should go smoothly and without trouble. It mattered to me that they should trust me and not suspect that I was trying to cheat them or do them down. Instinctively we, the staff, knew that if these three senior students signed the rest would follow suit. I tried to will them to accept our word and sign their names.

They pulled the piles towards them. Painstakingly and slowly they went through each document, checking spellings, dates, signatures. They counted the money. They studied the receipt-forms. They made their own calculations. No-one spoke.

I tried to chatter nonchalantly, about their holidays, their families, our next year together on the staff and how much we were looking forward to having them back. I reminded them of our 'Big Day' and urged them to make every effort to start their return journey in time to be with us. All the time I was praying for them to sign.

We could feel the tension. They didn't look at each other. They didn't speak to each other. They listened to my patter and I almost believed that they were going to sign.

'Please, please sign,' my heart was urging them. I feared whatever would happen if they refused. As always I was uncertain of my ground. I knew that what we were doing was in accordance with Government guide-lines. I knew that it was absolutely honest, and that the students were getting more, not less, than others would have given them. Yet if there was a show-down with Government officials called in, in the present climate of an African country, with feelings running high against white foreigners, the whole situation could very easily be turned against us.

They wouldn't sign.

Each had been meditatively chewing the tip of his ball-point pen, checking and re-checking each form. I felt that each one was waiting to see if one of the others would give in and sign. Slowly each one put down the pen and pushed the money back towards us. As I remember it, they said nothing. Their very silence was a bit uncanny and unnerving.

Carefully and patiently I went through all our reasoning again. I had the account books there and all the relevant Government correspondence. I offered to show them anything they wanted to convince them that not only were we acting in accordance with their own Government's wishes, but actually being generous over and above. Perhaps that was the mistake. The fact that we indicated that we could be generous to a certain degree made them question our ultimate honesty in saying that we couldn't give them all the money.

Still they refused to sign.

I know I was beginning to feel desperate. These were our best students, both academically and also spiritually. If they could be convinced that it was right that they sign, that they were making a mistake to refuse, the rest of the student body would probably accept their lead without too much difficulty.

They offered no explanation, no reasoning. However, we knew instinctively that they had made up their minds to accept nothing less than 100% of the back-pay scholarship money to January, and that probably they would consent to pay school fees the next year out of what followed. These first three were all graduating, so there would be no 'future payment'. I guessed that as soon as they had heard, via the African grape-vine, that the money was coming, £10 each month for the past six months, they had already decided what they would buy — a new suit, a transistor radio or a bicycle. What we were offering, 20% of it, simply made these purchases impossible and they felt cheated.

Perhaps they tried to reason about the rightness of their attitude and the wrongness of mine, though they said nothing.

'You've already fed us for these six months, so why take the money now? It's the same with clothes and housing and schooling. Why are you asking us to pay you back what you've already given? If you wanted it back, why didn't you say so last January, that it was only a loan?'

But they maintained a rigid, stony silence.

We sent the three away and called in other students, one by one.

With each one we had exactly the same situation. A careful perusal of everything, a silent reading and studying of the explanatory notes, an acceptance of all their papers and roadpasses — but a complete refusal to sign for and accept the money.

After about three or four more students, we called a halt for breakfast. During the break we gathered the other members of staff together and told them what was happening. Together we prayed that God would break the deadlock. We were almost certain that this was some kind of *likilimba*, an agreement between them all, like a trade union strike, plus threats of brutality for anyone who 'gave into the whites' and signed for and accepted their partial monies. It was a determined, concerted action by all of them to stand out for 'their rights', and to have the 100% of that back-pay scholarship money.

We decided to start again, and to call each of the three seniors separately and give them a chance to yield to our request without the direct hindrance of losing face in front of another. We promised that no-one should know who signed and who didn't. Apparently this was another wrong move and only hardened their resolve to resist our efforts. We were not exactly skilled in the art of strike-breaking, nor of conciliation between management and floor!

When Albert came in, he very nearly gave in to our earnest pleading and exhortation. He had been mission- and church-trained all his life, and all his school and college fees had been paid by his local church and missionaries. Deep in his heart, he knew he was throwing away something of lasting value by refusing to trust us. He took the pen from me and drew the form towards him. He read it all again and bent over it, poised to sign. Then suddenly, abruptly, he pushed it from him and said: 'No, no, I can't.' Looking up at me, he continued in a self-defensive, almost pathetic whisper: 'What's the good of one signing, anyway?' and with this cryptic remark he rushed from the room.

We sensed, rather than understood, that fear had ruled him, a fear which perhaps we staff could barely appreciate. He knew what awaited him outside if he broke the oath that they had taken together to refuse to accept our terms, and he just couldn't face the consequences. It was no good my telling him that no-one need know. He knew that they would know at once when he joined them: he just couldn't bluff them all. And he was deeply afraid.

Throughout that Monday we saw, individually, each of the students due for the first holiday shift. We treated each one similarly, patiently, prayerfully. We refused to accept the situation. We prayed earnestly for a crack, that perhaps just one would have the courage of his convictions and stand out against the crowd. We had no real idea of what might be involved in the 'oath of allegiance' or of the threats employed by the ringleaders.

Girl students were also being asked to sign a request-form to return to do midwifery studies in their third year, instead of public health studies as the male students did. In asking this, we had known that we were throwing down a gauntlet. Only one second-year girl student out of the four, though five first year students out of the six, signed willingly, and then she pleaded with us not to let the others know that she had signed. This gave us even greater certainty that strong threats were being employed by the directors of the revolt.

On Tuesday we started all over again. We asked Dr Becker to come and speak to the assembled college, to explain that what we were doing was absolutely in accord with the directions from their own leaders in Government authority; and that either they signed and accepted the money they were being offered, or else they could go home without the money, which would be returned to the Government. We were not free to choose what we would do with it: it belonged to the Government. Obviously we could not hold the money, even though it was sent for college funds, unless the students signed for it, as the Government receipt-forms were all made out in each individual's name.

We spent another seemingly long day, re-interviewing each student. We refused to give in half-way: we felt each one must be given the opportunity in private to change his mind following Dr Becker's words. No-one changed his mind. No-one signed his receipt-form.

I went to bed at midnight on Tuesday with a very heavy heart. I had discussed the situation carefully with our African members of staff, and with Africans in the local education offices. They all advised us to stick to what we had said, though they were obviously becoming nervous. If the students went to report the situation to local 'Party' headquarters, nobody was quite sure how the situation would look to an outsider. My heaviness of heart was not only caused by the impasse we were in, but also because these were *our* students. I loved them. I cared for them. For three years I had taught the seniors, preparing them for their future life-service, as medical evangelists in the service of the church and their fellow countrymen. They were like sons to me. Now I felt that they had turned on me, at the last moment — the moment of our apparent triumph with Government recognition. Later, when I heard them arraign me publicly, I really felt that they had rejected me, but already I sensed their almost-callous spurning. They appeared to have put up with me, my leadership, my administration and all the work we had slaved to do on their behalf to get the recognition; but now that it had come, they didn't want us any more. They wanted to show their independence of us. Even worse, I sensed that they didn't really trust us. All our reasoning was just words to them, easy words from the white foreigner to show once more how good and generous we were. It was as though all the daily radio brain-washing to beware of the deceit of the 'hated imperialist westerner' was suddenly bursting into fruit. They believed it, and so they did not believe us.

On Wednesday morning Dr Becker rang me and asked me to go down the hill to see him. By now the whole college was involved, not just the half going on vacation. All but ten of the first-year students were on strike. There was hardly a student nurse in the whole 250-bed hospital nor any to help with the thousand outpatients. Everybody at the Centre knew of the deadlock, and they were all watching closely.

'All right,' Dr Becker said to me as I entered his little office. 'We'll have the committee at six this evening.'

Uncertainly I looked at him for some explanation.

'I beg your pardon, Sir?' I queried.

'The committee can meet this evening,' he repeated, looking at me with obvious sorrow in his eyes.

'I don't quite understand, Sir. Which committee?'

He now looked puzzled and pushed a letter towards me.

'But you have asked for the executive committee to take over and sort out the problem in the college.' He spoke quietly, but there was a mild reproachfulness in his tone, at what must have seemed to him my deliberate obtuseness.

I picked up the letter, a piece of college note-paper, and read the short line of request for the executive committee to take over 'as we are unable to reach an acceptable solution', and then I read the several signatures. Dr Becker had not noticed that mine was not among them.

A lump rose in my throat. So my own staff felt I couldn't cope. I suppose I was unreasonable in my sheer weariness with the affair, but I felt that not only the students, but now also the staff had rejected my leadership. Doubtless this wasn't true in the slightest, but I was touchy. I guess that I was proud of being a good and fair and competent leader. I had led a para-medical training school all my twenty years in Congo/Zaire, and felt I really knew how to cope and handle affairs on all levels. And this was my last term, my last chance in a sense to show my colours. I didn't stop to think, or to ask the staff why they had taken this step. I had been ill only four months previously and this was probably a considerate action in order to save me too much involvement in sorting out the strike: but it just didn't register like that to me at that moment.

'O.K., Sir. I'll see everything is ready,' I answered Dr Becker politely, as I stumbled almost blindly from his office, wrapped in my own wounded feelings.

The day was spent preparing. There was a lot to do. All members of an extended executive committee had to be notified, including members of the local education office as they were closely involved with the college, particularly where finance was concerned. Certain local church elders were also invited, as the affair might well develop into a disciplinary one.

The annual financial statement was rushed through, simplified, duplicated and made available in French and in Swahili for each committee member to examine and to compare with the statistical reasoning involved in the employment of the scholarship money. All this was also carefully laid out and explained on the large blackboards in diagrammatic form. A brief concise history of the application for the scholarship money was compiled, and copies made available of all the correspondence of the previous six months as it related to the affair in hand.

At six o'clock everyone assembled, but they immediately rearranged the room from usual committee procedure, to resemble a lawcourt. Dr Becker took the chair and I was asked to sit on his right. Then three representative students were allowed to enter, to present their case against me.

It was unbelievable, really. To me it was the climax of twenty years of service. If I hadn't been leaving Africa in three months' time, I might have been able to look at things a little less passionately, a little more objectively. But, nevertheless, the shock of hearing my own students give a carefully-prepared, reasoned attack on me would have been humiliating at any time. I was basically accused of stealing college funds. They reasoned that, since the staff were subsidized, this proved that the college was recognized and that therefore we had been receiving student subsidies from the same date. That I had continued to demand £50 per annum per student, despite receiving Government grants, was plainly stealing. I was accused of lying, in denying these facts; of duplicity in being able to argue my way out of the situation every time it had been approached. They also stated that I had falsified the accounts and report-sheets sent to the Government so that they would not know that I was systematically misappropriating college funds.

The whole, long, twenty-minute tirade was recorded on cassette. It sounded even worse when I listened to it again the next day. The final cruelty was that the chosen spokesman for the students was Albert Amuli, our senior student, a man brought up in our own church schools and whose school fees had been consistently paid by church and missionaries.

By midnight we had achieved nothing. Much abuse had flowed. Mud was flung at many others besides myself, particularly anyone who tried to reason with them or show them how stupid they were being. We all separated and went to our various homes wearied, dispirited, discouraged. I couldn't sleep. I just felt utterly dejected, with a growing sense of personal failure.

I picked up my Bible and sought God's guidance. It didn't come easily. I prayed, but felt as though I was talking to myself, or, at best, to the ceiling. I wept, mostly out of self-pity. I tried the Bible again, re-reading the passage for my next day's regular reading, straight through the four chapters of the book of Jonah. I seemed to get nothing from it at all, no consolation, no strength, no guidance. I cried out in desperation to God to give me something to meet my need. I read Jonah for the third time that night, and began to see some sense.

The storm that shook Jonah awake, that upset a vast crowd of people, the sailors, passengers, those who sent cargo, those who were waiting to receive the cargo, other ships with their crews and passengers and cargo in the immediate vicinity, was all became God wanted to speak to one man, Jonah. When he jumped overboard the storm stopped, the ship reached its destination, and there is no particular indication that anyone was permanently affected. The sailors made a passing act of acknowledgment of the power of this God of Jonah by the offering of a sacrifice of appeasement: that was all.

'O.K., Lord, you want to speak to *me*, and my deaf ears have caused this storm in which everyone — all the students and staff of the college and medical centre, all the 250-bed patients and over one thousand outpatients — is becoming involved. O.K., I'll jump overboard — then what?'

So I wrote a letter of resignation as college director and sent it down to Dr Becker for the executive committee early the next morning. Probably, deep down in my heart, I didn't expect such a letter to be accepted, even though I had specifically asked that no-one question it. Wasn't I indispensable to them? How could they run and handle the college without me? So my heart reasoned, hoping against hope that they would refuse to accept my resignation.

They accepted my letter, presumably gratefully. I chewed my heart out in private chagrin and allowed my self-pity to make an enormous mountain out of the rapidly growing ant hill. Not only students and staff, but now fellow committee members were glad to get on without me.

My home help, Benjamin, kept me in touch with events. All the second- and third-year students were sent home, having received 80% of their scholarship money, the college retaining 20%, all receipts having been duly signed. They were not to be invited to return unless they apologized for their behaviour and language, accepted a period of discipline from their local churches for having involved patients in their strike action, and signed a statement with regard to the allocation of future scholarship money.

They left on Saturday. Not one came to say good-bye or to shake hands. There were no photos of this qualifying class, my last group of students. There was to be no diploma day. All August festivities were to be cancelled — including the choir, despite five months of hard practising, and no recordings to take home. I went into Bunia, to give a report to the Government education office, as we were directly responsible to them. I had to tell them and Dr Biki that there would be no graduation day celebrations as previously planned, to which they had already been invited. I felt very small. I wrote to the regional inspector of education at Kisangani, who had become a personal friend over the last two or three years and who had also been invited to our diploma day, both to represent the Party and also to present the diplomas. I told him briefly of the recent events and the reason for the cancellation of our graduation celebrations. By then, my pride was truly laid in the dust and trampled upon.

'Is it really worth while?'

The niggling question that I wouldn't look at, that I didn't want to hear, kept pressing up into the level of conscious thought.

'O.K. Right now, after all your philosophizing and encouraging others, just answer: has it all been worth it?'

11
Was It All Worth While?

The question had to be answered, I knew, and it really must be answered in Africa before I left, but for a few weeks I couldn't bring myself to face it squarely.

I knew of course that the staff and committee had not really rejected me. As I have said, I had been in hospital only four months earlier with complete nervous exhaustion after six months of intense activity. During that time I had had to make three trips from Nyankunde to Ibambi and Nebobongo, two by lorry, involving twenty or more hours of hard driving in each direction. Each trip had involved emotional, medical and spiritual commitments. The first had been for the triumphant funeral of our field leader, Jack Scholes, whom I had loved as a father through eighteen years of co-operation; the second had been for the Christmas and New Year conferences of church and mission, probably my last in Africa; and the third had been with regard to establishing our church medical services within the new Government framework of a national service, with the tremendous amount of documentation needed.

Apart from these journeys there was all the routine work of the college, with more than twenty hours a week in the classroom, preparation for classes, marking of test papers, keeping of student report-files and general college administration. Again, special extra work was being put in preparatory to handing over the leadership of the college to the two new doctors. Add to all this the growing tensions of a changing political climate, with increasing uncertainty as to the popularity of the white foreigner on African soil, and the scene had been well set for some sort of physical reaction. There was a limit, I suppose, beyond which I had just no right to push my body to keep up with my more ambitious mind and spirit; but I hadn't heeded the warning light. So a week in hospital had been essential, followed by four weeks of slow convalescence in the home of one of our kindly American nurses at the centre.

With this in their minds, it was hardly surprising that the team felt that they ought not to allow me to try to carry the load alone when the strike started. In fact, it would have been extremely surprising if they had sat back and left me to cope! It wasn't as if the college was mine (even though the way I spoke and acted might indicate that I thought it was): it was part of the whole medical centre, and we were all involved.

The staff knew my peculiarly stubborn streak, and that my pride would not let me give in to student pressure to lower the standard, as I saw it. Yet they could also see that there was another side to the problem. Looked at through African eyes, things were often not as clear-cut as they seemed to us foreigners. True, the scholarship money was given for the running of the college, but then the college had run for the past six months. The students had been fed from January to June and the food paid for, so why take the money for that now? They were clothed, and the tailors' salaries had all been paid, so why take money for that?

I was allowing myself to think that they, the staff and committee, had compromised by giving in to the students' blackmail: 'We'll report you to Party headquarters if you don't....' And yet, deep down, I knew this couldn't be so. They had clearly felt that a difference could and should be made between back-pay and future scholarship moneys. An agreement had been reached between management and workers, financially acceptable to both. To us, as college administrators, this was obviously unsatisfactory, as we had to plan ahead: get in stocks of food, books, cloth; prepare a budget for the coming year and Government subsidies were notoriously unreliable. Yet through the previous seven years here at Nyankunde, God had never failed to provide all our needs. Couldn't He continue to do so? Did the coming of Government subsidies change our reliance on God as sole provider for our daily needs? If so, we would need to look closely as to the underlying motive in the seven-year struggle to obtain recognition.

Then I had to realize that the students were not mine. How they would have resented my thinking of them in this way! Student involvement should only have been a small part of my total involvement in the local church situation. These particular students were only a very few out of the two hundred and more who had passed through the college.

Living went on. The routine responsibility of the end of another college year, with all the Government forms to be completed and sent off by a certain prescribed date, kept me busy and occupied. The continued preparation for the arrival of Philip and Nancy Wood, both in the home and also in the school, filled most of my spare moments so that I hadn't too much time for morbid introspection. I had the opportunity to spend two weeks away from Nyankunde, at a neighbouring Christian village in the mountains with missionary friends, being much spoilt, and this did a lot to restore balance and perspective.

The Lord reminded me sharply of that traumatic night of 29 October 1964, and how I had gone home on furlough in 1965 and testified all over the United Kingdom to His sufficiency. It had been true. On that dreadful night, beaten and bruised, terrified and tormented, unutterably alone, I had felt at last that even God had failed me. Surely He could have stepped in earlier, surely things need not have gone that far. I had reached what seemed to me the ultimate depth of despairing nothingness. Yet even as my heart had cried out against God for His failure and my mental anguish taunted me to doubt His very existence, another reasoning had made itself felt.

'You asked Me, when you were first converted, for the privilege of being a missionary. This is it: don't you want it?'

Events had moved so fast: everything seemed to happen at once. Pain and cruelty and humiliation had continued in an ever-growing crescendo, yet with it, a strange peace and deep consciousness that God *was* in charge and knew what He was doing. Odd thoughts and phrases and impulses broke through, and later on were woven together to show the inner meaning of the events of that night, but it had not been orderly, in a way one could set down on paper or explain in a lecture.

'These are not your sufferings: they are Mine. All I ask of you is the loan of your body.'

Again the overwhelming sense of privilege, that Almighty God should stoop to ask of me, a mere nobody in a forest clearing in the jungles of Africa, something He needed. They had called Him 'a worm, no man'. I said I wanted to be identified with Him, yet did I really want to be a worm, trodden on, spurned, ignored? No! Yet this was the privilege He offered, the privilege of being a missionary, His ambassador, identified with Him among those whom He wanted to serve.

'You went home and told everyone that I was sufficient at *that* moment, in *those* circumstances. Isn't this true now, in today's circumstances?'

I tried to say: 'But of course, Lord. You know it's true.'

'No,' He quietly rebuked me. 'No. You no longer want Jesus only, but Jesus plus . . . plus respect, popularity, public opinion, success and pride. You wanted to go out with all the trumpets blaring, from a farewell-do that you organized for yourself: with photographs and tape-recordings to show and play at home, just to reveal what you had achieved. You wanted to feel needed and respected. You wanted the other missionaries to be worried about how ever they'll carry on after you've gone. You'd like letters when you got home to tell you how much they realize they owe to you, how much they miss you. All this and more. Jesus *plus* . . . . No, you can't have it. Either it must be "Jesus only" or you'll find you've no Jesus. You'll substitute Helen Rose-veare.'

A great long silence followed — several days of total inner silence. At last I managed to tell Him that with all my heart I wanted 'Jesus only'.

I went back to Nyankunde, sobered and humbled, and completed preparations for Philip and Nancy's arrival. They flew into Bunia airport early on Monday morning, 13 August 1973. It really was marvellous to welcome them and drive them out to Nyankunde, watching them drinking in the beauty of our hills and views across the valley. The tempo of events really speeded up now, as we had only six weeks together before I was due to leave for the United Kingdom: six short weeks in which to hand over, in orderly fashion, what it had taken twenty years to create, and in which they were also to learn as much as possible of the Swahili language.

After three days locally, meeting everyone, seeing over the Nyankunde Village, getting a quick bird's-eye view of the whole, collecting the necessary residence cards, opening a bank account and acquiring driving licences, we set off to drive to Ibambi and Nebobongo. It seemed right to introduce them the hard way to African transport problems! Within the first fifty miles we met our first major mudhole with an 8-ton lorry firmly entrenched across the narrow, one-track road. Surrounding crowds lined the route and watched interest-edly. No-one offered a hand, but everyone offered advice. A local church group pushed us through and enabled us to reach our immediate destination only two hours late. On Friday, the second day of our trip, the 300 miles took from 4.30 a.m. to 11.30 p.m. and involved the nego-tiation of some ten mud-holes of varying intensity, length and depth, but of unvarying nerve-racking interest.

Saturday we spent at Ibambi, meeting missionaries and national church leaders, and welcoming Nancy and Philip into the family. On Sunday we went to a local church, some 30 miles north-east of Ibambi, and spent a wonderful day with over 1,000 local Christians, gathered under a palm-frond shelter and overflowing it in every direction, worshipping God. The singing was whole-heartedly African. The crowd ebbed and flowed; children trotted in and out; chickens and goats wandered around unhindered and unnoticed. The sun beat down. Older men tended to doze after noon in their deckchairs, till a rousing hymn jerked them back into active participation. Different groups of children or women or youth took part with specially-prepared items. Several different speakers, using any one of the three main languages of the area, took turns in exhorting the crowd. There was no formal direction to the service, and yet all was obviously controlled and orderly. It certainly was an experience for anyone's first Sunday in the tribal areas of inner Africa.

On Monday we started our week at Nebobongo, the first of many for Philip, my last after twenty years of 'belonging'. Eleven of our para-medical workers had gathered, from as far afield as Malingwia, 250 miles to the north-west, and Opienge, the same distance to the south. The workers had cycled in, some taking as much as five days to reach us. This was their welcome to their two new doctors; it was a week of refreshment, medically and spiritually, with daily teaching sessions and demonstrations; and it was to be their farewell to me.

Each day was full and varied. It was obvious from the start that we would not achieve all that we had planned, but we did our best. The pervading spirit of joy and harmony made work a pleasure. The whole team pulled together. The desire to learn and profit from the week was in evidence right from the start: everyone put all they had into it, to make it a great success. I was tremendously happy. These were my people: I was one of them, accepted by them. Each day the soreness grew at the thought of tearing oneself away, leaving them, and starting to make a new life again elsewhere.

Particularly was this so where John Mangadima was concerned. For twenty years we had worked together. Of course there had been ups and downs, times when he maddened me, times when I irritated him, even times when we doubted and distrusted each other: but we'd come through, and were now very closely knit in spirit. My deepest joy in leaving was to know that John was appointed as assistant medical director to Philip Wood, for the running and supervision of our medical services in our church area. I had prayed and worked so hard for that. He had a Yamaha motorcycle to enable him to visit all our hospitals and dispensaries regularly, and I couldn't suppress a grin as I watched him setting off to Ibambi, with all the aplomb of one who had owned it all his life.

One afternoon, as he and Philip were operating together in the theatre, I had entered his office to glean a few facts before coming home. He had come in while I was there, peeling off his surgical gloves.

'Hi, Doctor. What are you doing in here?'

'Oh, just copying down a few facts and figures to tell folk back home.'

He leant over my shoulder and saw the last line I had written: 372 major operations in 1972 with only six surgical deaths.

'Oh, Doctor, don't bother with things like that. Just tell them that nearly 200 people found Christ as their Saviour through the medical services last year.'

I turned and hugged him, my eyes filling with tears of joy. And God said pretty plainly: 'Isn't My way better than yours?'

The journey back to Nyankunde the following Monday was more cruel than usual. At 5.30 p.m., after an extremely good thirteen hours of driving, we came upon the king of mud-holes, 400 yards of a churned-up sea of mud, at some places more than 6 feet deep, already with several large transport-lorries involved. It was 3.30 a.m. when Philip and Basuana eventually struggled through, to join Nancy and myself at a small village up the next hill. We'd gone ahead on foot, to dry out and rest after the first gruelling five hours of effort. We eventually dragged wearily into Nyankunde at midday, ready to start straight into a new school year the next week.

It was a little strange, as the first Monday morning in September dawned, when Philip and Nancy went down the hill to college at 6.30 a.m. and I realized that I really had handed over. It was theirs now, not mine. There were still many ways to help them in the remaining three weeks, particularly in the office and in language-study. We made the most of every available hour.

Suddenly my last week-end was on me and I could hardly bear to

297

consider all that was involved. On the Friday, the missionary family had arranged a farewell party for me. It was very touching. All my special African friends were there, as well as all the missionaries. Speeches were made. I felt choked and too full up to say much, and I knew it was sincere and not just laid on for the occasion.

On Saturday afternoon the Africans had a party for me down at the college. When I arrived at five o'clock and was led through the waiting crowd to the top table, I glanced round and saw all my friends of the past seven years, masons and plumbers, tailors and cooks, office workers and teaching staff, church elders and choir members, printers from the local press and gardeners from the school allotments. My eyes filled with tears as I sensed the love in their welcome to me.

A goat had been cooking over a spit for the past twenty-four hours, and Philip duly carved it. Food poured in, in steaming dishes and bowls from the kitchen, served by first-year students. Chatter was soon flowing in the usual free, happy way of Africa as everyone ate their fill. Two ludicrous skits followed from staff members and brought roars of laughter. Then the small group of third-year students who had returned after all the sadness of June, and who had asked to be taken back into college, had sung for me words they had written themselves, basically asking me to remember them as my sons who loved me, and to let God blot out from my memory the sore wound they had tried to inflict on me in their stupidity. Again, my heart was strangely moved and touched.

Philip made a short speech in Swahili, his first public usage of the language, much to everyone's delight, thanking me for all the service to the college over the past seven years. By then I had scribbled down all the thoughts that I wanted to express to everyone, in groups and individually, to say thank you to them for all their love and friendship over the years.

'Now it is over to you,' Philip concluded, addressing the more than sixty African guests. 'If you have anything you want to say, now is your chance.' Turning to me, he added in English: 'Not you; you just wait a bit.'

Then they started. For two hours it went on. I don't know how many spoke, probably more than twenty of them. I don't remember much of what was said. I cried: it was very, very moving. One I remember especially, but many others were like him: Nyelongo, our mason.

'You don't remember, Doctor, but one day when we were building the main school block I was late for work. I was scared: roll-call was over and you had already gone into school. When you came out at eight o'clock you came straight over to me and asked how my baby was. I didn't even know that you knew I had a baby!

' "The baby is very sick," I told you.

' "Where is the baby?" you asked.

' "Back at home."

' "But why not in the hospital?" and you sounded irritated.

' "We can't afford the hospital card and care," I replied.

'Then you really were mad! You went straight up the hill to your home, got into your Land Rover, came charging down on to the building site and shouted to me to get in. I'd never been in a car before. You told me to direct you to our village, but no car had ever been to our village before. You didn't seem to care, and we went, jolting and bumping over the mountainside. I called my wife and collected the baby, and you took us all to the hospital.'

I guess his child must have been very ill, as he said I told him not to return to work till we saw whether his child would live. He probably missed three or four days' work. He continued his story:

'At the end of the month, I came with the rest to be paid. I was trying to pluck up courage to ask you to spread my debt over several months, rather than take my whole month's pay. When you called my name, you passed me my wage-packet like everyone else. I just stared at you in unbelief. Then I rushed round the side of the house, laid the money out on the ground and counted it. It was all there.

'I ran all the way home. I called my wife. "Look, look, our money is all here. She hasn't taken any off, not even for the days' work I missed, let alone for our baby's care and treatment."

'We cried. Then we knelt down, and we suddenly realized all that you and Basuana meant when you told us day after day of God's love: and we asked God then and there into our hearts and lives and have followed Him ever since.'

I drew a deep breath as he sat down. I was deeply stirred. I wouldn't be surprised if, when I made up the wage-packets that month long ago, I had simply forgotten that Nyelongo owed money! I'm like that. But God had not forgotten. He used that little, almost insignificant, event in our daily relationship: not through a Sunday preaching engagement, but just an ordinary work job; and He had brought about His purposes, and I had merely been one of the links in the chain. This was it. This was what Evangelist Agoya had said to me years ago at Nebo-bongo; it was what Basuana had said to me much more recently here at Nyankunde: 'We can't all be the last link in the chain.' Being the last link may bring public acclaim and a sort of popularity: but being willing to be any link, however inconspicuous, brings happiness and lasting joy.

The question returned in my heart: 'Has it all been worth while?'

As others testified, my mind strayed round the north-eastern region of Zaire to our many regional hospitals and rural dispensaries. I pictured our many graduates working singly or in pairs, in far-off places, putting into practice all we had taught them. I began to count them, mentally ticking them off on a list. Tokpo and Ezo at Malingwia; Balani at Poko and the lovely small hospital he had built himself, loved and respected by everyone; Anizanga at Nala, Angola at Gamba. There was Jacqueline van Bever at Betongwe doing an excellent job; Sengi at Ibambi, Boloki at Buambi and Tahilo at Opienge. Then of course at Nebobongo, the whole team with John Mangadima, Asea, Namuniabangi and Bundayi. Way down to the south, Basetea had gone with his wife and children as a missionary nurse to another tribal area and culture. Each name conjured up a face and a story. I could think of each one through his schooling, his problems and difficulties, his first job after graduating, his settling down and now becoming a really valuable member of the medical team. Many had had their teething troubles; some had had to undergo fairly severe church discipline; but they had come back the stronger and more reliable. There were so many of them. Not only those in our own church area, but in each of the various church regions: Ngonda at Aba, Rabama at Todro, Rasereka and others at Oicha, Mukwesi and others farther south in the Ruanguba area, Mandro doing dentistry at Itendeyi.

My heart thrilled as I continued to tick them off. There were the two whom we felt were called and set apart as future staff members for our training college, whom we had been able to send for further education, Mandaboy to be a nursing tutor, and Madrato possibly to be a doctor if he could procure a place at university.

Then I remembered so many others who weren't nurses or medical workers, but who had been very much in the team since the beginning. Basuana had been such a good, close friend through nearly twenty years; Benj Gandisi the same. Church elders and pastors everywhere—

Ndugu and Tamoma, Agoya and Taadi, too many to name — had become such close friends that I never even thought of them as black or any other colour. They were just those I loved, and I realized, as perhaps never before, just how much I loved them and was going to miss them when I left and went back to Britain.

The evening drew to a close. I wended my way up the hill to my little home, as Philip and Nancy drove some of the folk back to their homes, and I suddenly knew with every fibre of my being that these twenty years had been worth while, very, very worth while, utterly worth while, with no room left for regrets or recriminations.

WEC INTERNATIONAL

WEC International was begun in 1913 by C.T. Studd. Studd had served as a missionary in China and India. At the age of 53, he felt God calling him to the "heart of Africa," and he obeyed. He spent the next 18 years in the Belgian Congo, and founded the mission that Dr. Helen Roseveare joined in 1953.

WEC has grown into a mission of more than 1500 workers from more than 40 countries, serving Christ in over 60 countries around the world. We have always sought to evangelize the unreached peoples, those to whom no one has previously gone with the gospel of Jesus Christ. Our aim is to establish among them fully-discipled, self-governing, self-supporting and reproducing churches able to fulfill their part in the Great Commission. In 1984 we changed our name from Worldwide Evangelization Crusade to WEC International.

Our Motto: If Jesus Christ be God
and died for me, then no sacrifice
can be too great for me to make for
Him.   C.T. Studd

For information about WEC International, write to:

WEC International
P.O. Box 1707
Fort Washington, PA 19034
U.S.A.

WEC International
37 Aberdeen Avenue
Hamilton, Ontario L8P 2N6
Canada

Council of Reference

Dr. Stuart Briscoe
Mrs. Jill P. Briscoe
Dr. Wade T. Coggins
Dr. Harvie M. Conn

Dr. Dennis F. Kinlaw
Dr. Robertson McQuilkin
Dr. Ted S. Rendall
Dr. Ralph D. Winter

EFMA Member Mission